SAS®

FOR

DUMMIES®

2ND EDITION

SAS®
FOR
DUMMIES®
2ND EDITION

by Stephen McDaniel and Chris Hemedinger

WILEY

Wiley Publishing, Inc.

SAS® For Dummies®, 2nd Edition

Published by
Wiley Publishing, Inc.
111 River Street
Hoboken, NJ 07030-5774

www.wiley.com

Copyright © 2010 by Wiley Publishing, Inc., Indianapolis, Indiana

Published by Wiley Publishing, Inc., Indianapolis, Indiana

Published simultaneously in Canada

For general information on our other products and services, please contact our Customer Care Department within the U.S. at 877-762-2974, outside the U.S. at 317-572-3993, or fax 317-572-4002.

For technical support, please visit www.wiley.com/techsupport.

Wiley also publishes its books in a variety of electronic formats. Some content that appears in print may not be available in electronic books.

Library of Congress Control Number: 2010922564

ISBN: 978-0-470-53968-2

Manufactured in the United States of America

WILEY

About the Authors

Stephen McDaniel has 20 years of experience as a teacher, a consultant, a leader, an innovator, and an author in the fields of visual analytics, business intelligence, data warehousing, and data mining. Stephen is the author of *Rapid Graphs with Tableau Software* and is the cofounder of Freakalytics®, LLC. Freakalytics offers public training, on-site training, and expert consulting that delivers "Rapid Analytics to Explore, Understand, Communicate & Act."

Previously, Stephen was the senior manager in charge of the SAS Enterprise Guide development team and the SAS Add-In for Microsoft Office development team at SAS. Stephen has been a SAS user for more than 20 years and has experience with more than 50 organizations as a statistician, statistical programmer, product manager, and manager of data warehousing and business intelligence. You can reach him at www.Freakalytics.com.

Chris Hemedinger is a senior software manager in the Research and Development division of SAS. Chris began his career at SAS in 1993 as a technical writer, creating such hits as *SAS Companion for the OS/2 Environment* (remember OS/2?) and *SAS Companion for the Microsoft Windows Environment.* In 1997, he became involved in a prototype project to make SAS easier to use for nonprogrammers, and that project evolved into the hugely popular SAS Enterprise Guide, a product that Chris has worked with ever since. Chris can be found performing entertaining SAS tricks at blogs.sas.com/sasdummy.

Dedication

I want to thank my wonderful wife and business partner, Eileen, for her patience, support, insights, and encouragement throughout the writing process!—Stephen McDaniel

For my beautiful (and patient) wife, Gail, and our inquisitive three daughters: Maggie, Evelyn, and Gwen. Listen up, girls: Despite what you hear from me, it's usually *not* polite to call somebody a "dummy."—Chris Hemedinger

Authors' Acknowledgments

The first edition of *SAS For Dummies* took years to assemble, even with the help of dozens of people. It proved popular beyond our wildest expectations. With such momentum, you might think that this second edition would be a piece of cake and practically write itself. Think again.

We, the humble authors, could not have planned and completed this book without the tremendous help of our editors at Wiley and at SAS Press. From Wiley, we relied on Jodi Jensen and Katie Feltman for their coordination and Susan Pink for her thoughtful editing. At SAS Press, Stacey Hamilton served as our acquisitions editor, with help and guidance from Stephenie Joyner and Julie Platt.

Especially for this second edition, we had great technical and content feedback from our panel of reviewers: Marilyn Adams, Marie Dexter, and Jennifer Tamburro at SAS and Eileen McDaniel at Freakalytics.

Publisher's Acknowledgments

We're proud of this book; please send us your comments at http://dummies.custhelp.com. For other comments, please contact our Customer Care Department within the U.S. at 877-762-2974, outside the U.S. at 317-572-3993, or fax 317-572-4002.

Some of the people who helped bring this book to market include the following:

Acquisitions and Editorial

Project Editor: Susan Pink

Acquisitions Editor: Katie Feltman

Copy Editor: Susan Pink

Editorial Manager: Jodi Jensen

Editorial Assistant: Amanda Graham

Sr. Editorial Assistant: Cherie Case

Cartoons: Rich Tennant
(www.the5thwave.com)

Composition Services

Project Coordinator: Patrick Redmond

Layout and Graphics: Yovonne Grego, Joyce Haughey, Christine Williams

Proofreader: Shannon Ramsey

Indexer: Steve Rath

Publishing and Editorial for Technology Dummies

    Richard Swadley, Vice President and Executive Group Publisher

    Andy Cummings, Vice President and Publisher

    Mary Bednarek, Executive Acquisitions Director

    Mary C. Corder, Editorial Director

Publishing for Consumer Dummies

    Diane Graves Steele, Vice President and Publisher

Composition Services

    Debbie Stailey, Director of Composition Services

Contents at a Glance

Table of Contents

Introduction

● ●

*U*nless you're a hermit, chances are good that your life is touched by SAS (pronounced "sass") almost every day.

Have you ever received an offer for a credit card in the mail? The bank might have used SAS to select you for the particular offer you received. Remember a recent news article that cited demographic trends in the United States? The Census Bureau uses SAS to crunch its numbers. Were you tempted to buy that new gadget in a big-name retail store? The corporate office might have used SAS to calculate the best price to set for that specific item on that specific week.

The rate you pay for life insurance, the analysis behind pharmaceutical drug trials, the quality of parts used to assemble your automobile — all these are determined by people who use SAS. You don't see SAS directly from day to day — but, like gravity, it's an invisible force that affects your life.

This book offers a prolonged glimpse into the multifaceted world of SAS software. Read on to discover how people use SAS to influence the world around you. Perhaps you'll see how to grab the reins yourself and use SAS to affect your own sphere of influence.

About This Book

Although this book is titled *SAS For Dummies*, 2nd Edition, you absolutely need some smarts to get solid results using SAS. However, the overarching message of this book is that you don't need to be an expert at using software. You just need to know what questions to ask, what data is needed to provide an answer, and how to interpret the results.

This book covers a variety of SAS products. We take a high-level look at some and dive deeply into those that you're most likely to use. The amazing fact is that SAS offers hundreds of software products covering dozens of industries and disciplines. No single person could possibly use them all and still have time for essential activities, such as sleep and personal hygiene. (Hmm, maybe that explains the smell around here.)

Like most software products, SAS products look and work differently from version to version. We describe SAS 9.2 and version 4.2 of the applications that we discuss most, including SAS Enterprise Guide, SAS Add-In for

Microsoft Office, and SAS Web Report Studio. If you have a different version of these SAS applications, many of the instructions and figures in the book will differ from what you see in your installation.

And, hey! Here's something cool about this book: You don't have to read it from stem to stern. Feel free to skip around, reading the sections that cover what you need to know.

This book does *not* address two popular SAS topics:

✔ **How to program in SAS:** SAS software has been around for more than 30 years, and you can find plenty of books about SAS programming. Indeed, one goal of this book is to show you how much you can do with SAS without having to become a SAS programmer. However, we provide several examples of SAS programs throughout the book, especially in Chapter 16, so you can at least recognize a SAS program if you meet one on the street.

✔ **Life at SAS Institute Inc., the makers of SAS software:** SAS, the company (along with its founder, Jim Goodnight), has had more than its 15 minutes of fame on TV shows (such as *60 Minutes* and *Oprah*) plus a big dose of coverage in business magazines (such as *Fortune* and *Forbes*). The stories are overwhelmingly positive (not featuring anyone trying to blot out the camera view with his palm). SAS is famous for being a great place to work. One of the authors holds a day job at SAS — and he really likes that job. That's all we'll say about that.

Conventions Used in This Book

This book contains lots of descriptive information about SAS software. Because a picture is worth — well, you know — this book has lots of figures of the software in action. (*Action* is a relative term; after all, this *is* business and analytical software, not *World of Warcraft*.)

✔ You'll find plenty of step-by-step instructions to accomplish specific tasks. You can follow along with these if you have the software handy; otherwise, you can use your imagination and pretend how much fun it is.

✔ When we show a URL, filename, path, data set, or code within regular text, we set it off in a monofont type, `like this`.

✔ When we want you to type something, we bold the characters you type (such as, **type this**).

✔ If you get the munchies while reading this book, it's because most of the examples refer to data with a candy theme.

   ✔ The data files discussed in the book actually ship with *SAS Enterprise Guide,* which is a SAS application that features prominently in this book.

What You're Not to Read

Occasionally, you'll see some sidebar topics or Technical Stuff icons in the margin that indicate an historical or a technical side point. You can skip those if you want, but reading them will give you that extra edge when SAS comes up in the discussion at the next cocktail party you attend. Study up and impress your friends!

Foolish Assumptions

To better manage the task of writing this book, we had to begin with some assumptions about you, the reader. Here they are:

   ✔ SAS software runs on many types of computer systems, but the majority of people experience it under Microsoft Windows. So, the examples are presented as if you're using a PC. We assume that you know your way around a PC, clicking the mouse, selecting menus, and so on.

   ✔ As we stated, we don't assume that you are a SAS programmer or that you even aspire to be one. However, if you are or if you do, you'll still find this book useful to round off your SAS knowledge.

How This Book Is Organized

Yes, this book *is* organized; the chapters don't simply appear in random order. There are six major parts, each of which includes some self-contained chapters. Don't feel as though you need to read them in order, though. Please, make yourself at home and read whichever chapters interest you the most. (Really, it's okay; we won't be offended.)

Part I: Welcome to SAS!

SAS, meet reader. Reader, meet SAS. In Part I, you get to know each other in this overview of what SAS software is about and what it can do for you. You'll find an introduction to SAS Enterprise Guide and some examples for getting quick results without having to be an expert.

Part II: Gathering Data and Presenting Information

Data is everywhere, but information is scarce. Part II shows how you can use SAS to take data and turn it into information you can use. And even better, you can see how to turn it into information that others will use and thank you for. You'll find out how to build basic reports and graphs that actually convey useful information.

Part III: Impressing Your Boss with Your SAS Business Intelligence

Part III is a whirlwind tour through the concepts of statistics and analytics. You get an overview of the basics, as well as some examples of how you can apply analytics to understand and predict behavior, as represented in data. Correlations, causality, forecasting — those topics and others are discussed here.

Part IV: Enhancing and Sharing Your SAS Masterpieces

Part IV could be titled "SAS: It's Everywhere You Want to Be" or "SAS: It's Not Just for Programmers Anymore." You'll see how you can use SAS from your desktop, on the Web, in Microsoft Excel, and even in Microsoft PowerPoint!

Part V: Getting SAS Ready to Rock and Roll

Part V provides a high-level view of how to install and configure SAS software. You might come away with an enhanced appreciation for the person who performs that task for you. You'll find a gentle introduction to the concepts and structure of SAS programs. And for the experienced SAS programmers in the audience, you can find a candid overview of SAS Enterprise Guide, your new friend.

Part VI: The Part of Tens

Part VI is where we stored the nuggets of knowledge that you can count on both hands (or feet!). Even if you already consider yourself a SAS expert, we promise that you will discover something new here. Check out Part VI for ten productivity tips for SAS Enterprise Guide users, ten must-know items for SAS administrators, and links to more resources.

Icons Used in This Book

All the information in this book is special; we wouldn't have included it otherwise. But some information that we provide is more special than the rest. To draw attention to its "specialness," we tagged it with some eye-catching little icons.

The Tip icon calls out a sentence or two that might prove to be a timesaver in your work. (You're welcome.)

Got a mind like a steel sieve? Well, you might want to reserve some space in your memory bank for the content next to the Remember icon. We use this icon as a way to emphasize an important point or concept.

Hear the voice in your head yelling "Danger Will Robinson! Danger!"? Is your "spidey sense" tingling? Well, there is little danger, really, as long as you heed the advice shown near the Warning icon.

This book contains many little gems of technical information. You can still use SAS if you don't read and understand this stuff, just like you can still enjoy watching hockey if you don't know what *icing* means. But, as any fan will tell you, it's more fun knowing what it all means.

Where to Go from Here

After you read through this book, you might crave more details about specific areas that we cover. (Or maybe those cravings are related to the candy-themed examples.) The best starting place for more information is the SAS support Web site at http://support.sas.com.

If this book transforms you into a card-carrying SAS user, your next step might be to seek out others like you. That will be easy because millions of people around the globe use SAS. And do you know what? They like to get together every so often in SAS user groups. User group meetings and conferences provide a great way to find out more from your peers about how to use SAS in practical and creative ways. User group information is available from SAS at `http://support.sas.com`.

Part I
Welcome to SAS!

The 5th Wave   By Rich Tennant

"This isn't a quantitative or a qualitative estimate of the job. This is a wish-upon-a-star estimate of the project."

In this part . . .

What exactly is SAS anyway? Is it really a Scandinavian airline (wrong SAS), or do those letters mean something else?

In this part, you discover how to see the world for what it is: a huge bucket of data. And we show you how you can use SAS software to pull some of that data together and draw useful information from it. We introduce you to some of the basic tools that will become your companions as you begin your journey toward SAS savviness.

Chapter 1

Touring the Wonderful World of SAS

*O*ne of the questions newcomers ask most frequently about SAS is "What does the name mean?" After all, those capital letters usually indicate an acronym, right? Today, SAS just refers to the name of a company. If you've been around the world of data analysis for a while, however, you may also be familiar with the old meaning of SAS, *Statistical Analysis System.*

SAS software was developed by a bunch of smart and inquisitive people at North Carolina State University (NCSU) in the late 1960s and early 1970s. Some of these people are still at the company as owners or executives: Jim Goodnight (the current company president), John Sall, and Herb Kirk (the first SAS user). Most of these SAS software pioneers were trained as statisticians or mathematicians and developed the SAS language to help analyze a variety of scientific experiments being conducted at NCSU and other research universities.

Over time, the software became as important as the experiments it was being used to analyze. The company now known as SAS Institute was formed in 1976, by a few people who were brave enough to leave the cozy world of academics for the then-unknown world of software. The first few years were a bit rough; but before long, word of this software and its capabilities began to spread, revenues increased, and the company began to grow. As of this writing, SAS has enjoyed 33 consecutive years of revenue growth and profitability. They must be doing something right.

This chapter is an overview of the power and flexibility of SAS for a range of applications and industries. SAS has expanded from being just a programming language for experts to meeting the needs of a wide variety of users in almost every industry and country in the world.

Isn't SAS Just for Gurus?

You might assume that you need to be a statistician or math guru to use SAS, but happily that's not the case. In the last few years, SAS has made a significant investment in making the unparalleled analytical and data management capabilities developed over 30-plus years available to almost anyone with a problem to solve in business, science, or government. With recent products such as SAS Enterprise Guide and the SAS Add-In for Microsoft Office, SAS has never been more accessible or flexible. These products provide user-friendly interfaces and wizards to maximize the heavy-duty capabilities that SAS has long provided to gurus!

Most of this book is dedicated to simple-to-understand principles that are full of possibilities and limited only by your situation and imagination. SAS offers so much potential that this book just scratches the surface and gets you up to speed on the basics.

Data, Data Everywhere — But Not Where I Need It!

The glamorous side of business intelligence and data analysis is all the gee-whiz reports, graphs, and impressive statistics you can present. (It must be true because my p-value says so! And don't worry if you don't know what a *p-value* is right now. That will come later.) The surprising secret of actually arriving at good results for decision-making is the huge amount of time that many people spend accessing, organizing, and preparing their data for a particular analysis. We've found a common theme in our visits to more than 50 major companies: the massive amount of resource and rework time spent on the data preparation aspect of business analytics.

One real-life data preparation story

At one prominent aerospace company, the Six Sigma black-belts report that 85 percent of their time is spent collecting, cleaning, and preparing their data for the business tasks at hand. Even worse, they realize this work is duplicated across various departments. They all end up doing the same preparation work with a given data source, such as data describing all products currently sold, their predecessor products, and the dates that products were discontinued.

This data resides on different platforms in various formats with a wide array of data rules.

Staff work with older data in text files on a mainframe computer, data from an acquired subsidiary in Oracle on UNIX, data in DB2 from a new ERP system (Enterprise Resource Planning system — SAP in this case) on a Windows server, or data in a spreadsheet on someone's PC. When each team brings this data together for its own projects, they often arrive at different results. Upper management wonders why teams can never agree on even basic metrics and the analyses needed to run the business.

As we mention earlier in the chapter, the first developers of SAS were doing real-world research projects and faced these very same data preparation and analysis issues. Consequently, they developed products that allow seamless access to more than 100 data sources on almost every computing platform currently in use. This capability was way ahead of its time back then and is still hands-down the best we have used. These data access products — SAS/ACCESS products — run on your SAS server. They allow fast, seamless access to disparate data sources for your analysis (see Figure 1-1).

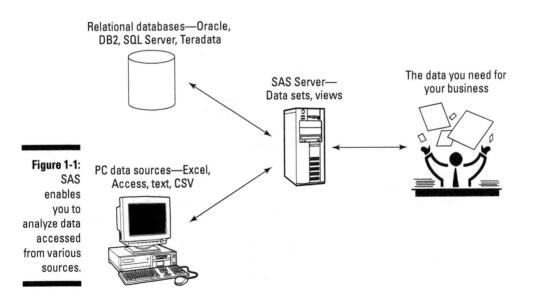

Relational databases—Oracle, DB2, SQL Server, Teradata

SAS Server— Data sets, views

The data you need for your business

PC data sources—Excel, Access, text, CSV

Figure 1-1: SAS enables you to analyze data accessed from various sources.

SAS can get to the data, but that's only the beginning. SAS also has excellent tools to enable centralized management of your data. Applications such as SAS Enterprise Guide have a wide array of data access, query, and management capabilities that enable you to slay your data-management dragons in a flexible and effective manner.

SAS also offers applications for power users to effectively access, manage, and aggregate your data. SAS Data Integration Server, in addition to other software products from DataFlux (a SAS company), focuses on the types of problems commonly connected to data warehousing and data quality. These tools allow you to have one integrated view of your data that is built on common rules and assumptions. The value here is in avoiding different answers to the same question by ensuring that everyone has access to a user-friendly, consistent data store. You find out more about this topic in Chapter 4.

Data Summaries and Reporting

If you've worked with traditional business intelligence tools from other software vendors, you might be familiar with data summarization and reporting. These tasks are critical to your ability to pull value from the data and knowledge inherent in your organization. Unfortunately, this immediate need for data is often the only area that people focus on when they ask for information to answer a particular question. If you can take a broader, long-term approach to your data management, reporting, and analysis needs, you can save money and time while yielding superior results.

One example to illustrate this point is a report of accounts past due. You could generate this information in Microsoft Excel and copy and paste subsets of the data to send to various sales teams. This is a very manual process. Or, you could design a report that can be easily updated with the latest data. This report can use subsets for accounts for each sales team and link to order details for each overdue account to show exactly what was in the overdue order. Imagine if this report could be delivered automatically over the Web, by e-mail, or directly into Microsoft Office. Now it is a much more flexible and powerful asset — all available from one SAS report!

Some simple forms of data summaries include sums, averages, medians, ranges, counts (sometimes called *frequencies*), and percentages. If you're interested in determining total sales by region, for example, the data source you have with this information might be a 50-million–row table. By using the summary functions of SAS, you can collapse this data to a small number of rows — one row per region, for example. Many functions in SAS automatically summarize the data for you. A pie chart of the sales by region would also automatically collapse the data to just a few rows before charting it.

Why summarize data?

Elsewhere in this chapter we give an example of reducing a 50-million–row table to just a few rows. Imagine, then, that you want to summarize that data in three forms: a pie chart, a listing, and a bar chart. By explicitly summarizing the large data source once (collapsing the 50 million rows down to 100 or so rows) and then creating the pie chart, listing, and bar chart from the summarized form, you get a much quicker generation of your results for your analyses.

SAS has a variety of powerful techniques to summarize your data, from basic counts, means, medians, minimum values, and maximum values to sophisticated algorithms that allow you to not just aggregate the data but also to actually find relevant confidence intervals around the aggregations you request.

The Secret Sauce: Analytics to Optimize the Present and Predict the Future

If you were familiar with SAS before you started reading this chapter, you may be aware that SAS was made famous by its analytic capabilities. And you may be wondering whether you can easily use the analytic capabilities that SAS offers. Even if they are easy to use, can they really make a difference in your business? We can almost absolutely, positively guarantee that the answer will be *Yes*! (Okay, legalese time. This is not some binding guarantee. Your results and mileage can vary, but we're 99.999% sure.)

Almost every analytic technique, statistic, and test is designed to help better identify the true state of something by analyzing limited information. Here are some examples of where analytics can come in handy:

- Did the Western sales region really have a better average sales number than the Eastern region?
- Do customers who buy our gum spend more money at retailers than customers who don't?
- What are the projected sales over the next year of CinnaPecans if I lower their price by 10 percent?
- Which customer demographic factors are useful in predicting customers' receptiveness to a direct marketing solicitation?

To answer any of these questions effectively, you first need access to data that is of high quality, familiar to you, and properly organized so that you can apply the appropriate analytic technique for the question at hand. Even after you apply the appropriate analytic technique, you need an integrated way to evaluate the success of the technique and a method of presenting (reporting) the results so that even managers (like us) can understand.

Table 1-1 offers a high-level view of some of the analytic capabilities of SAS, their potential applications, and which chapter tells you more about the technique.

Table 1-1	Example Applications of SAS Analytics	
Real-World Example	*Statistical Technique*	*Chapter*
An engineer wants to predict the mean time until failure for a new LED television based on 15 test models	Survival Analysis	Chapter 9
A manager wants to know the effect on projected sales next year if she doubles marketing spending	Forecasting	Chapter 9
A clinician wants to know the effect on patient response of doubling the dose of a new drug	Mixed Models	Chapter 8
A sales manager wants to know the projected profitability of a new customer based on the customer's demographic profile	Data Mining	Chapter 10
A taste tester wants to know whether people really prefer Fizzy Cola over Foamy Cola	Categorical Data Analysis	Chapter 9
A procurement team wants to test whether the new super-strong titanium bolts meet the specified strength specs for its new jet	Quality Control	Chapter 9
A sales promotion manager at OmniLoMart and her team want to know projected sales by country, store, and even SKU for the next week	High Performance Forecasting	Chapter 9
A hospital wants to predict patient stay length based on physician and nurse comments captured in the patient database	Text Mining	Chapter 10

Sharing the SAS Wealth

SAS has gone above and beyond its traditional market in the last few years to add an impressive array of tools and delivery mechanisms to make the lives of business analysts, managers, and executives easier and more productive. The following list describes just a few of the tools SAS offers:

- ✔ **OLAP (Online Analytic Processing):** Frequently referred to by lay people as a *pivot table*, provides a mechanism for large volumes of data to be summarized in advance and presented to users via customized tools designed to make exploring the data easy and fast. With OLAP, you can take a very large table, such as a sales history table for a large retailer, and predefine certain categories and metrics of interest that are run on a nightly basis. This results in a greatly collapsed data size with data stored in a specific format that enables very fast creation of summaries and exploration. Figure 1-2 illustrates a view of such a sales table in an OLAP hierarchical view.

- ✔ **SAS Add-In for Microsoft Office:** Provides you with seamless direct access to SAS reports, data engines, data management, reporting, and analytic tasks from Microsoft Excel, Word, and PowerPoint. The add-in enables you to avoid *spreadsheet hell,* the consequence of using a simplistic yet user-friendly tool such as Excel for complex data processing that should be performed with a better tool. SAS is well suited for this type of processing through the SAS add-in. When you use the SAS add-in, SAS content and data sources are centrally maintained and can be dynamically synchronized with your SAS server to ensure that all analysts in your company are accessing "one version of the truth." A simple example is illustrated in Figure 1-3: a centrally created and maintained SAS forecast analysis that is dynamically streamed and easily updated by end users from PowerPoint.

- ✔ **SAS Information Delivery Portal and SAS Web Report Studio:** Allows for simplified delivery of content over the Web and intuitive reporting for almost any level of user. Users access a centrally maintained view of their data to quickly create powerful and insightful reports that can be easily shared throughout the organization. Figure 1-4 illustrates just one of the many report formats that you can create in a matter of minutes with SAS Web Report Studio.

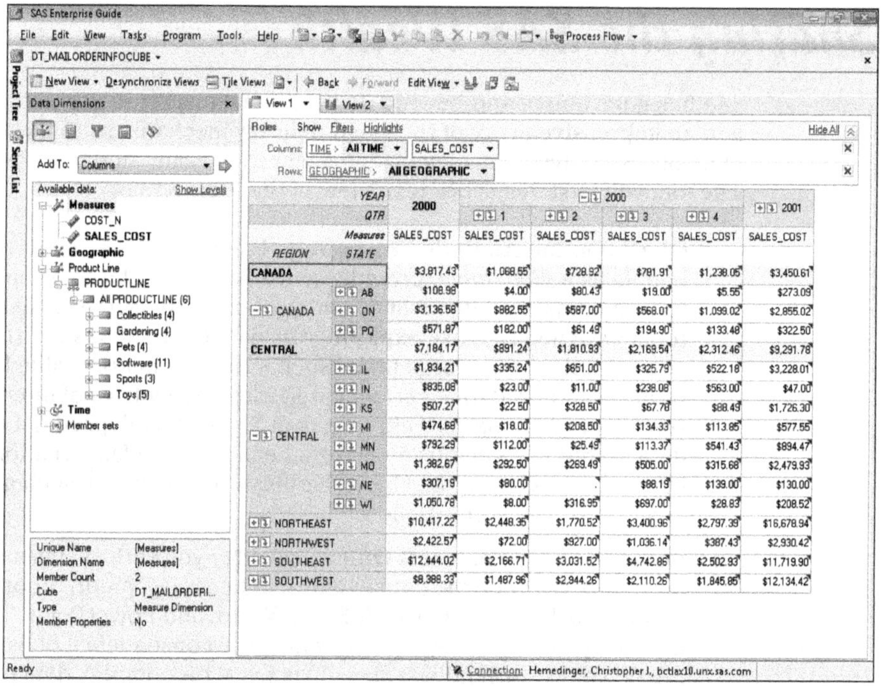

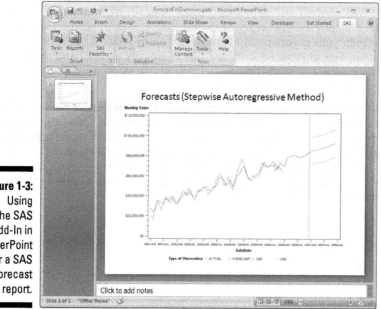

Figure 1-2:
Sales data
that uses
OLAP to
answer your
questions.

Figure 1-3:
Using
the SAS
Add-In in
PowerPoint
for a SAS
Forecast
report.

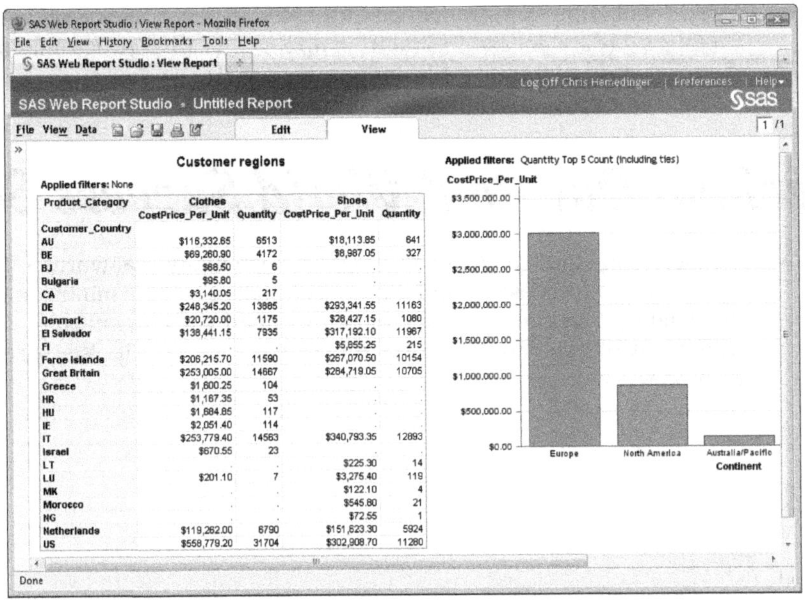

Figure 1-4:
Using SAS
Web Report
Studio for a
Web-based
report.

What the IT Department Needs to Know

The ease of use and the powerful analytical applications of SAS are great for the end user and number crunchers, but your IT folks will find SAS friendly to use as well. The good news for IT professionals is that SAS 9.2 provides a centralized approach for deploying software, managing security, managing user environments, creating content, distributing content, and controlling user access to data.

By using standard software packaging tools, administrators can prepackage the distribution of SAS software. Using SAS Management Console to maintain metadata in SAS Metadata Server, you can configure servers, server options, users, and user groups, manage data sources, and manage the content and capabilities available to users.

SAS Information Map Studio enables you to create dynamic data views based on administrator-defined Information Maps. These Information Maps hide the complexity and danger of accessing complex data schemas by presenting users with administrator-defined business views of the data. Based on user selections, SQL is dynamically created to provide them with just the data they need for their report.

More details that IT folks may be interested in reviewing are covered in Chapters 4 (data access), 15 (setting up SAS), 17 (SAS programming with the new world of SAS), and 19 (administrator tips).

Checking Out Real-World Success Stories

As users and employees of SAS, we have seen many real-world SAS success stories. From forecasting and data warehousing to data mining and business intelligence, SAS can meet just about any need you can imagine. To read a wide array of detailed SAS case studies, use your favorite Web browser and go to www.sas.com/success.

Chapter 2

Your Connection to SAS: Using SAS Enterprise Guide

. . . .

In This Chapter

▶ Seeing how SAS made its way to the PC

▶ Checking out your data access options

▶ Summarizing and otherwise compiling your data

▶ Reporting on-the-spot

. . . .

S AS has been around for a long time and has often been considered the province of math or programming experts. In the late 1990s, Dr. Goodnight (cofounder and CEO since the company was created in 1976) thought that this image needed to change and that the way to accomplish this was with a new interface that was both user-friendly and capable of delivering SAS power without programming. Thus, SAS Enterprise Guide was born.

SAS Enterprise Guide was the first application that SAS developed just for Microsoft Windows so that users could access, query, summarize, analyze, and publish results from their SAS server running almost anywhere. SAS servers can run from your PC, a Windows server, a UNIX server, or even on a good old mainframe (no funny-looking punch cards required!). And because SAS Enterprise Guide can run from a Windows desktop (for ease of use), yet interact with SAS on any computing platform, it is one of the most powerful user interfaces on the planet.

In this chapter, you see how to use this marvelous interface to the broad capabilities of SAS.

Using SAS Enterprise Guide, the Swiss Army Knife of SAS

Looking at the wide array of capabilities that SAS Enterprise Guide comprises, we can confidently call it the Swiss army knife of SAS. Just like a Swiss army knife, SAS Enterprise Guide is handy in lots of situations and offers a surprising array of options in a simple-to-learn package.

SAS Enterprise Guide is a ubiquitous SAS interface that almost every SAS customer has access to in one way or another. It is included with SAS for Microsoft Windows (sometimes called "PC SAS"), which is a local copy of SAS for your PC that works like your own personal SAS server. Universities teaching statistics courses and independent professionals learning SAS use SAS Enterprise Guide to access SAS OnDemand over the Internet, where SAS (the company) hosts the SAS server. Many companies also license SAS Enterprise Guide to allow their users to work with remote Windows, UNIX, or mainframe SAS servers that they configure and maintain. Whichever configuration of SAS you use with SAS Enterprise Guide, most of the functionality is the same; the difference is whether the processing is performed on your PC or on a remote computer.

Because this book addresses SAS 9.2, we assume that you are using SAS Enterprise Guide 4.2. If you're using an earlier version of SAS or SAS Enterprise Guide, you might have some trouble following along in these chapters. Our first edition of *SAS For Dummies* addresses those earlier versions.

Using SAS Enterprise Guide for the first time

When you first install and use SAS Enterprise Guide, the interface looks like Figure 2-1. This is the default, out-of-the-box view.

The interface has some familiar elements:

- **Menu bar**
- **Toolbars**
- **Workflow presentation:** Two panes — the tree-like Project Tree and the workflow-oriented Process Flow — show your workflow from two perspectives. More than one Process Flow can exist in a project; the large workspace area on the right is the overall "container" for all of them.
- **Resources pane:** This feature offers quick access to resources such as SAS servers and the data they host, task lists, administered SAS Folders, and prompts.

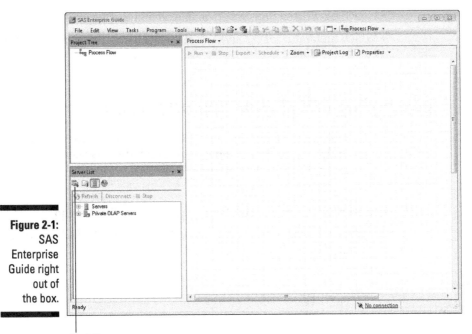

Figure 2-1:
SAS
Enterprise
Guide right
out of
the box.

Task list

Although the default view is a good general-purpose layout, we'll walk you through our preferred customizations in the next section. When you get ready to make SAS Enterprise Guide your own, you have a huge array of options for managing your workspace. You can

✔ **Customize the workspace:** Dock (hide or show) the interface panes so that you maximize the Process Flow and workspace viewing area.

✔ **Choose application settings:** Set a wide array of options for overall application behaviors by choosing Tools➪Options and making selections from the Options dialog box. For example, you can control the following:

  • What you see in the Process Flow

  • Your default output type (HTML, RTF, PDF, text, and SAS Report formats)

  • Whether you view your report output embedded in SAS Enterprise Guide or external to SAS Enterprise Guide by launching the relevant application with the report

  • How data is browsed

- How user-written SAS code is managed and displayed

- Which metadata server and SAS server you are using (if connecting to a remote SAS server)

Changing what you see onscreen

We simplified the screenshots in this book by making a few tweaks to the default options and window arrangement. Start SAS Enterprise Guide and follow these steps to set your interface to look like the screenshots you see in this book:

1. **Choose Start⇨SAS⇨Enterprise Guide 4.2 from the Start menu.**

   SAS Enterprise Guide appears, displaying the Welcome to SAS Enterprise Guide dialog box, as shown in Figure 2-2.

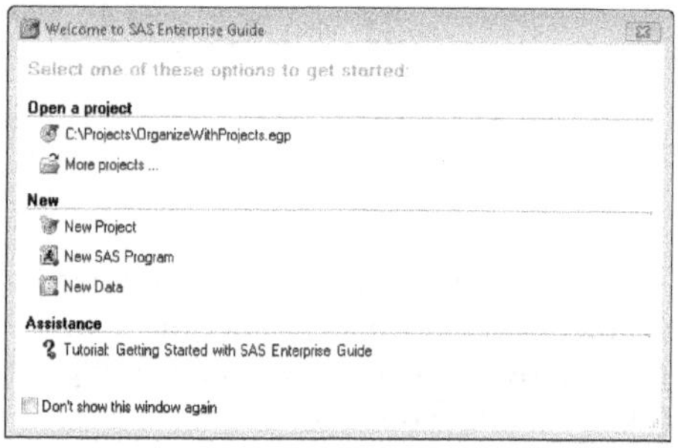

Figure 2-2: The Welcome to SAS Enterprise Guide dialog box offers several options.

Welcome to SAS Enterprise Guide

Select one of these options to get started:

Open a project
- C:\Projects\OrganizeWithProjects.egp
- More projects ...

New
- New Project
- New SAS Program
- New Data

Assistance
- Tutorial: Getting Started with SAS Enterprise Guide

☐ Don't show this window again

From this dialog box, you can choose to

- Open a recently used project

- Open a project by searching your computer drives or SAS server

- Create a new project

- Run the *Getting Started with SAS Enterprise Guide* tutorial

Our favorite choice is selecting the Don't Show This Window Again check box! You can always open or create new projects from the File menu.

2. **Click New Project to create an empty project.**

3. **Choose Tools⇨Options.**

   The Options dialog box appears.

4. **In the Results General section, under Managing Results, select Replace Without Prompting for the Replace Results option.**

   This enables you to rerun SAS tasks and programs without being prompted about whether you want to replace the last report created. The default value is Prompt Before Replacing.

5. **In the Tasks Output Library section, select WORK in the list of default library names and click the Up button until WORK is at the top of the list.**

   This tells SAS Enterprise Guide to use the temporary WORK location as the preferred location for output data generated by the SAS tasks that we'll run.

6. **Click OK to close the Options dialog box.**

7. **Click the Task List button in the lower-left pane (labeled as the Server List in the default view).**

   The Task List button is the farthest on the left. When you click it, the pane turns into the Task List pane and shows you a list of available tasks.

 You can click the small arrow at the top of the task list pane, or any similar docked pane, to control the docking behavior of the pane. You can select which edge of the application to dock to and whether the pane *auto hides* — that is, slides in to and out of view when you hover the cursor over it.

   Leave everything else in the default state.

 You can arrange your workspace differently at any time. If you don't like your changes and want to revert to the default layout, choose Tools⇨Options⇨ General and click the Restore Window Layout button.

Accessing and Managing Data

After setting up the application workspace, you're probably anxious to see SAS Enterprise Guide in action. A primary role of SAS Enterprise Guide is to give you access to and control over your business data. For example, you can open SAS data sources or import almost any type of commonly used data format for use in SAS Enterprise Guide. This section provides a brief glimpse into accessing and managing data with SAS Enterprise Guide.

Opening SAS data sets

SAS data sets are the building blocks of many reports and analyses in SAS. A *SAS data set* is the standard data storage format for data created with SAS.

The great thing about SAS data sets is that they're fast to open and analyze relative to other data storage methods, such as text files, comma-separated values (CSV) files, Excel spreadsheets, and even relational databases such as Oracle or DB2. By default, the output data created by your activities in SAS Enterprise Guide are SAS data sets.

To open a data set and create a project from scratch, follow these steps:

1. **Choose Start⇨SAS⇨Enterprise Guide 4.2.**

2. **Click New Project.**

   The Welcome dialog box closes, and the new project appears with a blank Process Flow pane. If you don't see the Welcome dialog box because you took our advice and turned it off, don't worry. A new project will be created automatically.

3. **Choose File⇨Open⇨Data.**

   The Open Data dialog box appears. The pane on the left displays options for the data location. Your choices are

   • **Local Computer:** Clicking this icon allows you to browse your local computer resources, such as Windows Explorer, to select a data source.

   • **Servers:** Clicking this icon takes you to predefined data libraries defined on your SAS server to select a server-based data source.

   • **SAS Folders:** Clicking this icon takes you to administered data sources. This option is useful only when you are lucky enough to work in an environment where an IT department organizes and maintains data sources for you.

4. **Click the Local Computer icon.**

   The file types that SAS Enterprise Guide can open appear in a standard Windows Open dialog box. If you want to examine only SAS data files, click the Files of Type drop-down list, as shown in Figure 2-3, and choose SAS Data Files.

   We're working with a sample SAS data set named Candy_Sales_Summary that comes with SAS Enterprise Guide. Our copy of this data set is at

   ```
   C:\Program Files\SAS\EnterpriseGuide\4.2\Sample\Data\
          Candy_Sales_Summary.sas7bdat
   ```

   If you want to follow along with this example, you may have to browse to a different location to find this file on your system.

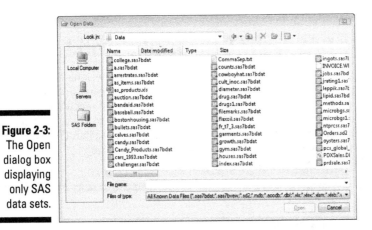

Figure 2-3:
The Open
dialog box
displaying
only SAS
data sets.

5. Click the Open button.

The data set opens in your project and appears in the data grid, as shown in Figure 2-4. You can easily browse the data by using the vertical and horizontal scroll bars.

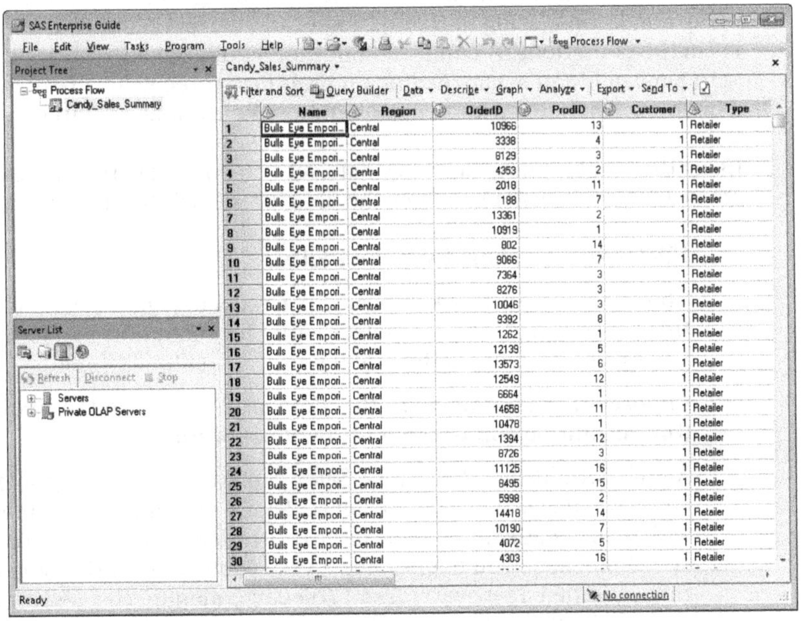

Figure 2-4:
The Candy
Sales
Summary
data set
browse
view via the
data grid.

Keep this data set open and continue to the next section to find out how to filter data in the data set.

What's a SAS task? Sounds like work!

SAS tasks in SAS Enterprise Guide are the wizards and dialog boxes that make your life easier. They logically present you with a variety of choices to enable you to perform the activity you requested just the way you want it. When you click Run (or Finish), the task automatically generates and submits to your SAS server the SAS program needed to perform the actions you requested. Some people use SAS tasks and the Preview Code button to teach themselves SAS programming. However, if you don't care about learning programming in SAS, you don't ever need to look at the code!

Filtering SAS data

Two of the most frequently used features of SAS Enterprise Guide are the Filter and Sort task (for simple filters) and the Query Builder task (for simple or more sophisticated filters). After you open a data set, these tasks make it easy to filter the data to analyze just the records that interest you. Filtering data can be as simple as organizing customer data based on country or the patients in a trial based on year of birth. Filtering can be based on one or many conditions, using and or or logic, and can even utilize complex formulas in the conditions. A complex condition could be "all patients born in 1968 with a mean blood sugar reading on their first three visits greater than 100 or a history of diabetes with at least two hospitalizations required."

Using the Candy_Sales_Summary data set you opened in the preceding set of steps, follow these steps to filter the data for records from the fiscal year 2003:

1. **Click Filter and Sort from the toolbar.**

   The Filter and Sort task appears, as shown in Figure 2-5. As the tabs in this task suggest, you can select variables (columns, in database parlance), create simple filters, and sort the result.

2. **Choose all the variables in this data set by clicking the double arrow (the second button in the middle of the window.)**

   All the variables in the Candy_Sales_Summary data set appear in the Selected space, as shown in Figure 2-6. By default, no variables are added automatically to your filter (no variables are in the Selected space) because you might have a very wide data set that you want to reduce to just a few variables. (You can configure this setting and many other defaults by choosing Tools⇨Options⇨Query.)

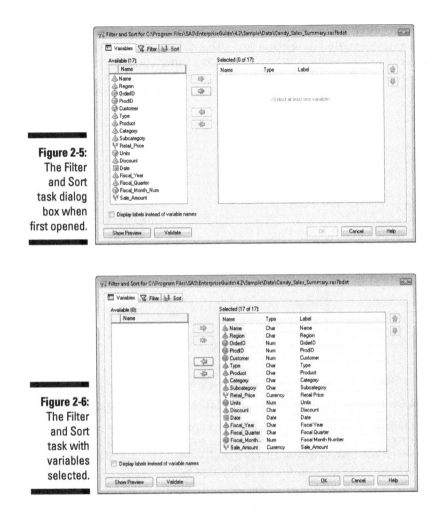

Figure 2-5:
The Filter
and Sort
task dialog
box when
first opened.

Figure 2-6:
The Filter
and Sort
task with
variables
selected.

3. **Click the Filter tab (to the right of the Variables tab).**

   The Filter tab appears, with an empty area for the Filter description.

4. **Click the first field in the Filter description to reveal the list of variables. Select Fiscal_Year from the list.**

5. **Click the second field to reveal the list of comparison operators. Select Equal to from the list.**

6. **Click the . . . button to reveal the list of distinct values for Fiscal_Year.**

   The Select a Single Value window appears with a list of values for Fiscal_Year, as shown in Figure 2-7.

The left side of the window shows the raw data value, and the right side shows the formatted data value (the value to present in reports). In this case, they're the same. A variable such as gender could have an *M* on the left raw value side and a value of *Male* on the right formatted side. You can click anywhere on the value row to select the desired value.

7. **Select 2003 from the list, and then click OK.**

8. **Click OK to close the Filter and Sort dialog box and run the task.**

    SAS Enterprise Guide automatically generates the SAS code needed to fulfill your request and submits it to your SAS server. The filtered data set, which the task labels as FILTER_FOR_CANDY_SALES_SUMMARY_S, opens in the data grid, as shown in Figure 2-8.

    SAS Enterprise Guide keeps a collection of useful information for each task that you run in the collection of tabs just above the data grid. These tabs provide quick access to the original input data, the SAS program (code) that the Filter and Sort task generated, the SAS program log that reports the technical details of how the program performed, and the output data.

9. **Click the Process Flow toolbar button to view the Process Flow built in this example.**

    SAS Enterprise Guide keeps an up-to-date process flow view of the data set opened, the query task built from it, and the resulting data set created when the query ran, as shown in Figure 2-9. Each view can be useful in quickly navigating your project. Double-clicking any item in the process flow automatically reopens the collection of results so that you can easily navigate to the part that interests you or modify the task to change some selections before running it again.

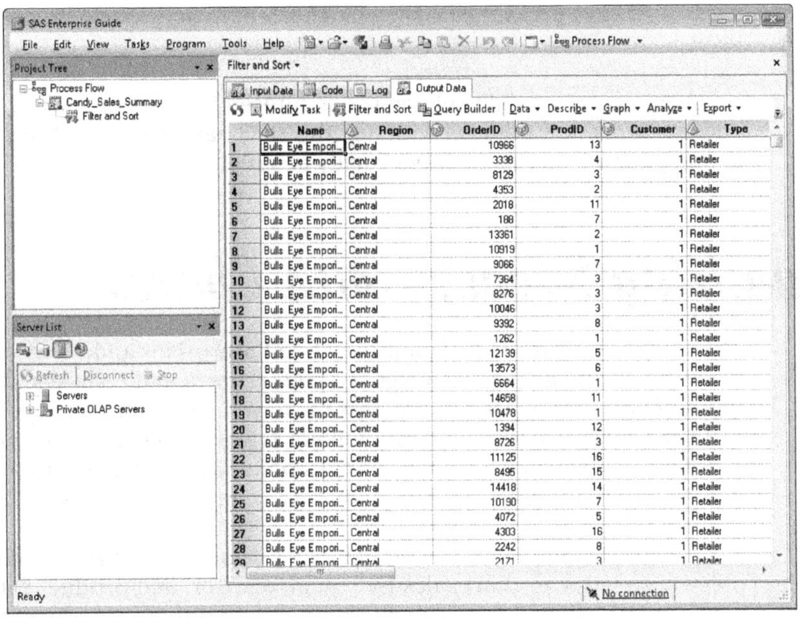

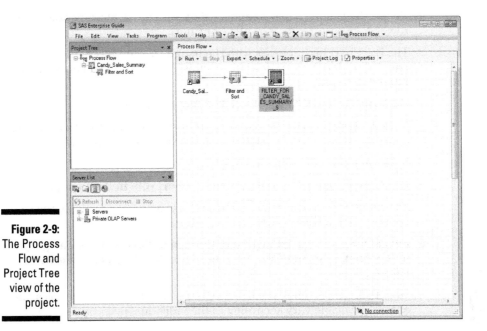

Figure 2-8:
The Candy Sales Summary data set filtered for fiscal year 2003.

Figure 2-9:
The Process Flow and Project Tree view of the project.

You can always press the F4 key as a shortcut to access the Process Flow view.

You have opened a data set, viewed it, filtered it based on fiscal year 2003, and created a new data set with just the 2003 data in it. The Process Flow shows your accomplishments visually at a high level.

Visualizing Success with Charts

The extensive charting capabilities of SAS Enterprise Guide give you the power to add new levels of insight to your reports and analyses. Different types of data and questions are best displayed with different types of charts, and SAS Enterprise Guide offers 13 major types and 60 subtypes of charts. This section provides a glimpse into graphing with SAS Enterprise Guide. To find out more about working with charts and graphs in SAS, see Chapter 7.

Bar charts are one of the most common and useful chart types. In this example, you see how to chart sales by region, quarter, and product category in one easy-to-read and interpret chart. To create this chart, follow these steps:

1. **To use the Candy_Sales_Summary data set you've already opened and filtered, choose Tasks⇨Graph⇨Bar Chart.**

    The Bar Chart task appears with the bar chart subtypes in the opening panel. The title in the task window shows that you're working with the filtered data set.

2. **Click the Grouped/Stacked Vertical Bar chart type.**

    Note the task tip near the bottom part of the task. Most tasks have this context-sensitive help available at all times, as shown in Figure 2-10.

3. **In the panel on the left, click Data.**

4. **Drag Fiscal_Quarter to the Column to Chart role in the Data pane.**

    Assigning variables to roles is part of the process of specifying the work the application will do after you click Run.

5. **Repeat Step 4 to assign Region to the Group Bars By role, Category to the Stack role, and Sale_Amount to the Sum Of role, as shown in Figure 2-11.**

    Most tasks have a similar structure to the bar chart task. The roles and options available vary according to the individual task.

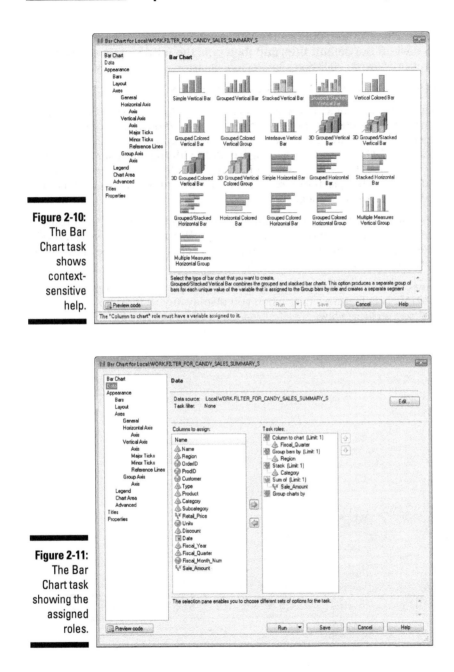

Figure 2-10:
The Bar
Chart task
shows
context-
sensitive
help.

Figure 2-11:
The Bar
Chart task
showing the
assigned
roles.

6. **Click Titles in the panel on the left, deselect the Use Default text box to turn off the default title, and then type the following in the Text for Section: Graph:** 2003 Sales by Region, Quarter, and Category.

7. **Click the Run button to run the Bar Chart task.**

The task dialog box closes and SAS Enterprise Guide instructs the SAS server to execute the submitted SAS code based on your requested specifications. After the code is executed, the graph opens in SAS Enterprise Guide, as shown in Figure 2-12. With this bar chart, you can see the importance of each region in overall sales, the differences in sales trends by quarter by region, and the contribution of each product category to overall sales.

To make it easier to see the entire graph without the rest of the project workspace visible, choose View⇨Maximize Workspace. When you finish viewing the output in the maximized mode, choose the same menu item to go back to the standard project view.

You can access the Maximize Workspace feature also by pressing Ctrl+M. This feature works when you display any report view, data view, or Process Flow view.

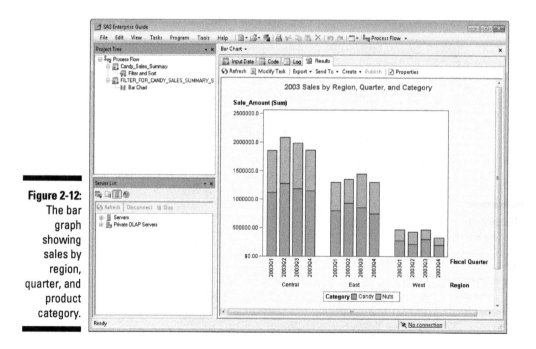

Figure 2-12:
The bar graph showing sales by region, quarter, and product category.

Creating Reports for Even the Crankiest Manager

When most software products refer to *reporting,* they mainly focus on bringing in data to a pretty layout or a cross-tabular report and controlling the layout, page numbering, and other appearance options such as formatting. SAS Enterprise Guide certainly lets you do this type of work, but it also gives you many other options. To help you make just the right presentation, SAS Enterprise Guide has an impressive array of SAS tasks, such as simple counts, descriptive statistics, complex cross-tabulations, graphs, and even advanced analytics and forecasting — all in one report! In this section, you see how to create a moderately complex cross-tabulation report and then enrich it to make a composite report featuring some of your graphs and the summary table.

Creating a list report with totals

List reports are a great way to summarize, or *aggregate,* data by categories or by groups. Summaries could include average sales amount, number of units sold, or maximum sales discount. Categories could be year, quarter, region, or product line. To create a list report of regional sales summary by subcategory and product, follow these steps:

1. **Choose Tasks➪Describe➪List Report Wizard.**

   The List Report Wizard appears, as shown in Figure 2-13. The first page of the wizard enables you to check that you're working with the intended data.

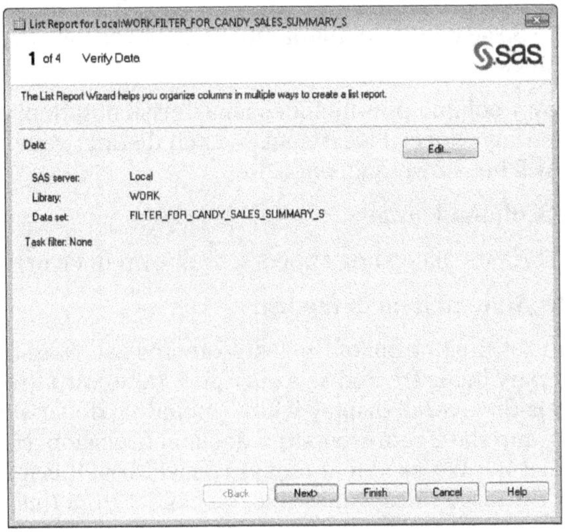

Figure 2-13: The List Report Wizard.

Most tasks in SAS Enterprise Guide provide this convenient opportunity to verify that you're working with the correct data source. If you launch a task with the wrong data, you can simply choose Edit to select a different data source. You can also specify a simple filter to apply to the data; that filter applies only within the scope of the active task.

Because we already filtered the data in a previous step, we don't need to specify an additional filter at this point. (But it's nice to know that we could, if we wanted to.)

2. Click Next.

The Define List page appears. By default, all the columns in the data source are added to the report and shown in the Preview area.

3. Delete the default columns and add just the four that we need for the report:

    a. Click Edit⇨Delete All Columns.

    b. Click Add⇨Subcategory.

    c. Click Add⇨Product.

    d. Click Add⇨Fiscal_Quarter.

    e. Click Add⇨Sale_Amount.

4. Click the Fiscal_Quarter column in the Preview area to select it, and then click Move⇨Position Above⇨Sale_Amount.

When you place a categorical column such as Fiscal_Quarter above a measure column such as Sale_Amount, you create an "across" relationship in the report. As a result, there will be one Sale_Amount column for each value of Fiscal_Quarter. The preview area in the task does not reflect these additional columns, so for now, you have to take a leap of faith that they're there. Trust us; the report is going to look great.

5. Right-click the Subcategory column and choose Display Type⇨Hide Repeating Values.

The Subcategory column now includes an asterisk notation, indicating that it's getting a special treatment — each distinct value for Subcategory will be shown only once.

6. Choose Edit⇨Column Formats.

The Column Formats dialog box appears, as shown in Figure 2-14.

7. Click the Sale_Amount item in the list.

Sale_Amount is at the bottom of the List Columns list. Note that Sale_Amount is already being treated as a currency value with the DOLLAR9.2 format. The 9 is the overall display width (including dollar sign, decimal, and commas), and the 2 represents the decimal precision. (Does that make cents? Get it?) We need to increase the width of this format so that it can display the large sales values that we expect from this report.

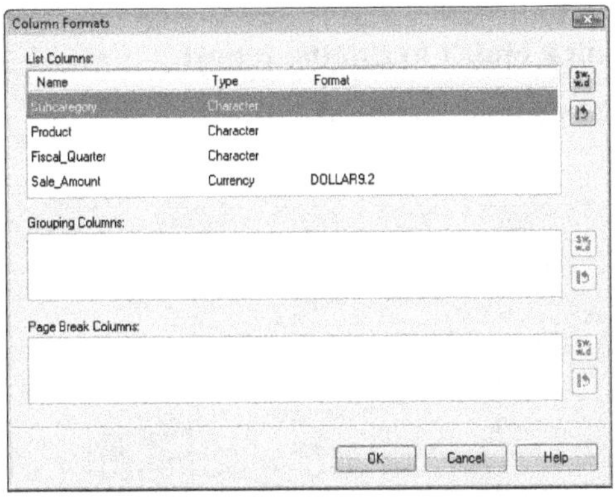

Figure 2-14:
The Column
Formats
dialog box.

8. **Click the Edit Format button (the upper-right button with the funny little characters).**

9. **In the Format for Sale_Amount window that appears, change the Overall Width field to 12 and the Decimal Places field to 0. Click OK to close the Format window.**

   In the Column Formats dialog box, Sale_Amount now shows the DOLLAR12. format.

10. **Click OK to close the Column Formats dialog box.**

11. **Choose Edit⇨Assign Columns.**

    The Assign Columns dialog box appears.

12. **In the Available Columns list, drag Region to the pane labeled Create a Separate Table for Each Value Of (in the bottom right). Click OK.**

13. **Choose Edit⇨Column Headings.**

14. **In the Column Headings dialog box, deselect the box labeled Display the Type of Statistic in the Column Headings and then click OK.**

    This suppresses the SUM label in the final report.

15. **Click Next.**

    The Specify Totals window appears. This window shows a preview of the report layout, but unlike the previous page, you can't click and interact with the preview area.

16. **Select the Sale_Amount box in the Select Totals area, and then click the Edit button.**

    The Type of Totals dialog box appears.

17. **Deselect the Grand Totals item, select the Totals by Region item (at the bottom of the list), and then click OK.**

18. **Click Next to move to the last page for titles and footnotes.**

19. **Change the Title text to** Regional Sales Summary by Subcategory and Product, **and then click Finish to run the report.**

Figure 2-15 shows the completed report.

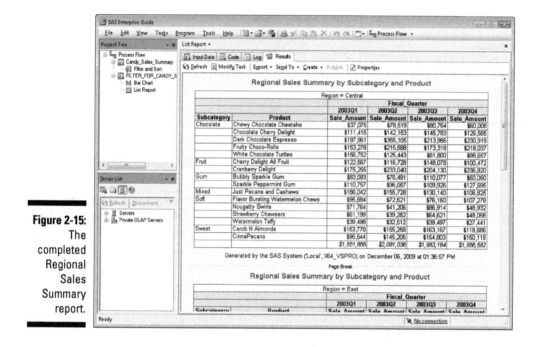

Figure 2-15:
The completed Regional Sales Summary report.

Getting your hands dirty with code

Sometimes, the recipe for a perfect report calls for something not on the menu. If you need to add some homegrown ingenuity to your SAS Enterprise Guide project, it's easy to do by creating your own SAS program.

To add a program that creates a fancy bar line chart in your project, follow these steps:

1. **Choose File⇨New⇨Program.**

    A new program editor window appears. It's empty, but we'll soon fix that with some feverish typing.

2. **Type the following program in the editor window:**

```
ods graphics / width=700 height=450;
title "Customer report: sales and volume";
proc sgplot
  data=work.filter_for_candy_sales_summary_s
  noautolegend;
```

```
vbar name /
  response=sale_amount
  transparency=.8
  fillattrs=graphdata1 ;
vline name /
  response=units
  lineattrs=graphdata2
  y2axis;
format
  sale_amount dollar12.
  units comma12.;
xaxis display=(nolabel);
yaxis label="Sale amount";
y2axis label="Units sold";
run;
```

Don't worry if you don't understand the content of the program. Many beginning SAS programmers start by running SAS programs written by other people, examining the results, and then tweaking the program code to see how it affects the output.

To save yourself some typing, you can copy and paste this program and other examples from `support.sas.com/sasfordummies`.

3. **Click Run from the toolbar at the top of the program editor window.**

    SAS Enterprise Guide submits the program to your SAS session and adds the results to your project. The result, shown in Figure 2-16, is a bar line plot, where the bar height shows the sale amount per customer and the line shows the volume of products each customer purchased (in numbers of units).

Putting it all together — no scissors or glue necessary

A *composite report* enables you to combine output from multiple tasks on one report for easy viewing and printing. Viewing data from a variety of perspectives on a composite report often makes it easier for decision makers to arrive at an effective conclusion.

You build a composite report from the pieces of output that already exist in your project. This report is linked to the original tasks and programs that it is based on. It is *dynamic,* meaning it will always be updated with new content if you rerun the tasks.

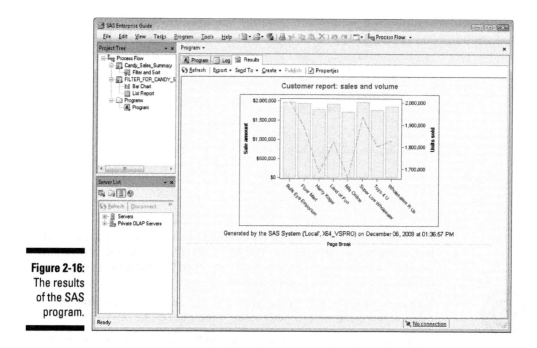

Figure 2-16:
The results
of the SAS
program.

To create a composite report using the summary report and the charts created earlier in this chapter, follow these steps:

1. **Choose File⇨New⇨Report.**

   The New Report window appears, as shown in Figure 2-17. This window is like a blank canvas, with your palette on the left and your work area on the right.

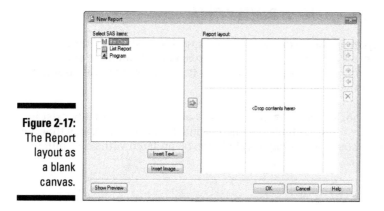

Figure 2-17:
The Report
layout as
a blank
canvas.

2. **Drag the SAS items from the list on the left and arrange them in the Report layout grid on the right, like this:**

   a. **Drag Bar Chart to the upper-left corner of the Report layout grid.**

   b. **Drag Program to the grid square just to the right of where you placed Bar Chart.**

   c. **Drag List Report to the grid square just below Bar Chart.**

   d. **Using the grabber handle on the right side of the List Report item in the Report layout area, drag the edge of the List Report item so that it spans the width of the two grid squares above it.**

   The result looks like Figure 2-18.

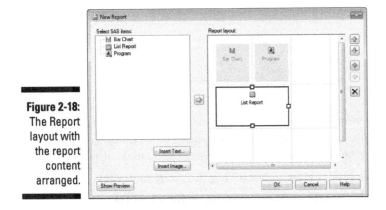

Figure 2-18: The Report layout with the report content arranged.

3. **Click Insert Text to add a title to the report.**

   The Insert Text window appears.

4. **Type** Sales Summary from 2003 **in the text field, and click the center alignment button in the toolbar to center the text.**

5. **(Optional) Change the font size, color, and typeface to further customize the title.**

6. **Click OK to close the Insert Text window.**

   The text element is added to the report layout, below the List Report output.

7. **Resize the title element (labeled Sales Summary from 2003) so that it spans two grid squares, similar to the way you resized the List Report item in Step 2.**

8. Drag the title element from the bottom of the Report Layout area to the top, above the Bar Chart element.

The title element moves to the top of the Report Layout area, as shown in Figure 2-19.

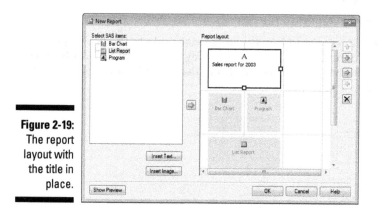

Figure 2-19:
The report
layout with
the title in
place.

9. Click OK to save the report definition.

SAS Enterprise Guide displays the composite report in the content area. It's really taking shape; just a few more tweaks will make it perfect.

10. Clean up the report view by removing the chart footnotes:

a. Click the Header & Footer button at the top of the report window.

b. In the Header & Footer dialog box that appears, click the Titles & Footnotes tab and deselect the Footnote check boxes for List Report, Program, and Bar Chart.

c. Click OK.

The report view updates to remove the footnotes.

11. Make this report printer-ready by changing the page settings:

a. Click the Page Setup button at the top of the report window.

The Page Setup dialog box appears.

b. In the Paper settings, select Fit Width for the Fit value.

c. Select Landscape for the Orientation value.

d. Click OK to save the Page Setup settings.

To see a preview of how this report will appear when printed, click the Page View button at the top of the report window. The report view appears as shown in Figure 2-20. (Note that we've maximized the view space for the report in this picture by choosing View⇨Maximize Workspace.)

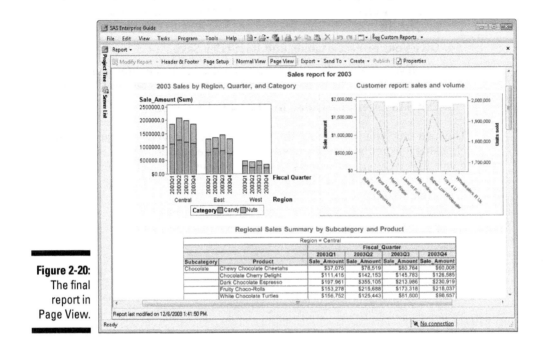

Figure 2-20:
The final report in Page View.

You can easily page through the report using your Page Up and Page Down keys. Notice how the report is "smart" enough to repeat table and column header information when a page breaks in the middle of the table.

You can choose File⇨Print Report to print this report, or you can choose File⇨Export to save the report as a PDF file or HTML file so that you can easily share it with a colleague in electronic format.

Now that you've invested so much time and creativity in producing a brilliant report, don't forget to save your SAS Enterprise Guide project! With a saved project, you can come back tomorrow and simply rerun the project, refreshing the report with any data updates that have happened in the meantime.

1. **To save your work, choose File⇨Save Project As.**

   The Save dialog box appears.

2. **Click the Local Computer Icon.**

   We won't do this right now, but you can use the Servers Icon to navigate to file storage locations on your SAS server.

3. **In the Save dialog box, navigate to a location that makes sense for you — for example, somewhere in My Documents — to save your project file.**

4. **Give your project a name, and then click Save.**

   If you've followed along with the examples in this chapter and want to save this project as-is, name this project **SAS for Dummies Chapter 2**.

5. **Exit SAS Enterprise Guide by choosing File⇨Exit.**

The next time you want to use the project you just saved, you can open it by choosing it from the recently used projects listed at the bottom of the File menu. The Welcome screen also lists recently used projects when you restart SAS Enterprise Guide — unless you turned off that screen as suggested earlier in this chapter!

Chapter 3

Six-Minute Abs: Getting Miraculous Results with SAS

A cornerstone of 20th century progress was the gain in economic efficiency and capacity. Americans, in particular, have been obsessed with making things faster, quicker, cheaper, or bigger. One of our favorite examples was a recent comedic movie in which a character had big plans to strike it rich with a product named Six-Minute Abs. He stated that this would provide the same workout as the one touted by the Seven-Minute Abs folks but in just six minutes — thus saving you a minute a day!

SAS Enterprise Guide is the Six-Minute Abs of SAS, only much better! As a statistician and programmer, Stephen used SAS for many years the old-fashioned way: programming in the SAS language. Mastering SAS Enterprise Guide, though, has made it possible for even a SAS programming guru like Stephen to be far more productive in accessing, managing, analyzing, graphing, and reporting in his daily work life.

In this chapter, you see more of the awesome capabilities SAS Enterprise Guide offers.

Knowing Where Your My Data Set Is Coming From and Going

SAS uses server *libraries*, which are the logical assignment of folders on your computer or server to simple but meaningful library names, such as WORK or SASUSER. Depending on your SAS configuration, you might use the WORK or SASUSER library by default because these are typically available on SAS servers.

For example, WORK is a special temporary library automatically assigned by the SAS server. WORK data exists only for your current SAS session and goes away when you close your SAS Enterprise Guide session. Data you place in the WORK library is not available if you close SAS and later reopen it!

If your data is required for a future SAS Enterprise Guide session, do not use the WORK library. You would have to rerun your analysis to re-create it each time. This isn't an issue for a table that takes just a few seconds to re-create. If a table results from a long-running task, however, you don't want to waste your time re-creating it unless the source data is constantly being updated and you want those updates every time you work on them.

Another automatic SAS library is SASUSER. Unlike WORK, SASUSER is a permanent library. Any data placed in SASUSER during your current session stays there until you overwrite or delete it.

Some organizations turn on a special option to prevent writing back to SASUSER, often because they have other standards regarding where your personal data and work project are placed. Other organizations don't even use SASUSER because of security concerns about shared data that may be restricted due to privacy and confidentiality policies.

You or your administrator will likely create numerous other libraries specific to your organization and needs. Some of these might be *read-only* (you can't save data sets there), and others allow you to write to them. Depending on your SAS configuration, you may be using the WORK or SASUSER library by default.

Organizations can create user- or administrator-created libraries that provide access to relational databases such as Oracle, Teradata, DB2, or SQL Server. These libraries let you seamlessly transfer data into and out of these databases at will. This ability is critical for companies because their key corporate data is often stored in these database systems.

Querying Your Way to Success

Of the many capabilities that SAS Enterprise Guide offers via SAS tasks, the Query Builder task is one of the most important for use across a wide array of users and applications. With the Query Builder task, you can

- ✔ Join data from separate data tables
- ✔ Filter data
- ✔ Sort data
- ✔ Create computed columns
- ✔ Summarize data
- ✔ Add dynamic run-time prompts to select filter criteria to apply
- ✔ Create basic listings
- ✔ Create output data sets from the selections made in the task

As you can see, the Query Builder task encompasses a broad range of functionality. The capability to access tables in a database, join them, and filter the results is often the first step in reporting or analysis. A simple example would be joining a sales history table with a products table to obtain a detailed sales and products table. You can also filter the sales data to a particular year and the products to a certain product line. Additionally, you may have several computed columns that compute the net sale price for each transaction based on the discount given and the full retail price.

When you master the basics of the Query Builder task, your success at accessing the data you need will know no limits! The following example touches on some of these features. For more in-depth coverage on working with your data, see Chapter 5.

Understanding all this talk of joining

Joining data is like getting married — bringing together two separate entities and making them one — except that joining data is a lot quicker and cheaper. When you have relevant data for a report or analysis in more than one table, you can merge that data by matching rows based on the columns they have in common so that all the relevant information is in one table. Examples of columns commonly used to join data tables are customer ID, date, product ID, product name, and location. Figure 3-1 shows a simple example of joining two tables. Here, the Students table is joined with the Grades table by the Student_ID column so that you have a unified table of student information and their grades.

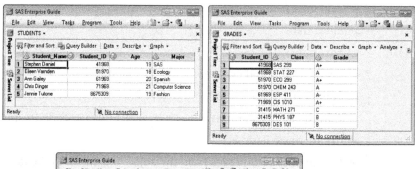

Figure 3-1: An example of a simple two-table join.

Joining data from multiple tables

To examine the power of the query task, follow these steps to see how you can join data sources:

1. **Launch SAS Enterprise Guide and create a new project.**

   If you need a refresher on how to create a new project, see Chapter 2.

2. **Choose File⇨Open⇨Data and click the Local Computer icon.**

3. **Navigate to the folder with the sample data files for SAS Enterprise Guide, and open the following data sets:**

   - **Candy_Customers**

   - **Candy_Products**

   - **Candy_Sales_History**

   - **Candy_Time_Periods**

   Remember that the sample data folder can be found at `C:\Program Files\SAS\EnterpriseGuide\4.2\Sample\Data`.

   Just as you can in Windows Explorer, you can select multiple items in an open dialog box by pressing Ctrl+click to select individual noncontiguous items or by pressing Shift+click at the beginning and end of a list of files to select a contiguous block.

   All the data sets open in your project; the last one opened appears in the data grid, as shown in Figure 3-2.

   If the Candy_Time_Periods data set does not appear in your data view, double-click its table name in the Project Tree to open it.

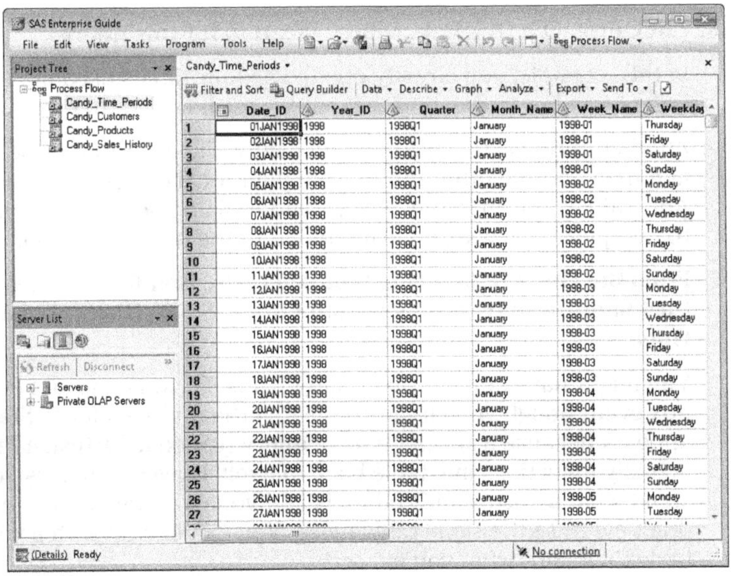

Figure 3-2:
Browsing the Candy data set via the data grid.

4. Click Query Builder from the toolbar above the data view.

The query task appears with the Candy_Time_Periods table already selected.

5. Click Add Tables.

The Open Data dialog box appears, as shown in Figure 3-3.

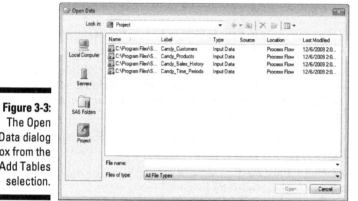

Figure 3-3:
The Open
Data dialog
box from the
Add Tables
selection.

6. Click Project as the data source location for this query.

In this example, you already opened all four tables used in the project before you began creating the query, which added them to the project.

Another option is to open only the Candy_Time_Periods table in Step 3 and then add the other tables from your local computer by using the Add Tables button in the Query Builder dialog box. When you add tables to the query this way, they are added to the project for you.

7. From the Open Data dialog box, select the first three tables (Candy_Customers, Candy_Products, and Candy_Sales_History) and then click Open.

You might have noticed that Candy_Time_Periods appears in this dialog box even though you already have it in the query (refer to Step 4). It appears because a special type of query (called a Cartesian Product) actually joins the same table back to itself! However, unless you understand what a Cartesian Product is and you're certain that you need it, don't ever use the same table twice. You can end up with a very large table that's not what you expect!

After clicking Open, you receive a warning message, as shown in Figure 3-4; but don't worry about this right now. The warning message is informing you that you have some work to do in the next window.

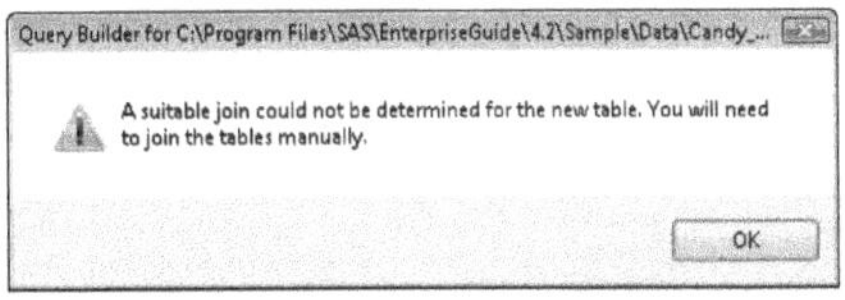

Figure 3-4:
For now,
don't worry
about this
suitable join
warning
message.

Query Builder for C:\Program Files\SAS\EnterpriseGuide\4.2\Sample\Data\Candy_...

⚠ A suitable join could not be determined for the new table. You will need to join the tables manually.

[OK]

8. **Click OK to dismiss the warning message.**

The Tables and Joins dialog box appears, and Candy_Products is auto-matically joined to Candy_Sales_History via the ProdID column. SAS Enterprise Guide automatically joins tables by columns with identical names because it assumes that identically named columns in different tables contain the same information. The connecting lines between the tables show the columns that will be used to join the various tables. You can exercise some control over the joins:

- If you don't like the auto-join feature, you can turn it off by choosing Tools⇨Options.

- You can easily delete joins by clicking the join connectors between the tables and pressing the Delete key.

9. **To add joins that weren't automatically determined based on identical column names, perform the following:**

a. **Drag the CustID column from the Candy_Customers table to the Customer column in the Candy_Sales_History table. When the Join Tables dialog box appears to confirm the join settings, click OK.**

b. **Drag the Date_ID column from the Candy_Time_Periods table to the Date column in the Candy_Sales_History table. Click OK.**

We cover more about join types in Chapter 5.

When you've added the joins, the Tables and Joins dialog box is similar to Figure 3-5. Note that we've arranged the tables in this figure to make it easier to see the join relationships.

You can also rearrange the table layout for easier reference in the Tables and Joins dialog box. Typically, you have one central table that the other tables join with. Putting the central table (often called the *fact table*) in the middle and the supporting tables (often called *dimension tables*) around it can make your join much simpler to understand at a glance. In our example, Candy_Sales_History is the fact table.

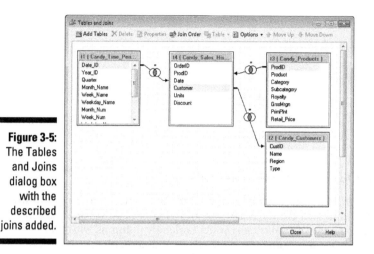

Figure 3-5:
The Tables
and Joins
dialog box
with the
described
joins added.

10. **Click the Close button to close the Tables and Joins dialog box.**

    Now you're back to the main dialog box for the Query Builder task. The table join details just added are a vital step that you should always perform when you build a new query with multiple tables. If you neglect this step with multiple tables in a query and one table unjoins the others, the application warns you about possible performance issues before it runs the query.

11. **From the main dialog box of the Query Builder task, select the variables that will be in the output table created by the query.**

    For this example, click and drag the following variables to the blank space on the Select Data tab labeled Drop a Column Here to Add It to the Query:

    - **Quarter, from Candy_Time_Periods**
    - **Name and Region, from Candy_Customers**
    - **Product and Retail_Price, from Candy_Products**
    - **Units and Discount, from Candy_Sales_History**

    When you're finished, the task looks like Figure 3-6.

12. **(Optional) To make the variable names in the output data set more meaningful, you can rename them. Here's how to rename the Name variable to Customer Name:**

    a. **Double-click the Name variable in the Select Data pane.**

       The Properties dialog box opens.

    b. **Type** Customer Name **in the Alias text box and then click OK.**

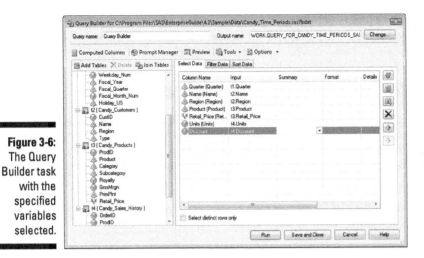

Figure 3-6:
The Query
Builder task
with the
specified
variables
selected.

13. **(Optional) To make the name of the output data set more meaningful, rename it. Here's how to rename the output data set to Quarterly_ Sales_Summary:**

   a. **In the upper-right corner of the Query Builder window, click the Change button (beside the Output Name field).**

      You can see this button in the upper-right corner of Figure 3-6. The Save File dialog box opens.

   b. **In the File name field, enter the new data set name** Quarterly_ Sales_Summary, **as shown in Figure 3-7.**

   c. **Click Save.**

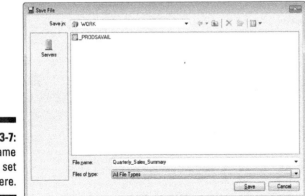

Figure 3-7:
Rename
a data set
here.

After your join is set the way you want it, you can create computed columns with your data, a topic discussed in the following section.

Creating computed columns

One of the most powerful features the Query Builder task offers is the capability to create computed columns based on your current needs. Computed columns allow you to create new variables from your data. For example, you can use a computed column to calculate net sales based on the gross sales and returns columns in your source data.

For the running example used here, you want to review the net sales amount for each record. The net sales amount can be expressed as

```
Net_Sale_Amount = Retail_Price x Units x (1-Discount)
```

To create the computed column Net_Sale_Amount (the left side of the preceding expression), do the following:

1. **Click the Computed Columns icon in the upper-left corner of the Query Builder task.**

   The Computed Columns dialog box appears.

2. **Click New to create a new computed column.**

   The New Computed Column Wizard appears.

3. **Click Advanced Expression, and then click Next.**

   The Advanced Expression Editor window appears, as shown in Figure 3-8.

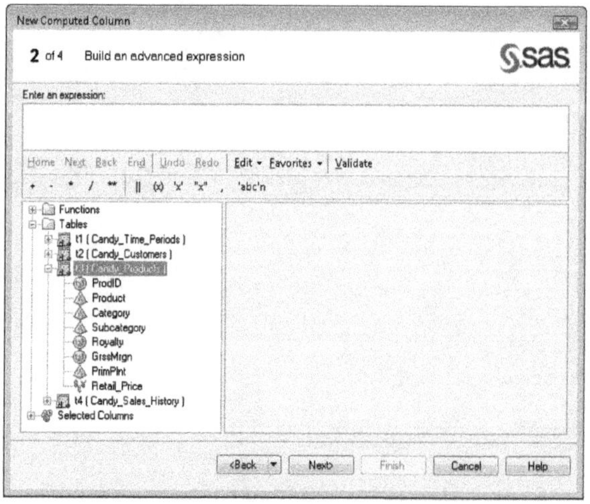

Figure 3-8: The Advanced Expression Editor awaits your input.

4. **In the list of tables in the bottom-left pane, double-click the Candy_ Products data set symbol to expand the list of variables in that table.**

5. **Double-click the Retail_Price variable.**

   Retail_Price appears in the Enter an Expression field.

6. **Click the single asterisk (*) multiplication button, which is just below the Enter an Expression field.**

   The multiplier symbol is added to the Enter an Expression field (see the result in Figure 3-9).

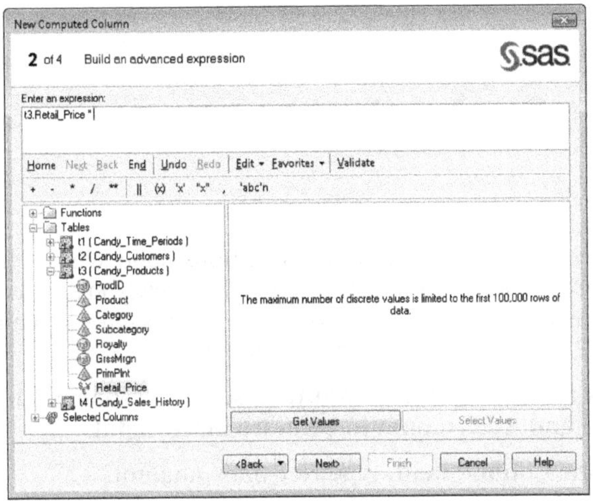

Figure 3-9:
The
Advanced
Expression
Editor
with the
net sales
amount
calculation
partially
completed.

At any time, you can click inside the Enter an Expression field and type or edit. You can also use the standard Windows copy and paste functions to rearrange your expression.

7. **In the list of tables, expand the Candy_Sales_History data set.**

8. **Complete the expression as follows:**

   a. **Double-click the Units variable to add it to the expression.**

   b. **Click the multiplier symbol (*).**

   c. **Click once in the Enter an Expression field and type (1-.**

      Type an open parenthesis, the number 1, and a hyphen.

   d. **In the tables list, add the Discount variable by double-clicking it.**

   e. **Type a closing parenthesis —) — at the end of the expression in the Enter an Expression field.**

See Figure 3-10 for the completed calculation.

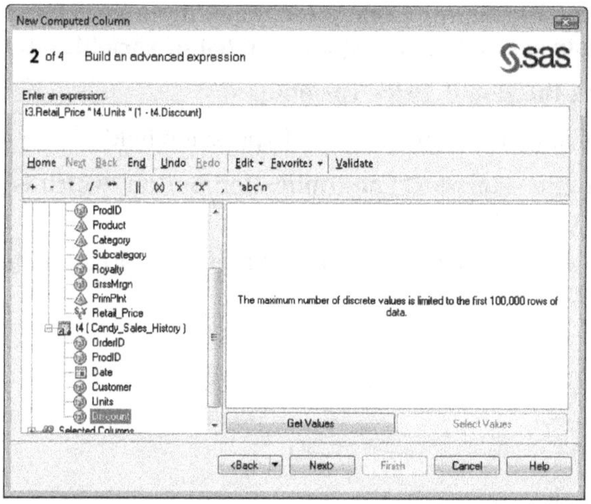

Figure 3-10:
The
Advanced
Expression
Editor
with the
completed
net sales
amount
calculation.

9. **Click Next.**

You are now at the Modify Additional Options page, which lets you refine the properties of this new column. The newly created computed column name defaults to a standard name: in this case, Calculation1, or Calculation2 if Calculation1 exists, and so on.

10. **The name Calculation1 is not intuitive, so we'll rename it by changing the Column and Alias names to be more meaningful:**

    a. **In the Column field, type** Net_Sale_Amount.

    b. **In the Alias field, type** Net_Sale_Amount.

With the changes so far, the Modify Additional Options page looks like Figure 3-11.

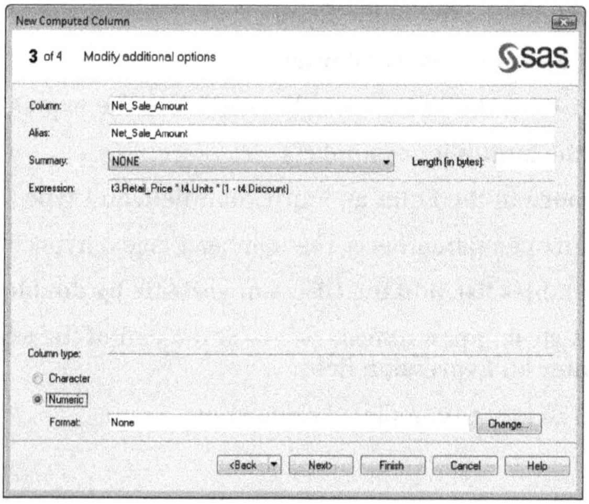

Figure 3-11:
The Modify
Additional
Options
page.

You may have noticed that the computed column has no format. But don't worry. In the following section, you find out how to format your computed columns.

Formatting your computed columns

Formats are an important concept to understand if you want to get the most out of your SAS reports and analyses. Data is typically stored as either a character value (for example, *New*) or a numeric value (for example, *18701*). A format can change data in many ways, from shortening how your data is represented, to changing the use of commas and decimal points for numbers, to recoding values from system codes to human intelligible words. Table 3-1 shows examples of the many formats available in SAS.

Table 3-1		SAS Formats	
Raw Storage Value	**Format Applied**	**What You See**	**Description**
New	$1.	N	The dollar sign means that this is a character variable, and the 1 shows the variable with just the first character.
New	$3.	New	Shows the variable with the first three characters.
New	$20.	New	Shows the variable with the first three characters; because there are only three characters, this is all you see.
New	$QUOTE5.	"New"	Allows five spaces of output and automatically adds double quotes to the raw value.
New	$MyTrans.	New York City	User-defined format that acts as a lookup for abbreviated city names; in this case, New translates to New York City, Ne2 might translate to New Haven, and so on.

(continued)

Table 3-1 *(continued)*

Raw Storage Value	Format Applied	What You See	Description
18701.5	5.	18702	The simplest numeric format; it adds no commas to your number.
18701.5	8.2	18701.50	Allows eight spaces of length and two decimal places to show more detail.
18701.5	4.	19E3	Allows only four spaces, so SAS shows a rounded version in scientific notation; 19 X 10^3, or 19,000, is the closest value it can display with the format specified.
18701.5	Best8.	18701.5	Best is a special SAS format that tries to use the precision in your data to determine the appropriate detail to display.
18701.5	Comma8.1	18,701.5	Adds a comma as the thousands separator and the decimal point with one level of precision.
18701.5	CommaX8.1	18.701,5	Adds decimal points as the thousands separator and commas with one level of precision (for European partners).
18701.5	Dollar10.2	$18,701.50	Uses standard American currency formatting with the dollar sign, commas as thousands separator, and decimal points.
18701.5	Dollar8.2	18701.50	Strips the dollar sign and the comma to show the numeric amount when not enough space exists to show the full currency default.

Raw Storage Value	Format Applied	What You See	Description
18701.5	MMDDYY10.	03/15/2011	One of many date formats; translates the number in the variable to the number of days from January 1st, 1960 and formats it as month/day/year.
18701.5	MMDDYY8.	03/15/11	Same as preceding entry but uses a two-digit year.
18701.5	ENGDFDWN8.	Tuesday	English word for the day of the week for this date.
18701.5	MMDDYY10.	01JAN60:05:11:42	One of many date time formats; translates the number in the variable to the number of seconds from January 1st, 1960 and formats it as month, day, year, hours, minutes, and seconds. This format assumes your data is in seconds, not days.

SAS enables you to change the display format of data values in the storage table (SAS data set) as an associated attribute of the column. If you need to see both the formatted and unformatted output, or if the data has not already been formatted for you, SAS allows you to format a column in a particular task for a particular application. As a continuation of adding a new computed column, follow these steps to format a column of data in SAS:

1. **Continuing from the preceding section (from the Modify Additional Options page), click the Change button next to the Format field.**

   The Formats dialog box opens, with the current selection set to None.

2. **Apply a U.S. Dollar currency format to the Net_Sale_Amount column:**

   a. **Click Currency in the Categories scroll box.**

   b. **Click DOLLARw.d in the Formats scroll box.**

   c. **Change the Overall Width from 6 to 12, as shown in Figure 3-12.**

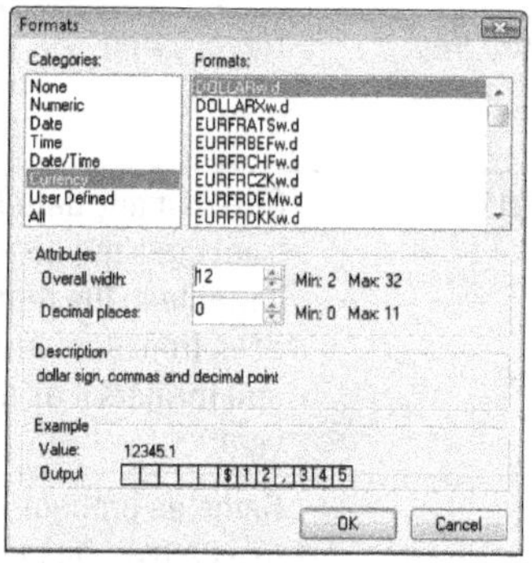

Figure 3-12:
The Formats
dialog box
with the
DOLLAR12.0
format
specified.

3. Click OK, and then click Next.

You see a summary of the computed column definition, as shown in
Figure 3-13.

4. Click Finish.

You see the list of computed columns that you've defined so far —
just one.

5. Click Close.

The new computed column is added to the Select Data list as an output
column.

6. Click Run.

Within a few seconds, the newly created data set Quarterly_Sales_
Summary opens, as shown in Figure 3-14. The Net_Sale_Amount
computed column appears as dollars with no decimal point, but the
detailed precision of the calculations has not been lost. This is simply
a function of the currently applied format. If you were to add all the
Net_Sale_Amount records, you would see that the column is calculated
based on the precise values.

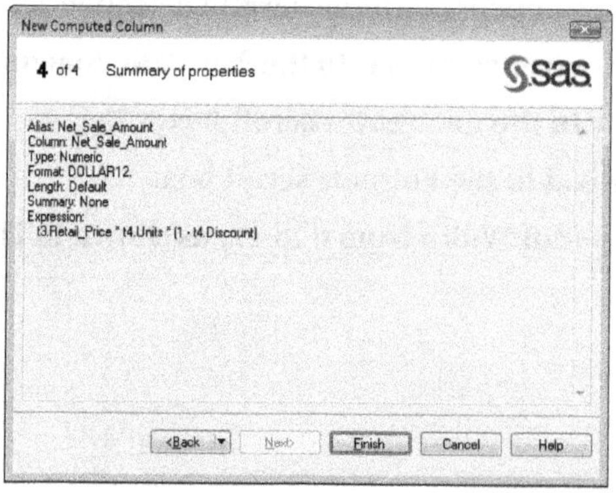

Figure 3-13:
The
summary
of the New
Computed
Column
Wizard.

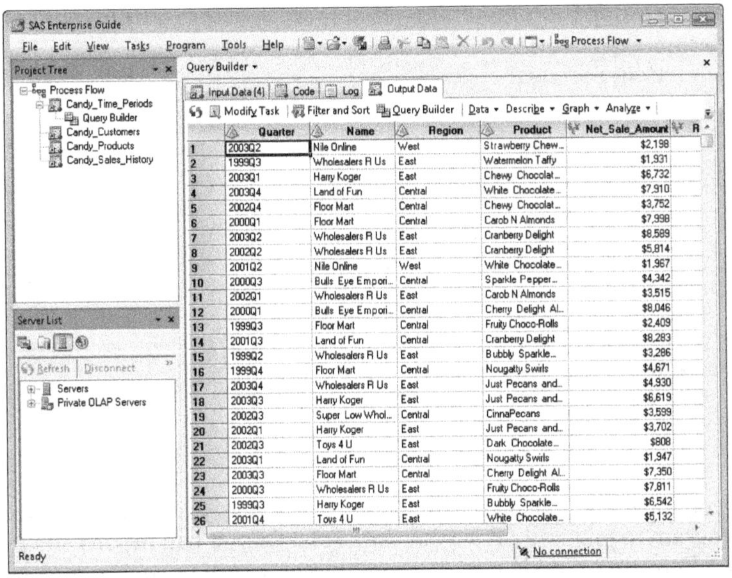

Figure 3-14:
The newly created quarterly sales summary data set.

Getting your hands dirty with SQL

Like all tasks in SAS Enterprise Guide, the Query Builder task creates a SAS program to do its work. In the previous steps in this section, you didn't see the program, and you certainly don't have to understand the program to benefit from the output.

But if you're the sort of person who likes to peek under the hood, don't be afraid to click the Code tab while you're viewing the Query Builder results. You'll see the SAS program that was submitted to SAS. (If you're really brave, you can also click the Log tab and see how the program performed.)

The Query Builder task generates an industry-standard dialect called *SQL* (*structured query language*). Here are the SQL statements that represent the work that we covered in this section. The SQL section is wrapped in the SAS SQL procedure (PROC SQL) so that SAS can process it.

```
LIBNAME Candy "C:\Program Files\SAS\EnterpriseGuide\4.2\Sample\Data";

PROC SQL;
CREATE TABLE WORK.Quarterly_Sales_Summary AS
SELECT t1.Quarter,
    t2.Name AS Customer_Name,
    t2.Region,
    t3.Product,
```

```
/* Net_Sale_Amount calculation*/
  (t3.Retail_Price * t4.Units * (1 - t4.Discount))
    FORMAT=DOLLAR12. AS Net_Sale_Amount,
t3.Retail_Price,
t4.Units,
t4.Discount
FROM
/* Tables to join */
Candy.Candy_Products AS t3,
Candy.Candy_Sales_History AS t4,
Candy.Candy_Customers AS t2,
Candy.Candy_Time_Periods AS t1
/* Join conditions */
WHERE (t3.ProdID = t4.ProdID
  AND t2.CustID = t4.Customer
  AND t1.Date_ID = t4.Date);
QUIT;
```

If you have SQL skills and you want to practice, you can create your own SAS program to join and filter your data sets. Or you can modify the program that SAS Enterprise Guide generates to suit your own purpose. See Chapter 16 to discover how to "take the wheel" and write your own programs.

Many long-time SAS programmers are not as familiar with SQL as they are with another mainstay in the SAS language, the DATA step. So why does SAS Enterprise Guide generate SQL statements instead of DATA step statements? It turns out that SQL is more efficient than DATA step code when your data resides in third-party databases, such as Oracle or Teradata, because SAS can push most of the intense processing to these powerful database servers. With large data sources, efficiency is paramount (just ask any database administrator). Using SQL can ensure the most efficient processing, and the resulting output is the same.

Summarizing the Data

SAS Enterprise Guide presents you with many task choices to summarize and aggregate your data. Table 3-2 presents choices by task. As you can see, almost any summary statistic you can imagine is available.

Table 3-2		The Many Ways to Summarize Data in SAS				
Task	Menu	Output Data Set Option?	Printable Report Option?	Statistics Available	Optional Graphs?	Notes
Query Builder	Data	Yes — default behavior	Yes — optional	Sum, average, count, distinct count, N, max, min, range, number missing, variance, standard error, and about 20 others	No	Statistics are calculated for each distinct value of your summary group. If your data source is a relational database, the calculations are performed on the database before being sent to your SAS Server session.
List Report Wizard	Describe	No	Yes	Sum, mean, mode, min, max, percent sum, range, variance, and others	No	This task supports totals and sub-totals, and also "across" variables to categorize summary calculations.
Rank	Data	Yes — default behavior	No	Ranked order of records, percentile ranks of records, decile ranking of records, quar-tile	No	A specialized task for creating output data sets that have ranked a variable with one of the specified methods for further analysis, report-ing, or graphing.

(continued)

Table 3-2 (continued)

Task	Menu	Output Data Set Option?	Printable Report Option?	Statistics Available	Optional Graphs?	Notes
				ranking of records, ntiles ranking of records, percentages, and six advanced ranking methods		
List Data	Describe	No	Yes — default behavior	Totals and subtotals	No	The most limited task in terms of statistics available.
Summary Statistics	Describe	Yes — optional behavior	Yes — default behavior, can be suppressed	Mean, standard deviation, standard error, variance, minimum, maximum, range, sum, weighted sum, N, N missing, median, quartiles, percentiles, and five advanced statistics	Yes — histograms and box and whisker plots	This is one of the easier to use general-purpose summary tasks. This task offers some of the most common statistics for quick review.

Task	Menu	Output Data Set Option?	Printable Report Option?	Statistics Available	Optional Graphs?	Notes
Distribution Analysis	Describe	Yes — optional behavior	Yes — default behavior, can be suppressed	Mean, standard deviation, standard error, variance, minimum, maximum, mode, range, sum, weighted sum, N, N missing, median, quartiles, percentiles, and many advanced statistics for checking goodness of fit with various statistical distributions — normal, lognormal, Exponential, Weibull, Beta, Gamma, and Kernel	Yes — histograms, probability, quantiles, box and whisker, and stem and leaf plots	A specialized task for graphically and statistically checking the fit of a variable to a user-specified statistical distribution. This task is often used to determine whether data needs to be standardized to fit a specified distribution before further statistical analysis.

(continued)

Table 3-2 (continued)

Task	Menu	Output Data Set Option?	Printable Report Option?	Statistics Available	Optional Graphs?	Notes
Characterize Data	Describe	Yes — default behavior, can be suppressed	Yes — default behavior, can be suppressed	Count, N, N missing, total, minimum, mean, median, maximum, and standard mean	Yes — default behavior, can be suppressed, bar charts	A specialized wizard that analyzes every variable in a data set or every data set in a library and prints a concise report and analysis of every variable for quick data review.
Summary Tables	Describe	Yes — optional behavior	Yes — default behavior	Mean, standard deviation, standard error, variance, minimum, maximum, range, sum, weighted sum, N, N missing, median, quartiles, percentiles, and other advanced and table statistics	No	A task focused on creating multidimensional tabular reports. One of the most complex tasks to master in SAS Enterprise Guide.
One Way Frequencies	Describe	Yes — optional behavior	Yes — default behavior, can be suppressed	Frequencies, percentages of total, cumulative percentages, and Chi-square and binomial proportions tests	Yes — horizontal and vertical bar charts	A specialized task for creating one-way frequency (incidence) tables of your data.

Task	Menu	Output Data Set Option?	Printable Report Option?	Statistics Available	Optional Graphs?	Notes
Table Analysis	Describe	Yes — optional behavior	Yes — default behavior, can be suppressed	Frequencies, percentages of total, cumulative percentages, many table statistics such as Chi-square, exact p-values, CMH, Jonckheere-Terpstra, Cochran-Armitage, and various scores	No	A specialized task for creating n-way frequency (incidence) tables of your data. Has a plethora of statistical options available.
Various graph tasks	Graph	No	Yes — default behavior	Frequency, cumulative frequency, percentage, cumulative percentage, mean, sum, median, and percentiles depending on chart type	N/A	The graph tasks automatically aggregate your data for the graph type selected. They typically provide several statistical choices depending on the chart type in use.

For many customers of SAS Enterprise Guide, the most commonly used task for summarizing data is the Summary Statistics task. In the following two examples, you use this task and a few others to create some useful summaries of the Quarterly_Sales_Summary data you created in the preceding section.

With SAS, you can easily summarize every variable in a data set or summarize only specific numeric variables. The following steps use the Query_Sales_Summary example to summarize every variable in a data set:

1. **Choose Tasks⇨Describe⇨Characterize Data.**

   The Characterize Data Task Wizard appears with Quarterly_Sales_Summary as the input data source, as shown in Figure 3-15.

   If you want to use additional data sets as input to the task, click Add. This task is able to summarize one or more data sets at once in one concise report.

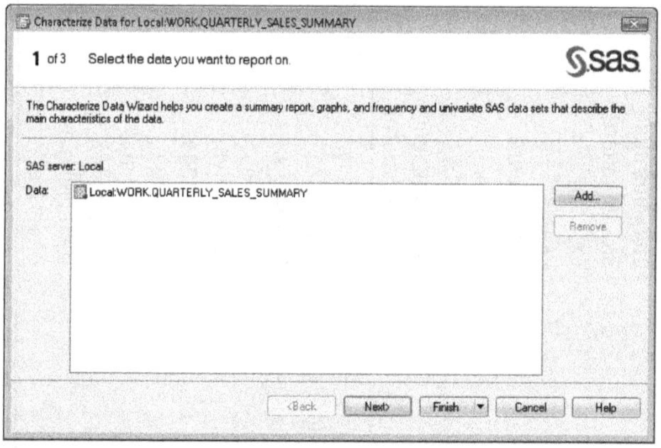

Figure 3-15: The Characterize Data Wizard.

2. **Click Next.**

3. **Deselect the option for generating SAS Data Sets.**

4. **Click Finish.**

   The task runs, and the summary report opens in a few seconds, as shown in Figure 3-16.

   The report automatically creates sections based on the various data types for each variable in the data set: character, numeric, currency, and date. These are presented in frequency count and numeric variable summary tables for each variable. Using this task is one of the quickest ways to summarize many variables.

Here's something to keep in mind when you use the Characterize Data task: Because it analyzes every record and every variable, if you have very large tables or have selected many tables, running the task may be time-consuming.

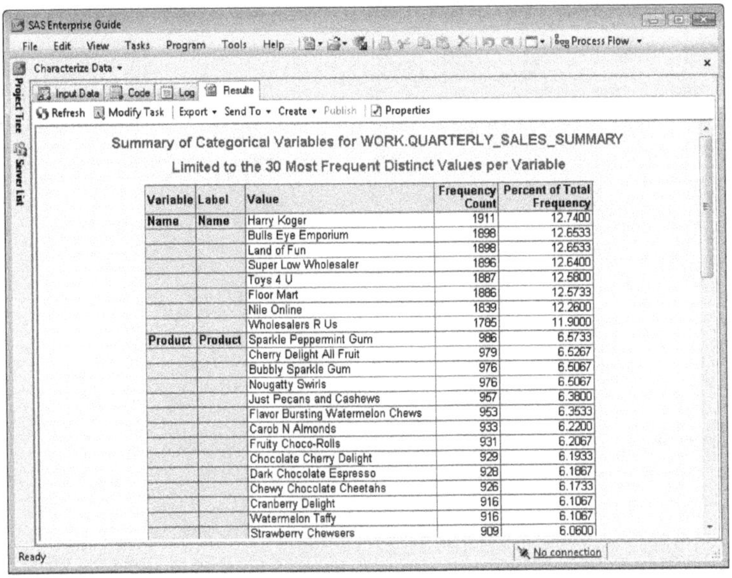

Variable	Label	Value	Frequency Count	Percent of Total Frequency
Name	Name	Harry Koger	1911	12.7400
		Bulls Eye Emporium	1898	12.6533
		Land of Fun	1898	12.6533
		Super Low Wholesaler	1896	12.6400
		Toys 4 U	1887	12.5800
		Floor Mart	1886	12.5733
		Nile Online	1839	12.2600
		Wholesalers R Us	1785	11.9000
Product	Product	Sparkle Peppermint Gum	986	6.5733
		Cherry Delight All Fruit	979	6.5267
		Bubbly Sparkle Gum	976	6.5067
		Nougatty Swirls	976	6.5067
		Just Pecans and Cashews	957	6.3800
		Flavor Bursting Watermelon Chews	953	6.3533
		Carob N Almonds	933	6.2200
		Fruity Choco-Rolls	931	6.2067
		Chocolate Cherry Delight	929	6.1933
		Dark Chocolate Espresso	928	6.1867
		Chewy Chocolate Cheetahs	926	6.1733
		Cranberry Delight	916	6.1067
		Watermelon Taffy	916	6.1067
		Strawberry Chewsers	909	6.0600

Figure 3-16: The Characterize Data Wizard report.

Summarizing specific numeric variables

As mentioned at the beginning of this section, SAS lets you focus on only the variables you need to evaluate from a data set instead of summarizing every variable. Follow these steps to summarize specific numeric variables in the Quarterly_Sales_Summary data set:

1. **Choose Tasks⇨Describe⇨Summary Statistics.**

   The Summary Statistics task appears.

2. **Drag Net_Sale_Amount from the Data pane to the Analysis Variables role. Then drag Region to the Classification Variables role, as shown in Figure 3-17.**
3. **In the far left pane, select Percentiles. Then select the Median Statistic check box.**
4. **In the far left pane, select Plots to show the Plots page, and then select the Box and Whisker check box.**

5. Click Run.

The analysis runs, and the summary report opens in a few seconds. The report is shown in Figure 3-18.

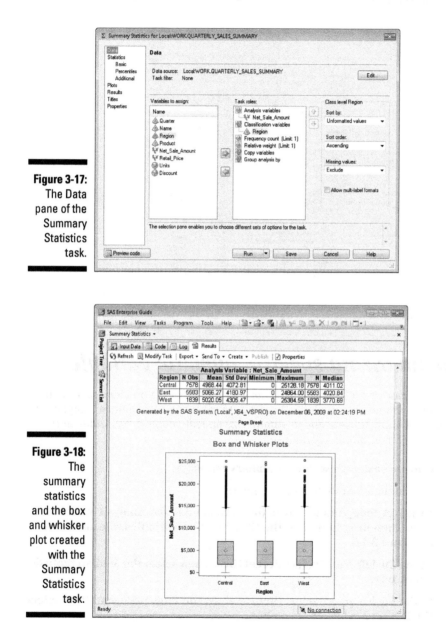

Figure 3-17:
The Data pane of the Summary Statistics task.

Figure 3-18:
The summary statistics and the box and whisker plot created with the Summary Statistics task.

The Summary Statistics task produces a report with a table, so that you can see the precise numbers that represent the calculated statistics. The task also produces a chart, which makes it easy to visualize the characteristics of these statistics.

In the box and whisker plot for this report, you can see how the data is distributed in quartiles, with the line near the center of the box representing the median value. The median for the West region is slightly lower than the other two regions. The values for Median in the table show you exactly how much lower. Also, the dots above the top line (above $15,000 or so) represent outlier values. What does that mean? We cover more about the field of analytics in Chapters 8 and 9, but in a nutshell we can interpret this report as saying: We have a lot of high-dollar transactions, but they are not the norm. By far, most of our Net Sale Amounts fall under $10,000.

Building a Forecast

SAS Enterprise Guide adds the capability to create forecasts to your arsenal of reports and presentations. Although forecasting is probably one of the easiest areas of statistical analyses to understand, it's also one of the easiest to oversimplify, resulting in answers that are just plain wrong. To ensure that you have a solid grasp of forecasting principles, be sure to read Chapter 9.

Forecasting can take on several levels of complexity. For example:

✔ Use the data on the historic variable of interest as the sole predictor based on the historic trend of just this variable (for example, net sales for candy)

✔ Add additional variables of relevance and their historic effect on the variable of interest (for example, marketing spent and monthly weather conditions)

The Basic Forecasting task uses the simple single variable approach to obtain a forecast for your variable of interest. Follow these steps using the SAS Enterprise Guide sample data set beer_sales_minimal (found in C:\Program Files\SAS\EnterpriseGuide\4.2\Sample\Data, just like the candy data sets earlier in this chapter):

1. **Open the beer_sales_minimal data set, as shown in Figure 3-19.**

   Note that all the tasks that we used earlier in this chapter are displayed in the Project Tree pane. The beer_sales_minimal data set has several years of monthly beer sales data for a fictional company.

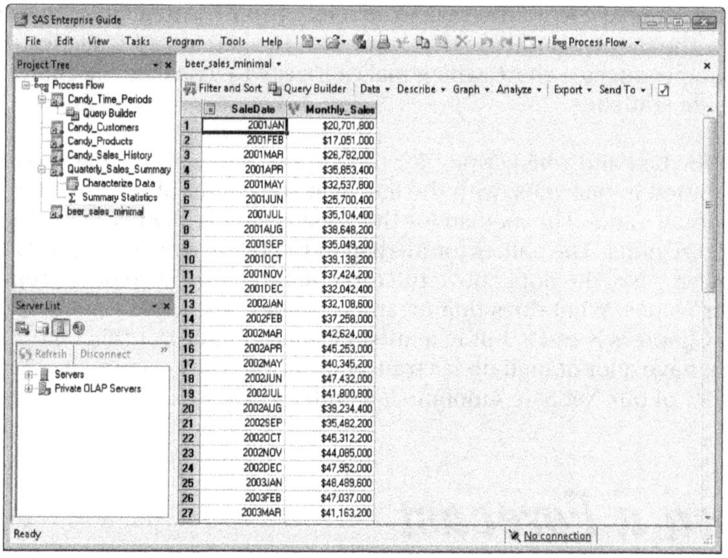

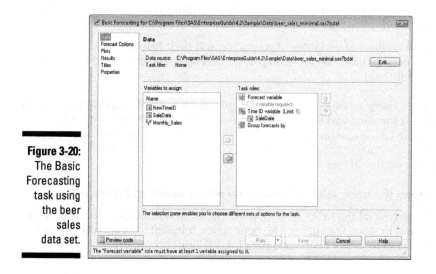

Figure 3-19:
The beer sales data set.

2. **From the toolbar in the data view, choose Analyze⇨Time Series⇨Basic Forecasting.**

   The Basic Forecasting task appears, as shown in Figure 3-20. Note that the task automatically added the date variable — SaleDate — to the Time ID Variable role. It also created the new task-specific variable NewTimeID, which you can ignore in this example.

Figure 3-20:
The Basic Forecasting task using the beer sales data set.

3. Drag Monthly_Sales from the list of variables to the Forecast Variable role.

4. In the left pane, select Forecast Options. Then do the following:

   a. Change the drop-down selection for Forecasting Method from Stepwise Autoregressive to Winters Additive Method.

   b. Change the drop-down selection for Time Interval Between Observations from Number of Units to Monthly.

   c. Change the drop-down selection for Seasonal Cycle Length from Number of Intervals to Three Months.

   See Figure 3-21 for all the settings in this step. For further details on forecasting, see Chapter 9.

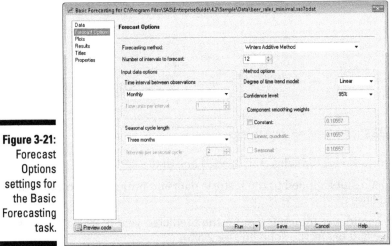

Figure 3-21:
Forecast
Options
settings for
the Basic
Forecasting
task.

5. Click Run.

   The forecast runs, and the forecast plot opens in a few seconds, as shown in Figure 3-22.

6. To save the work you performed in this chapter, choose File⇨Save Project As and then save your work to either your local computer or your SAS server.

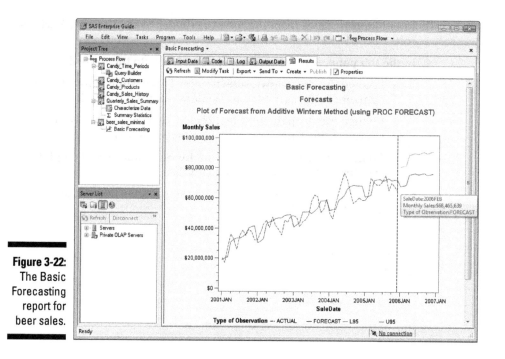

Figure 3-22:
The Basic
Forecasting
report for
beer sales.

Figure 3-22 shows you several things:

- ✔ Historic values for sales (the dashed line to the left of 2006)

- ✔ Model results applied to the historic data and projected into 2006 (the solid line)

- ✔ 95% confidence intervals just for the predicted year of 2006 (the lines above and below the solid line for 2006)

You can quickly see that the model appears to match up with the historic data pretty well. However, because you use only historic sales as a predictor of future sales, the confidence intervals are wide for the 2006 forecasts (from $55 million to $81 million for 2006/01.) This implies that we can probably improve the accuracy of the forecast by adding other variables — such as average high temperature and marketing dollars spent. Still, you can obtain some insight into what next year might look like. After all, this is just the basic forecast, which is far more than you get with many other business intelligence tools.

Part II
Gathering Data and Presenting Information

The 5th Wave   By Rich Tennant

"And tell David to come in out of the hall. I found a way to adjust our project budget estimate."

In this part . . .

In this part, you see how you can pick up spare data that you find from almost anywhere and make it usable in SAS. After you have a hold on the data, you can begin "massaging" it. That might sound like a treat, especially from the data's point of view, but really it's all about getting data into a usable form that's suitable for analysis and reports.

Every data source has a story that it's itching to tell. Simple listings, summarizations, and cross-tab reports begin to tease apart that story. And graphs? Well, when you do graphs right, they can make your data sing.

Chapter 4

Accessing Data: Oh, the Choices!

The fact that SAS can meet just about any of your reporting and analysis needs is of little use if you can't quickly and efficiently access your data wherever it exists. SAS has the broadest set of data access options available from any business intelligence or analytic product. Whether your data is in a Microsoft Excel spreadsheet, a relational database, or a legacy location such as a mainframe text file, you can access and use it as a source for your data reports and analyses.

SAS offers two approaches to accessing data:

✔ Opening a local data file or connecting to a data source from your local PC and moving it to your SAS server

✔ Accessing the data source directly from your SAS server

Using your local PC as a conduit to opening your data is more convenient than accessing the data directly from the server; but it is also a slower method and not intended for accessing large data sources. *Large* is a relative term, but any source with more than 10,000 records (also referred to as *rows, observations,* or *data points*) of data can probably be considered large for this purpose. Thus, using SAS server connections to your data sources is much more efficient than accessing data from your PC and is therefore the preferred way to access data sources that you use frequently. In this chapter, we present your data access options as well as points to consider with each one.

Accessing the Data Hidden on Your PC: Microsoft Excel, Microsoft Access, and Text Files

Using applications such as Excel and Access to manage important data is common in almost every organization, regardless of whether the IT department approves such activities. IT groups frown on the use of these products to manage important data for many valid reasons:

- ✔ **Undocumented data management methods:** People often build various rules into their local spreadsheets or databases that can vary significantly from those in the corporate systems, resulting in different results when using various sources.

- ✔ **Systems may not be backed up on a regular basis:** Although your local PC may be backed up, do you keep an audit of the transactions?

- ✔ **Isolation from central naming schemes:** For example, one Excel spreadsheet might define net profit differently than another.

- ✔ **Privacy and security concerns:** Excel passwords are notoriously easy to break. Don't delude yourself into thinking that they secure your spreadsheet.

Errors can occur quite easily in applications such as Excel and Access because these applications lack the centrally maintained, automated data integrity checking commonly available in relational databases.

Despite the potential problems just listed, users often have valid reasons for maintaining their own personal databases. For example, you can start and complete some short-term projects more quickly with Excel or Access. You also may decide to use Excel as a staging area before loading the final results of a subset of the overall project into the centralized corporate system. The good news is that SAS can easily access, manage, and analyze the data from these sources at will. Here are the locally stored PC file types that SAS Enterprise Guide can import:

- ✔ SAS data sets on your PC
- ✔ SAS views of data on your PC
- ✔ Microsoft Excel worksheets
- ✔ Microsoft Access tables
- ✔ dBase tables
- ✔ Lotus 1-2-3
- ✔ Paradox database tables

✔ Text files (fixed-width, tab-delimited, and comma-delimited)

✔ HTML documents

✔ Files from other analytical products such as JMP (from SAS), SPSS, and Stata

SAS Enterprise Guide leverages the vendor-specific data providers automatically installed with your relevant data source application (for example, Excel or Access) for each data source to optimize the accuracy of your data import. For example, if you use the local import functionality of SAS Enterprise Guide with an Excel spreadsheet, Microsoft Excel native capabilities are automatically called to acquire the appropriate translation method for converting the data into SAS data sets.

SAS Enterprise Guide translates your data like this:

1. The spreadsheet (we assume you're using Excel) is converted into a specially delimited text file (typically consisting of columns of data separated by commas called a *comma-delimited* file).

2. SAS Enterprise Guide copies this text file to your SAS server.

3. SAS imports your data based on definitions extracted in the process (from Excel, in this scenario).

SAS Enterprise Guide performs this data translation service as a default behavior. But it's possible that your SAS server is equipped with the capabilities to read these data files in their native format, if you have a product called SAS/ ACCESS Interface to PC File Formats. When your SAS server has this capability installed and configured, it can be more efficient to move the data file (for example, the XLS file) to the SAS server and allow SAS to do most of the work using the SAS IMPORT procedure. If SAS/ACCESS is available when you import your data, the Import Data Wizard in SAS Enterprise Guide will offer it as an option.

Data storage and SAS Enterprise Guide projects

SAS Enterprise Guide offers many ways to access your relevant data. As a rule, you never embed and store data in your SAS Enterprise Guide project. Instead, SAS Enterprise Guide stores the needed information on how to connect to your data source in the future. Any data changed using the native table editor in SAS Enterprise Guide is immediately written to the data table source, assuming that you have write permissions to the data source.

The conversion and copying processes can be slow when using large sources, so consider how large your data is before importing it directly with SAS Enterprise Guide. As mentioned earlier, *large* is a relative term, but anything with more than 10,000 rows is large for our purposes.

Importing an Excel workbook

Importing data from most applications is easy and the process is similar regardless of the type of document you're importing from. For this reason, we won't waste pages discussing how to import each file type; instead, this section shows you how to import from one of the most popular spreadsheet formats: Microsoft Excel. If you want to play around with other file formats later, SAS Enterprise Guide includes many sample files in the sample directory (typically `C:\Program Files\SAS\EnterpriseGuide\4.2\ Sample\Data` if your installation used the standard directory) for you to import. The sample files include Access databases and text files. The process for importing other file types is similar to the process outlined in this section, with slightly different functionality depending on the file type.

Here's an example of importing data from a local Excel spreadsheet for use with SAS:

1. **Choose File➪Import Data.**

   The Open dialog box appears, as shown in Figure 4-1.

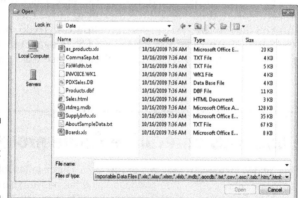

Figure 4-1: Start importing data here.

2. **Click the Local Computer icon.**

   You can now navigate the standard Windows file system.

3. **Navigate to the SAS Enterprise Guide sample data folder (`C:\Program Files\SAS\EnterpriseGuide\4.2\Sample\Data`), select the `SupplyInfo.xls` file, and then click Open.**

As we mention at the beginning of this section, many sample files are available for importing from this directory, including Access databases and text files. Feel free to try these later; the process is similar with slightly different functionality, depending on the file type.

The Import Data Wizard appears, as shown in Figure 4-2. The first page allows you to confirm your data source and the output data destination. The output will go to your default SAS server (if you have more than one) and the default output SAS library. If you want to target a different SAS server or library, now is the time to make those changes. In this example, we're sticking with the default values.

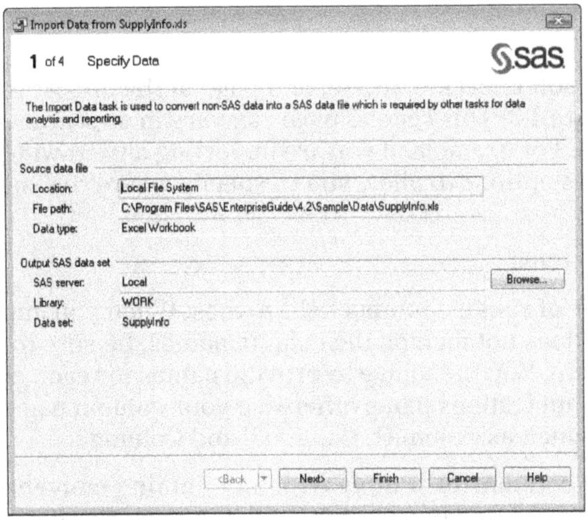

Figure 4-2:
The opening page of the Import Data Wizard.

4. **Click Next.**

The Select Data Source page appears, as shown in Figure 4-3. The Suppliers worksheet is selected by default.

If Microsoft Excel is installed on your PC, a status window might appear briefly with the message "Starting Microsoft Excel." When SAS Enterprise Guide imports a Microsoft Excel file, it uses your local installation of Microsoft Excel to determine attributes of the data in the spreadsheets. This approach yields the most accurate results to guide you in later steps of the wizard. If you don't have Microsoft Excel installed, don't worry; SAS Enterprise Guide can still determine the basic attributes of the data and import almost any spreadsheet.

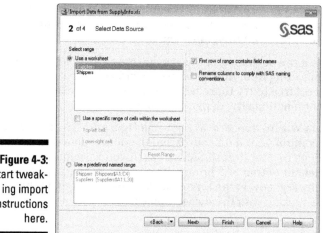

Figure 4-3:
Start tweaking import instructions here.

For this Microsoft Excel file, the second page of the Import Data Wizard looks like Figure 4-3. This second page can vary in appearance for different data types. For example, if you are importing a fixed-width text file, this page offers options to allow you to specify where the column breaks should occur.

Note these options:

- **First row of range contains field names:** When you import a file that does not include the column names, be sure to deselect this option. You then have to provide names for each column in the Column Options pane; otherwise your column names will be generic, such as Column1, Column2, and Column3.

- **Rename columns to comply with SAS naming conventions:** Spreadsheet data often contains column names that contain spaces or special characters (such as "Profit & Loss"). SAS can handle these names without a problem, but the SAS programming syntax for referencing these names is clunky. If you know that you want to use this data in a SAS program later, you might want to select this check box (to turn "Profit & Loss" into something like "profit_loss").

5. **Click Next.**

   The Define Field Attributes page that appears (see Figure 4-4) is where you typically spend most of your time tweaking import definitions. The Inc selector (short for "Include/Exclude") is useful when you are paring large data files of unneeded variables. For this example, you don't need to adjust any SAS Enterprise Guide selected details.

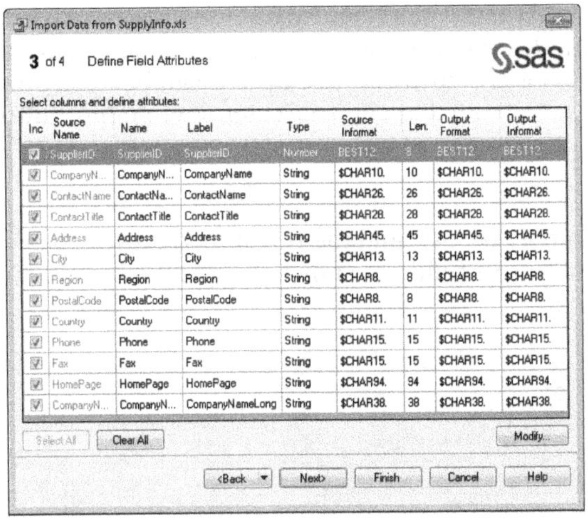

Figure 4-4:
Tweak
more import
instructions
here.

You can adjust the properties of any data columns from this page. To change the property of an individual column (for example, Name), simply click the current value in the list and provide a different value. If you want to adjust the properties for a range of columns (for example, to change the Output Format for several columns), hold the Shift or Ctrl key as you click each column. Then click Modify. A Field Attributes dialog box appears, and you can change the common attributes to a new value that applies to all selected columns.

6. Click Next.

The Advanced Options page appears. We don't need to change any advanced options for this example.

The Advanced Options page offers just three options, each of which has a significant effect on how SAS Enterprise Guide generates the SAS program to import your data. Here are brief descriptions of the options and their effects:

- **Embed the data within the generated SAS code:** Select this box to see the actual data values included in the SAS program (using a `DATALINES` statement). By default, this option is not selected, and the data values are included in a separate text-based file that you don't see in your project.

- **Import the data using SAS/ACCESS Interface to PC Files whenever possible:** This option tells SAS Enterprise Guide to use the `IMPORT` procedure if available on your SAS server, as described earlier in this section.

- **Remove characters that can cause transmission errors:** If you work with data in primarily one language, you will probably never need this option. However, this option can be handy for coercing data values encoded in one character set to import into SAS using a different character set.

7. **Click Finish.**

   The data set import occurs, and the resulting data set opens automatically in SAS Enterprise Guide as shown in Figure 4-5.

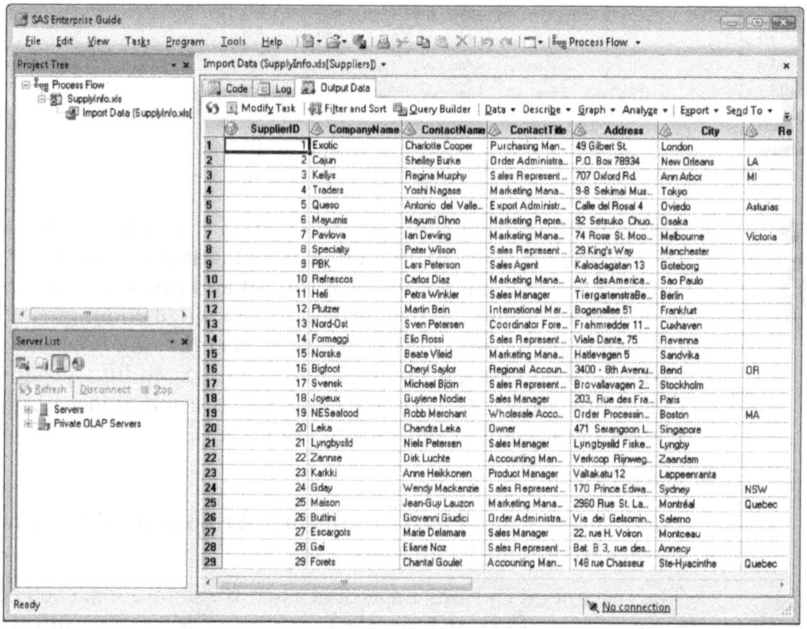

Figure 4-5:
The data imported from Microsoft Excel, now in SAS.

Accessing your data with OLE DB and ODBC

As we mention earlier in this chapter, SAS Enterprise Guide takes full advantage of the varied data sources accessible from a PC. The last section discussed using SAS to import data from your PC to the SAS server. Following are two common methods for connecting to local and remote data sources:

- **ODBC (Open Database Connectivity):** This method is a standard means for accessing data from multiple data sources from a variety of software products.

✔ **OLE DB (Object Linking and Embedding for Databases):** This newer technology from Microsoft attempts to extend ODBC capabilities to various nonrelational databases and spreadsheet formats that otherwise could not be accessed with ODBC.

In this section, you use your local PC-based ODBC and OLE DB data connections to retrieve the data from your PC and automatically send the data to the SAS server. Both technologies are commonly used to access various databases such as Oracle, DB2, or SQL server. If an ODBC driver or OLE DB provider is available for your data source, SAS can access it and use it via SAS Enterprise Guide. Hundreds of data sources are accessible using these two technologies.

SAS Enterprise Guide provides the capability to use local ODBC or OLE DB connections for convenience in accessing smaller or infrequently accessed data sources. When you use native SAS Enterprise Guide access to these data sources (instead of SAS server-based SAS/ACCESS Interface to ODBC or SAS/ACCESS Interface to OLE DB), importing processes can be much slower than reasonable for very large data sources. The reason for this is simple: SAS Enterprise Guide first reads the data table results from your database to your PC and then must transfer the data table to your SAS server as a data set to allow your SAS analysis to occur. Therefore, we recommend limiting use of this feature to small tables — 10,000 rows or less. Although using very large tables will work, you could wait a long time. (Bring your knitting.) See Chapter 15 for more information on how to set up data sources for efficient access.

Importing an Access database table with ODBC

ODBC data sources can be local files or remote databases on other PCs or servers. ODBC drivers that you configure to access various data sources provide an easy and consistent way to access the desired data through one configuration to multiple applications, including SAS. In this example, we use the sample Access database to demonstrate how you access an ODBC data source. (Note that you can use the Import Data Wizard to read this same data source; we're using this only to illustrate the ODBC steps.)

1. **Choose File⇨Open⇨ODBC.**

   The Performance Warning dialog box appears. (Now you can't say you weren't warned.)

2. **Click OK to dismiss the Performance Warning dialog box.**

   The Select Data Source dialog box appears, as shown in Figure 4-6.

3. **Click New to define a new ODBC data source.**

4. **In the Create New Data Source Wizard that appears, select Microsoft Access Driver (*.mdb) as your driver type and then click Next.**

5. **For the file data source, type a meaningful name, such as** SAS Dummies Example.

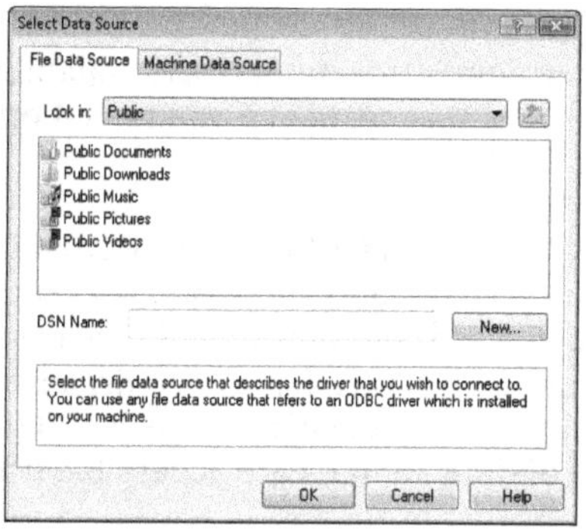

Figure 4-6:
The ODBC
Select Data
Source
dialog box.

6. **Click Next, and then click Finish.**

   The ODBC Microsoft Access Setup dialog box appears, as shown in Figure 4-7.

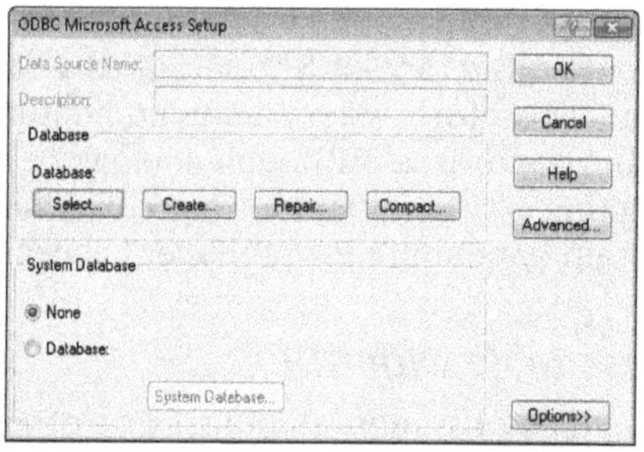

Figure 4-7:
The ODBC
Microsoft
Access
Setup
dialog box.

7. **Click Select.**

8. **In the Select Database dialog box that appears, navigate to and select the file that you want. Click OK.**

   For this example, navigate to the supplied sample data directory supplied by SAS Enterprise Guide and click the stdreg.mdb file.

9. **Click OK to close the ODBC Microsoft Access Setup dialog box.**

10. **Click OK to close the Select Data Source dialog box.**

    The Open Tables dialog box appears, as shown in Figure 4-8.

11. **Select the tables you want. For this example, select the following check boxes to make a report of course enrollment by instructor:**

    • **Course**

    • **Enrollment**

    • **Instructor**

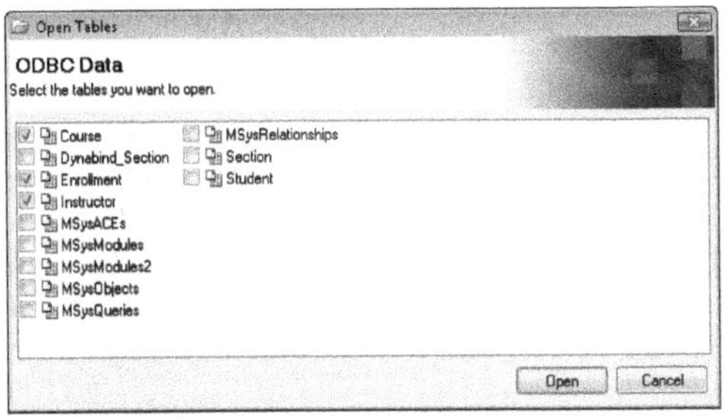

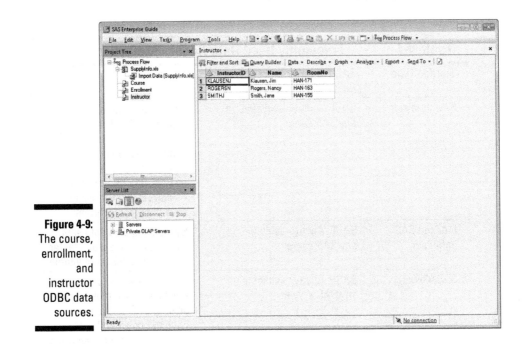

Figure 4-8:
Select
tables here.

12. Click Open.

The three tables open in your project, as shown in Figure 4-9. You can use these tables as input to tasks and wizards in your project. When you use them with a task in SAS Enterprise Guide, they are converted into SAS data sets just prior to the analysis task running. You won't be aware of this conversion occurring or see the SAS data set that is created because this conversion happens behind the scenes every time you access one of these tables. The conversion is performed each time you access one of these tables because your source file can change at any time.

Figure 4-9:
The course,
enrollment,
and
instructor
ODBC data
sources.

Importing an Access database table with OLE DB

Importing an Access database table by using OLE DB is similar to using ODBC except that you use an OLE DB provider to access your data source. To configure an OLE DB data source, consult the documentation included with your OLE DB provider. OLE DB is a newer technology developed by Microsoft that expands on the capabilities of ODBC. Whether you choose OLE DB or ODBC to access your data is not a critical point in this chapter. Use the one that is available for your data; even better, use whichever one is already installed on your PC!

Supersizing with Server-Based Data

Using technologies on the SAS server is by far the fastest and most efficient way to access large data sources. And SAS has a plethora of choices for accessing data from SAS servers. Often, you can ask your SAS administrator to add direct server-based access to key data sources if you don't already have this in your organization. In addition, with products such as SAS Enterprise Guide, you can easily add server access libraries to open almost any data source directly from the SAS server. A summary of frequently used data access methods is in Table 4-1.

Table 4-1	Frequently Used Data Access Methods	
Storage Type	SAS Server Product Required	Notes
SAS data sets	BASE: Always available on any SAS server.	The default storage method of libraries in SAS. This is optimized for very fast sequential reading of data. You can easily make a library on your SAS server with the Assign Library Wizard to save data in this format.
Indexed SAS data sets	BASE: Always available on any SAS server.	By indexing SAS data sets, you can achieve much faster retrieval of subsets of a table.
SAS views	BASE: Always available on any SAS server.	Views allow you to make virtual lookup of a table accessible to SAS so you don't have to copy it and take up additional storage. Views are typically slower than direct data set access.

Storage Type	SAS Server Product Required	Notes
Relational databases	Relevant SAS/ACCESS product. Examples include Oracle, DB2, Teradata, ODBC, and OLE DB.	SAS/ACCESS engines allow SAS to "speak" with almost any data source in an efficient way. It is even possible to make multiple connections concurrently to accelerate storage and retrieval to these systems.
SAS OLAP	SAS OLAP server (included with SAS Enterprise BI Server).	A very fast way to access your data in presummarized form. Business analysts seeking unusual trends or quick answers to questions often favor this technology.
Other OLAP servers	SAS Enterprise Guide can access SAP BW and SQL Server Analysis Services OLAP data sources.	Use other OLAP servers if you have to, but why deal with the hassle and lower performance when SAS OLAP Server is available?
SAS Scalable Performance Data Engine (SPDE)	SAS Scalable Performance Data Server (SPDS).	By using multiple hard drives to store your large data tables, SAS Scalable Performance Data Engine (SPDE) can greatly accelerate storage and retrieval of very large data sources. Support was recently optimized to leverage several of the most common data warehouse storage structures.
XML Engine	BASE: Always available on any SAS server.	XML Engines allow you to read directly from XML data sources. This is a common format for data exchange among companies and organizations.
Text files such as `.txt`, `.csv`, and tab-delimited files	BASE: Always available on any SAS server.	Text files are an old way to get data, but this method is still common!

Make like a library and book

A SAS library is like a virtual pointer to your data source that you reference by a simple name. Libraries enable you to change the route used to access your data at any time. As long as you keep the library name, all your SAS processes will still work with the data sourced from the new location. The library map might be a simple access description, such as a folder name on a server. Or it might be more complex, such as a database connection with required user credentials and specialized data connection software installed on your server.

After you define a library, using it from SAS Enterprise Guide is seamless if you choose File⇨Open⇨Data and click the Servers location. A sample dialog box is shown in Figure 4-10. To switch libraries, use the up-one-level-folder icon to the right of the Look In box. If you have multiple servers in your environment, you can switch servers by clicking the Servers icon in the left panel.

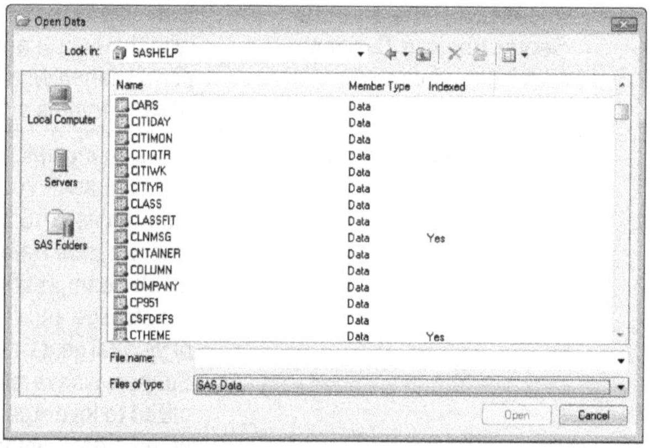

Figure 4-10:
Choose a
library.

A common need among users is the capability to create a library specifically for a current project. SAS Enterprise Guide makes this easy with the Assign Project Library Wizard. The following example shows this in action:

1. **Choose Tools⇨Assign Project Library.**

   The Assign Project Library Wizard dialog box appears, as shown in Figure 4-11.

2. **Enter a name for the library.**

   In this example, you can use CHAPTER4 for the name.

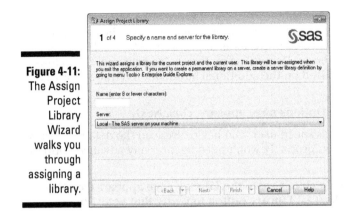

Figure 4-11:
The Assign
Project
Library
Wizard
walks you
through
assigning a
library.

3. **Select the SAS server on which you want this library to be available and then click Next.**

   The Specify the Engine for the Library page appears, as shown in Figure 4-12.

   The SAS server you select must be able to reach the data you're trying to access. In this example, the SAS server is local, so we can use the local file system. On a remote server (for example, running on another Windows machine or a UNIX machine), the data must be accessible using that machine's file system.

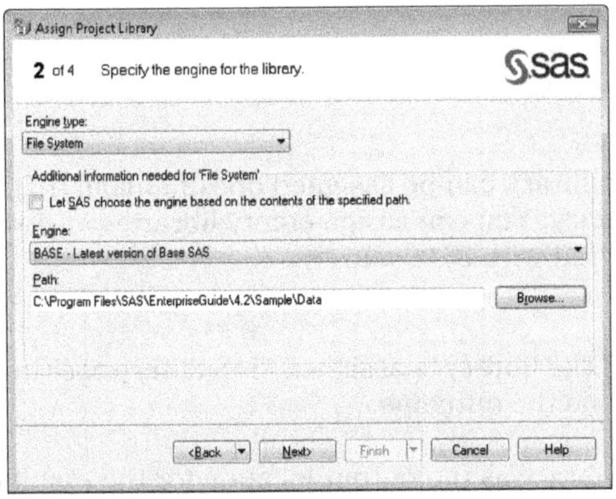

Figure 4-12:
Enter the
path where
your data is
located.

4. **Type the file path for a directory on your server holding the data of interest and then click Next.**

   In Figure 4-12, the location entered in the Path box is where the SAS Enterprise Guide sample data is installed. The default engine is BASE, which is used in this example. You could browse this drop-down list to see the complete set of engine types. Some of these choices come with Base SAS, but others require the appropriate SAS/ACCESS engine on your selected server. Depending on the engine selected, the following screens vary based on the additional information required for that engine's library.

5. **When the Specify Options page appears, click Next.**

Unless you're an advanced user who has referenced the detailed library documentation, you probably won't need to enter any advanced options here.

6. **When the Press Finish to Create the Library page appears (see Figure 4-13), click the Test Library button to verify that your library can be assigned.**

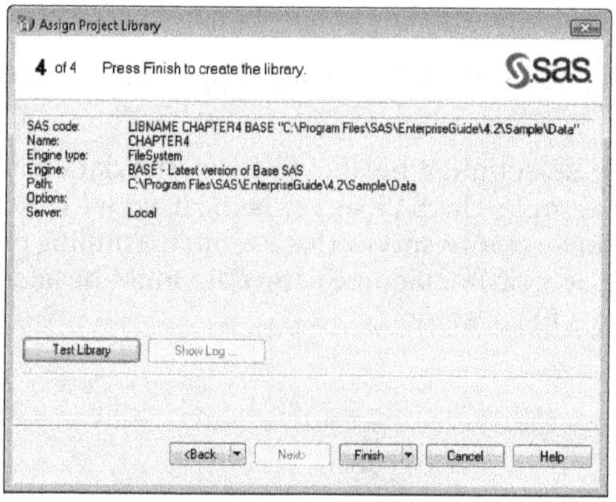

Figure 4-13:
The Finish page with a Test Library button.

Just because your library can be assigned doesn't mean that you have any data in the library. You can assign empty libraries or libraries that are already populated with data sources.

7. **Click Finish.**

The task runs, and the library is assigned. SAS Enterprise Guide displays a log file to show you the outcome.

If you want to use this library as the output location for the result of the Excel import task, you must update the Process Flow to ensure that the library is assigned before the import data task is run. To achieve this automated processing order, follow these steps:

1. **In the Process Flow pane, click and drag from the corner of the Assign Project Library task to the middle of the SupplyInfo.xls node.**

This creates the link shown in Figure 4-14.

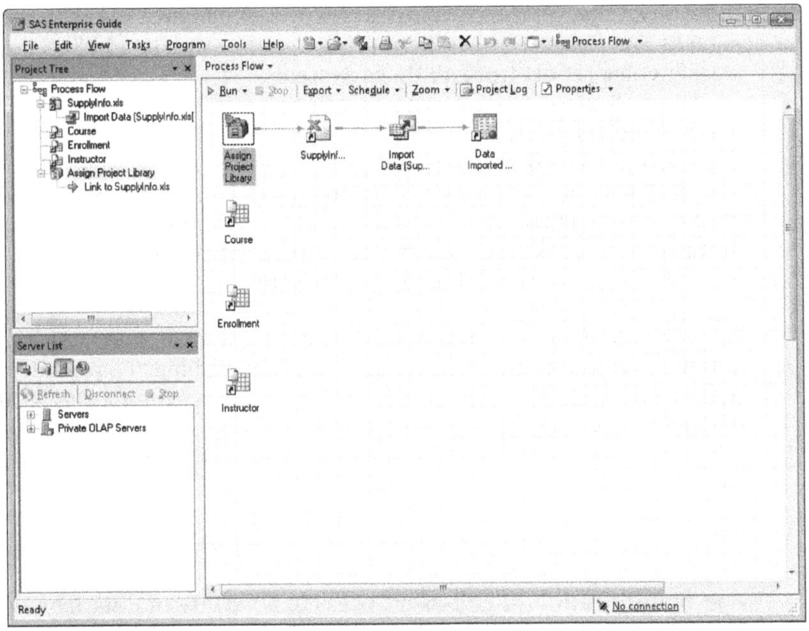

Figure 4-14:
The updated
process
flow for
the project
with added
dependen-
cies.

2. **Right-click the Import Data task and then choose Modify.**

   The Import Data task reappears, displaying the settings that you selected previously.

3. **Click Browse and select the CHAPTER4 library (instead of the default WORK or SASUSER).**

4. **Click Finish to rerun the import task.**

   Manually connecting the Assign Library task to the Excel import flow ensures that the right order of events occurs the next time you open and run the project.

Administered data: One version of the truth

Consider a simple report of sales invoices, which includes data from customer, shipping, and returns systems. At many companies, the sales department maintains the customer systems, the shipping database is in operations, and returns are in finance. All these systems are often independent databases with different rules and assumptions about the data stored in them, even though the data is describing a single process. You can use a tool such as SAS Enterprise Guide to bring together the data in SAS and create the sales invoice report from all these systems.

Suppose you created 15 versions of a report in 15 different SAS Enterprise Guide projects so that you could meet the widely varying needs of various decision makers and users in your company. Now also assume that others in your company used other applications to create their own specialized forms of this report. This array of projects and systems still sounds maintainable — but only with a lot of work and coordination.

Disparate data sources maintained by different groups are called *data silos*, and they are generally regarded as Not a Good Thing. To remedy the situation, companies often turn to the concept of *data warehousing* — the process of collecting and organizing all critical data in an enterprise so that many groups can use it for different purposes, thus providing them with "one version of the truth."

Here are some reasons to consider using data warehousing at your company:

- ✔ **Simplification of end-user access to a variety of data from a single source rather than from many systems:** Users don't need to learn all the systems providing the data. Instead, they learn how to use only the data warehouse.

- ✔ **Simplification of long-term maintenance of reports and analyses:** You isolate users from the source systems and use a consistent data structure (from the data warehouse) for reporting and analysis.

- ✔ **Virtual elimination of performance and maintenance effect on end users who directly access operational systems:** Your shipping team no longer has to wait around on Friday afternoon for the system to take their shipping orders because you're running a big analysis against that database!

- ✔ **Seamless integration of business rules used to combine data from various systems into one process when the data warehouse is updated:** Structured rules help avoid confusion around which report or analysis is correct. This integration also provides an easy mechanism to transparently update the underlying assumptions used in your corporate reporting and decision making. Want to change the calculation for the estimated amount of returns for international customers, for example? Just update the data warehouse rules.

- ✔ **Improvement of performance for end-user ad hoc analysis and reporting:** Data warehouses are structured for such purposes. Most systems that feed the data warehouse aren't designed for optimal performance when reading the data; instead, they are designed for optimal perfor-mance for updating and adding new information. The shipping system is optimized to process new orders, not to run your big query to access all ship events from 2008.

✔ **Uncovering significant quality problems in and among the various operational systems in the company:** Data mismatches can occur when various areas of the company attempt to support all their reporting and analysis needs from the centralized data warehouse and discover that they have applied different rules and assumptions to the data in the vari-ous systems.

SAS and its subsidiary company, DataFlux, offer products to build data ware-houses and ensure data quality. We don't cover these products in detail. But if you're lucky enough to work in a company that provides managed data repositories, your primary method of accessing data may be through admin-istered data sources. Administered data sources can include:

✔ **Tables in SAS libraries:** These are just like the SAS library that we defined earlier in this chapter, except that a database administrator is in charge of what's in them and who can access them. You can use them in SAS Enterprise Guide by choosing File⇨Open⇨Data and then selecting the Servers location.

✔ **Tables in SAS Folders:** These are data sources registered in the SAS Metadata Server. They reside in SAS libraries but are also organized logically within a folder structure, similar to the way you might orga-nize documents on your PC. You can access these data sources in SAS Enterprise Guide by choosing File⇨Open⇨Data and then selecting the SAS Folders location.

✔ **SAS Information Maps in SAS Folders:** SAS Information Maps represent a business view of your data. They remove you from having to under-stand the physical structure of tables and columns in a database, and instead present you with useful column names, predefined filters, and even prompts. You can access Information Maps by choosing File⇨Open⇨Information Map.

SAS Information Maps are the primary way that users of SAS business intelligence applications, such as SAS Web Report Studio, access data sources. (SAS Web Report Studio is covered in Chapter 14.)

Chapter 5

Managing Data: I Can Do That?

. . . .

. . . .

*I*f you have only a passing familiarity with SAS, it might bring to mind images of fancy statistics, cool graphs, and complex analyses — things your college professors created to earn their tenure. But behind every glamorous graph lies a boatload of data preparation, propping it up with meaning.

One of the reasons why SAS is an unparalleled system for accomplishing work in so many industries is because of its impressive data management capabilities. People sometimes find that most of their analysis time is spent trying to get their data into a form that lets them perform the needed analysis. At your service, SAS Enterprise Guide offers you frequently used forms of data management, right at your fingertips!

Managing your data can include the following tasks:

✔ Filtering your data

✔ Creating new computed columns in your data

✔ Manually editing data values

✔ Taking a sample of your data

✔ Comparing a new version of a data set with a previous version

By putting a little upfront thought into what you want to accomplish, you can simplify the tasks you perform in SAS and have an easier time creating effective projects. Think about these things:

➤ Results you want to create in your SAS Enterprise Guide project

➤ Data sources you have at hand

➤ Steps required to arrive at your results

Based on the data sources at hand and your desired outcome — and with practice — you can mentally sketch out the steps you must take to get the results you want. You can accomplish many of these steps by using the functionality discussed in this chapter. Let the following sections be your guide.

Bringing Your Data Together and Making It Sing (or at Least Hum) with Queries

The Query Builder task in SAS Enterprise Guide provides a tremendous amount of power in one task. This task enables you to

➤ Join two or more tables into a single output table

➤ Filter the rows of your input tables

➤ Select a subset of columns for your output data set

➤ Create computed columns based on an extensive array of functions, including aggregations across groups

➤ Recode a column's values

➤ Sort output data

➤ Parameterize your query filter so that you're prompted each time you rerun the query to get just the output data you want in your project

SAS Enterprise Guide also offers the Filter and Sort task, which is a simpler method for filtering data. This task has fewer features than the Query Builder task, but new users might find it easier to navigate. The Filter and Sort task allows you to work with just a single table, select columns to use, apply basic filter conditions, and specify how to sort the output. It does not support joining multiple tables, calculating new columns, or prompted filters.

With the Query Builder task, you can filter candy sales by product type, join the sales table with a sales discount table (to have all the needed columns in one table), create a computed column of net sales based on the original transaction price multiplied by the updates sales discount, sort the sales data by date, and recode the date column to a quarter/year column — all in one task!

The following sections tell you more about each of these activities.

Joining table data

Joining data allows you to combine two or more related tables by specifying the columns that they have in common — often referred to as *keys*. Matching rows are combined, and the new table has the columns you specified from each source table.

The columns used in a join may be named identically or similarly but must be of an identical type (for example, character or numeric) and typically be the same format (for example, date). There are four join types between two tables: inner, left, right, and full outer. Joins occur between two columns in two separate tables, but you can have many join specifications in one task, so you could be combining two or more tables at one time.

Joins can be simple (joining data from the sales and product table into one table by the product ID column, for example) or complex (such as joining sales, product, customer, customer state, and salesperson tables using multiple columns and join types). Columns used in a join don't have to be included for the output table created, nor do all columns in the tables need to be in the output table.

Figure 5-1 illustrates the use of two data tables and is the basis for the next four figures, which illustrate the results of the four most common join types. The circle on the left represents all students. The circle on the right represents all courses. The two tables are joined by the student ID number. Students with no courses are off on the far left (they must be in Cancun partying for the semester). A few courses have no students enrolled (too bad for the underwater basket-weaving instructor). Finally, the intersection of the two circles shows the students enrolled in courses. In reality, this would likely be the majority of the data, but this figure represents it as a rather small section.

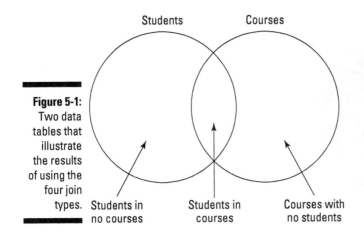

Figure 5-1: Two data tables that illustrate the results of using the four join types.

Students   Courses

Students in no courses   Students in courses   Courses with no students

The following list describes the four types of joins:

- **Inner:** Most of the time, you want matching rows or an inner join, which returns only those rows that have rows with a matching key in each table (see Figure 5-2). With this type of join, rows that have no corresponding matching row are left off the output table.

- **Left:** This join returns all rows from the table to the left of the join symbol and all data from the right side table that has a matching key value (see Figure 5-3). An example of a left join is if you need data on all students and the matching courses they have taken.

- **Right:** This join is like a left join except that it is reversed for the right table (see Figure 5-4).

- **Full outer:** A full outer join returns all rows from both tables regardless of whether a matching row based on the key value is in the other table (see Figure 5-5). The result of this join is all students (including those who never took a course) and all courses (regardless of whether a student ever enrolled.)

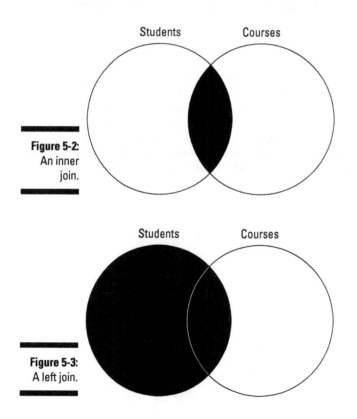

Students   Courses

Figure 5-2:
An inner
join.

Students   Courses

Figure 5-3:
A left join.

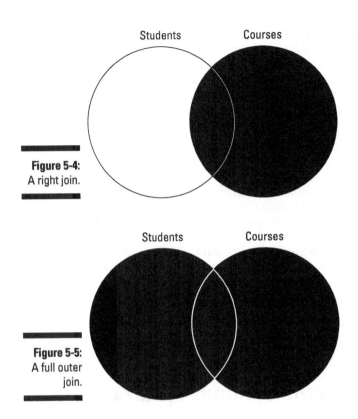

Figure 5-4:
A right join.

Figure 5-5:
A full outer join.

Imagine two simple tables:

- ✔ On the left side of the query is the Student table with join column Student_ID and values of 001, 003, and 004.

- ✔ On the right side of the query is the Courses table with join column Student_ID and column values of 001, 002, 004, and 005.

Here is how the different joins and their results play out:

- ✔ Inner join: Student_ID row values of 001 and 004 (two rows)
- ✔ Left join: 001, 003, and 004 (three rows)
- ✔ Right join: 001, 002, 004, and 005 (four rows)
- ✔ Full outer join: 001, 002, 003, 004, and 005 (five rows)

To access the join feature, click the Join button in the upper left of the main task window. There is no need to use this feature unless your output table requires data from more than one input table.

SAS Enterprise Guide offers one more class of join types called the natural join. A natural join tells SAS (or the underlying database) to decide how to match the data in the different tables based on common column names and types. It saves you from making some decisions but the results and performance may be unpredictable, especially if your table structure is subject to change. This is one case where it can be dangerous to let nature take its course.

Filtering table data

When you filter data, you reduce the rows returned in your output table based on conditions that you set. Filtering your data can significantly improve your query processing time and greatly speed the tasks downstream of your data.

Filter conditions can be simple (say, chocolate candy sales) or complex (chocolate candies sales with a discount greater than 30 percent or a total sale amount more than $9,000). Columns used in a filter don't have to be selected for the output table.

To use the filter option, click the Filter Data tab in the upper right of the main task window; then drag columns to this area from the tables area.

Selecting specific columns of data

Your input tables might contain columns irrelevant to the question at hand. By selecting specific columns of interest, your output table gives you exactly the information needed for your analysis and can greatly decrease your overall processing time.

When you select columns, you can also specify formats for the column, rename the column, or specify an aggregation for certain columns. When you select an aggregation for a column (Sum, for example), the output table automatically includes one row for each unique set of nonaggregated columns. For example, the sum of sales by quarter and region has only one row per unique combination of quarter and region.

To select specific columns of data, drag columns from the tables area to the Select Data tab.

You can specify an aggregation after you add a column to the Select Data tab.

Creating a computed column

Computed columns let you create a column based on either of the following:

- A simple expression

  ```
  Net_Sales = Revenue - Expenses
  ```

- A more complex expression

  ```
  Net_Sales = Gross_Sales X (1-Discount) - Expenses -
          Gross_Sales*
          (1-Sales_Commision)
  ```

Expression Builder in SAS Enterprise Guide can help you build and validate your new column. You access Expression Builder by clicking the Computed Columns button in the upper left of the main task window, choosing New, and then choosing Advanced Expression from the New Computed Column Wizard. Expression Builder has many powerful functions, including:

- Text-parsing and manipulation functions
- Many statistical and financial functions
- The capability to look up column values
- The capability to utilize data quality functions in SAS

Computed columns are automatically added to your selected columns list.

Recoding a column

The Query Builder task gives you the capability to rename (or *recode*) data value abbreviations or numeric codes for a couple of handy purposes:

- To rename data abbreviations to something understandable by average humans (for example, you can set a gender identifier of 1 to appear as Female)
- To collapse a range of values to one category (for example, you can set test scores of 90–100 to appear as an A)

To access the recoding function, click the Computed Columns button in the upper left of the main task window, choose New, and then choose Recoded Column from the New Computed Column Wizard.

Sorting data

You can sort your output table by one or more columns. Data can be sorted in either *ascending* order (1, 2, 3; or A, B, C) or *descending* order (9, 8, 7; or Z, Y, X). Sorting data affects only your output table, not your input table, unless they are the same! Common uses for sorting include quickly finding records occurring on a particular date or finding a particular range of customers in the sorted output table.

Adding prompts to the query filter

Queries that filter your data in a frequently changing manner can be *parameterized.* This means that each time you run the query, the user is automatically prompted to specify the exact data filter conditions (also called *prompts*) to apply.

Suppose that a sales report you frequently run for other people in your company is filtered each time by product and region. You can add prompts to the product and a region filter condition so that you can select the appropriate values each time you run the report. One time you might select chocolate candy in the West region; the next time you run the report, you might select hard candy in the Central region.

To use the prompting option, click the Prompt Manager button in the upper left of the main task window. Click Add to add a new prompt value. Use this prompt in the Filter Data dialog box.

When you add prompts to a filter in a query, or to any task, SAS Enterprise Guide uses a SAS programming element called a *macro variable.* Experienced SAS programmers can use their knowledge of macro variables to do some fancy tricks with these prompt values. We cover SAS macro variables and programming in Chapter 16.

In the following multipart example, we build a query that combines data from three data tables in the Sample Data directory supplied with SAS Enterprise Guide:

- Candy_Customers
- Candy_Products
- Candy_Sales_History

In part one of this example query, you join the Candy_Customers, Candy_Products, and Candy_Sales_History tables. The output table includes the region column and a new computed column named net sales.

In part two, you add prompts to the query with the product column. By adding this parameter, the query prompts users each time they run this query to select a particular product for analysis.

In part three, you use the resulting table from this query with the Bar Chart Wizard to create a graphical summary of net sales by region using the user selected product filter.

Example query: Part one

Follow these steps to join the three sample tables and create an output table that includes a new computed column:

1. **Click the Candy_Sales_History table in the Process Flow to specify the initial table used in your query.**

2. **Choose Tasks⇨Data⇨Query Builder.**

   The Query Builder dialog box appears, as shown in Figure 5-6.

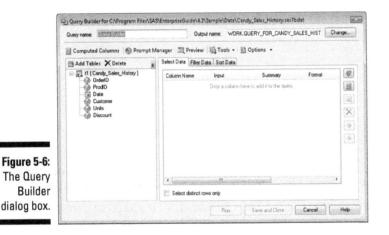

Figure 5-6:
The Query Builder dialog box.

3. **On the left side of the dialog box, just to the left of the Select Data tab, click the Join Tables button.**

   The Tables and Joins dialog box appears.

4. **Click the Add Tables button to add the Customers and Products tables to this query.**

   (The Add Tables button is on the same row as the Join Tables button.) The Open Data dialog box appears.

5. **Select Project as the source for the tables to add.**

   The list of available tables in the project appears. This window also allows you to add new tables to the project from other locations, such as your local computer or the SAS server.

6. **Press Ctrl and click the Candy_Products and Candy_Customers tables; then click Open.**

   A warning message appears stating that a suitable join can't be found. This means that the tables can't automatically be associated by a variable with an exact name match.

7. **Click OK to dismiss this warning.**

   See Figure 5-7 for the current state of the Tables and Joins dialog box. Note that ProdID is a variable common to Candy_Sales_History and Candy_Products, so an inner join is added automatically between these two tables by using this column.

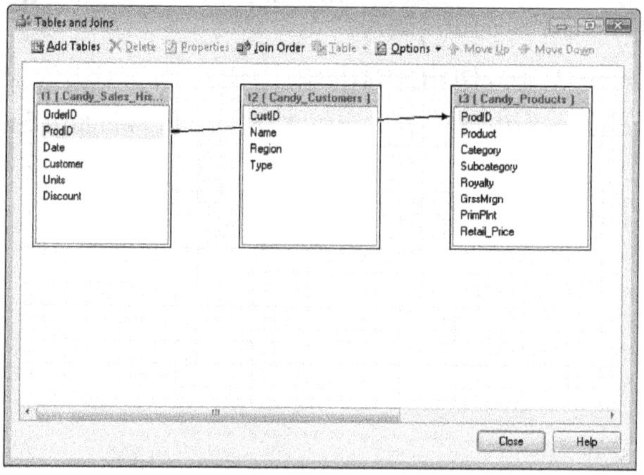

Figure 5-7:
The Tables
and Joins
dialog box.

8. **Click the Candy_Customers table to select it. Then click and drag it down the screen about half the length of the other two tables.**

   You can see that Candy_Sales_History is now joined to Candy_Products by the identically named column ProdID.

   Rearranging the tables in this view can be tricky. To select the table so that you can drag it with the mouse, move your cursor near the top of the table outline until it turns into a four-way grabber arrow, and then drag it to move the table.

9. **Click the CustID column (in the Candy_Customers table) and drag it on top of the Customer column in the Candy_Sales_History table.**

   The joins between columns in tables default to an inner join. (You can read about inner joins earlier in this chapter.) Figure 5-8 shows this new layout.

   If you find the drag operations tricky, you can create the join a different way by right-clicking the CustID column and choosing Join [t2.CustID] with⇨t1⇨Customer.

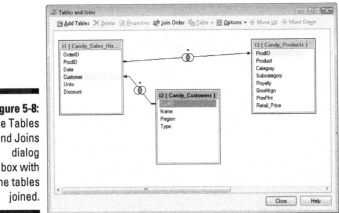

Figure 5-8:
The Tables
and Joins
dialog
box with
the tables
joined.

The symbol in the middle of each join line provides a quick reference to the type of join being used. You can double-click the join line to access the Modify Join dialog box (see Figure 5-9), which presents you with detailed join information and options.

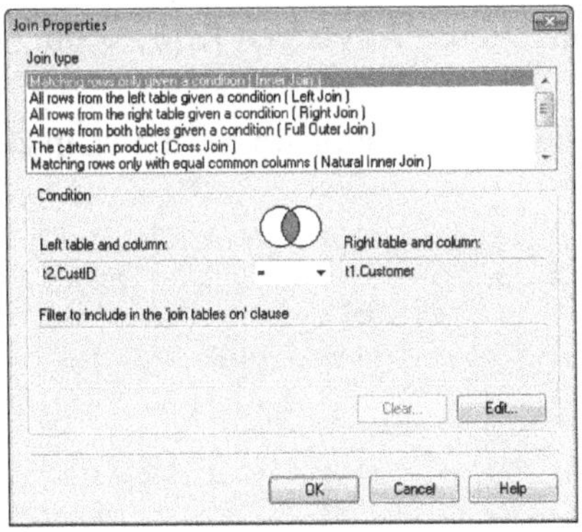

Figure 5-9:
The Join
Properties
dialog box.

10. **When the Join Properties dialog box appears, click OK to close it. Click Close to dismiss the Tables and Joins dialog box.**

    All three tables now appear in the main query dialog box (see Figure 5-10) based on the work you did in the Tables and Joins dialog box.

11. **Click the Region column in the Candy_Customers table and drag it to the Select Data tab on the right. Do the same with the Product column in the Candy_Products table.**

    If you want to add all the columns from a particular table, just drag the table name to the Select Data region.

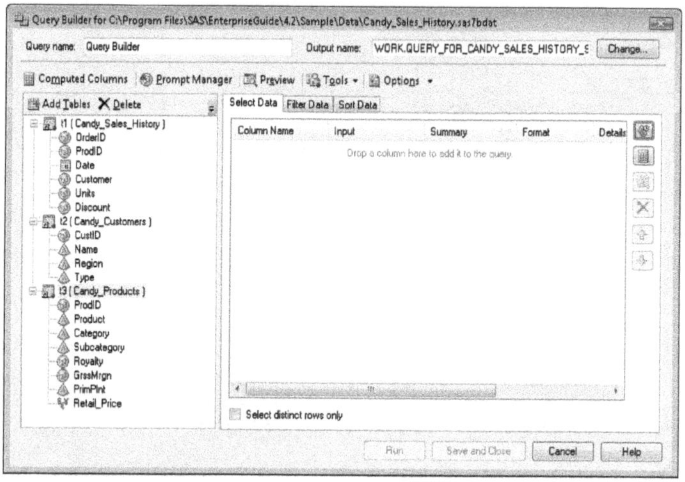

Figure 5-10:
The main
query dialog
box now
listing the
three tables.

12. **To calculate net sales, follow these steps:**

    a. **Click the Computed Columns button.**

    The Computed Columns dialog box appears.

    b. **Click the New button, choose Advanced Expression, and then click Next.**

    The Advanced Expression page appears, as shown in Figure 5-11.

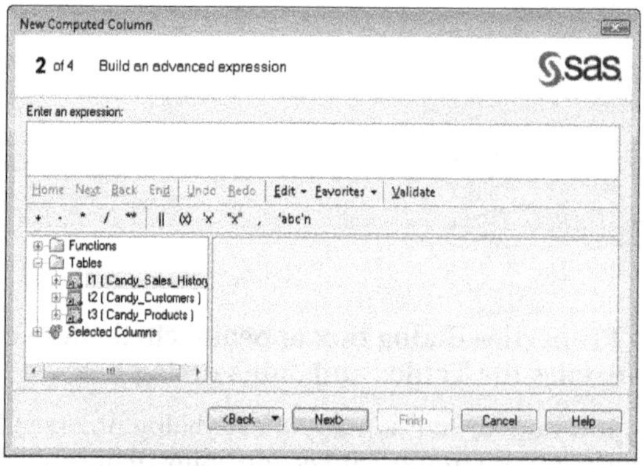

Figure 5-11:
You can
use the
Advanced
Expression
Builder
to create
computed
columns.

In this example, net sales is calculated as the units sold times the retail price. For example, if an order has 100 units of a product sold at a retail price of $2, the net sale amount for that order is $100 \times \$2$ ($200). And for this example, the general formula we need is

```
t1.Units * t3.Retail_Price
```

We'll create this formula over the next few steps.

13. **In the box on the left, double-click t1 to show the columns in Candy_ Sales_History, and then double-click Units.**

    t1.Units appears in the Expression Text at the top of the dialog box.

14. **Click the button showing the asterisk (*) just below the Expression Text box.**

    The multiplier symbol now follows the variable.

15. **Scroll down the tables list and expand the t3 (Candy_Products) table, and then double-click Retail_Price.**

    t3.Retail_Price appears in the Expression text field, completing the expression.

16. **Click Next.**

    The Additional options page appears.

17. **Change the column name and alias to a more meaningful name, such as Net_Sales.**

18. **In the Format field (at the bottom of the window), type DOLLAR12. Be sure to include the period at the end!**

    This specifies a U.S. currency format instead of a plain number. The completed Additional Options page looks like Figure 5-12.

    If you don't remember the exact name of the SAS format you want to use, click the Change button and point-and-click your way to the correct format.

19. **Click Finish to return to the list of Computed Columns, and then click Close.**

Aliases: A table by any other name

As you use the Query Builder task, you might notice that it refers to tables and computed columns using names that are different than you expect. For example, instead of the Customer_ Sales_History table, the Query Builder might show t1. This is called an *alias*, and it's like a nickname for the table. An alias can be handy for reducing a long, complex name to something simple to remember and type. For folks who create queries the hard way (writing their own programs), using aliases can help insulate their programs from table and column name changes, because then the names need to change in just one place instead of throughout the program. SAS Enterprise Guide generates queries that use aliases because it's generally regarded as good practice and makes those generated programs reusable in other situations.

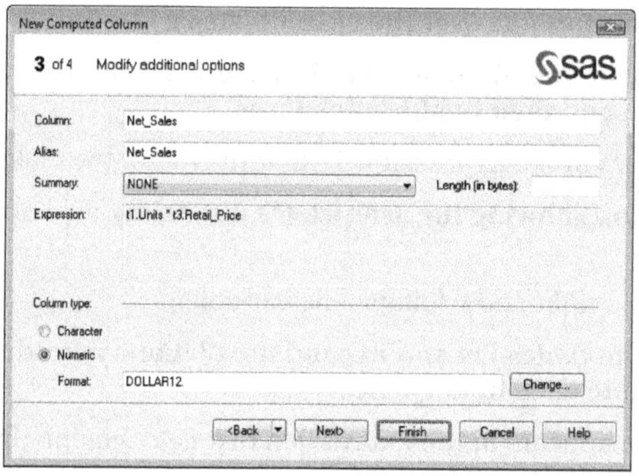

Figure 5-12:
The completed Additional Options page, with a useful alias and format.

This is the end of part one of this example. You can click Run to see the table shown in Figure 5-13, or you can continue with the next part. If you run the task now and want to continue with part two of this query example, reopen the Query Builder task from the Process Flow by right-clicking and selecting Modify Query Builder.

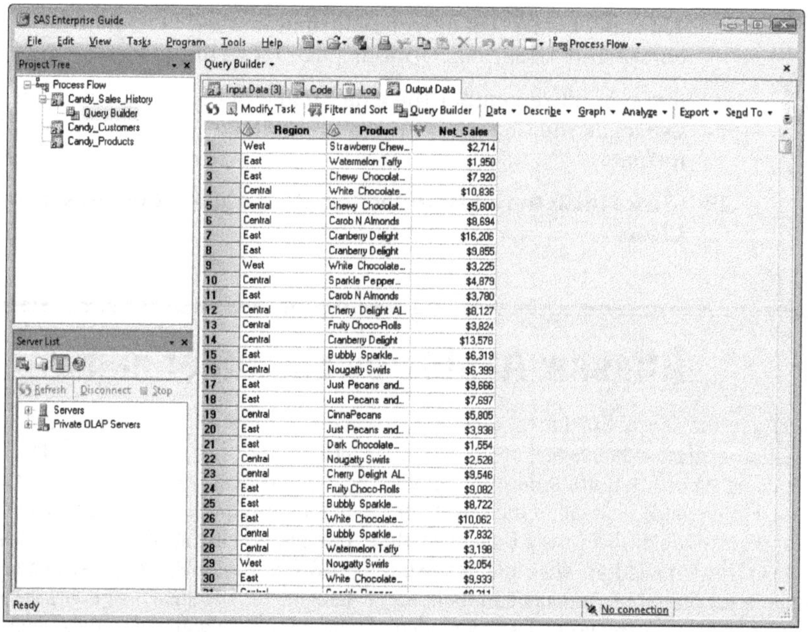

Figure 5-13:
The Query Builder output table.

Example query: Part two

In part two, you add a prompt to the query using the product column. By adding this prompt, the query asks the users to select a product for analysis each time they run the query:

1. **For the prompts filter, create a prompt containing the list of products:**

   a. **Click the Prompt Manager button in the upper left of the main Query Builder dialog box.**

   The Prompt Manager dialog box appears.

   b. **Click Add.**

   The Add New Prompt dialog box appears, as shown in Figure 5-14.

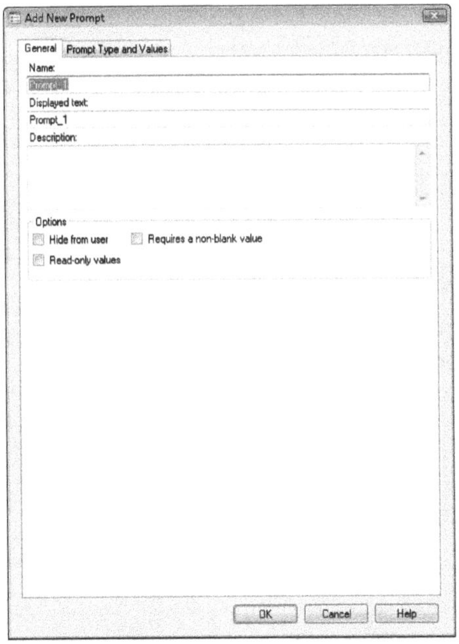

Figure 5-14:
The Add New Prompt dialog box.

2. **In the Name box, type** Product; **then click the Prompt Type and Values tab.**

3. **In the Prompt Type drop-down list, verify that Text is selected.**

4. **In the Method for Populating Prompt drop-down list, choose User Selects Values from Static List.**

   The fields in the window change automatically to provide options that are appropriate for this type of prompt.

5. **Click the Get Values button (in the middle-right edge).**

   The Get Values dialog box appears.

6. **Click Browse, and then click Project in the Open File dialog box.**

7. **Click Candy_Products, and then click Open.**

   The Get Values dialog box now shows Candy_Products as the active data source.

8. **In the Unformatted Values section, select Product in the Columns drop-down list.**

9. **In the Available Values section, click the Get Values button.**

   The list of available values is updated with the list of products from the Candy_Products data, as shown in Figure 5-15.

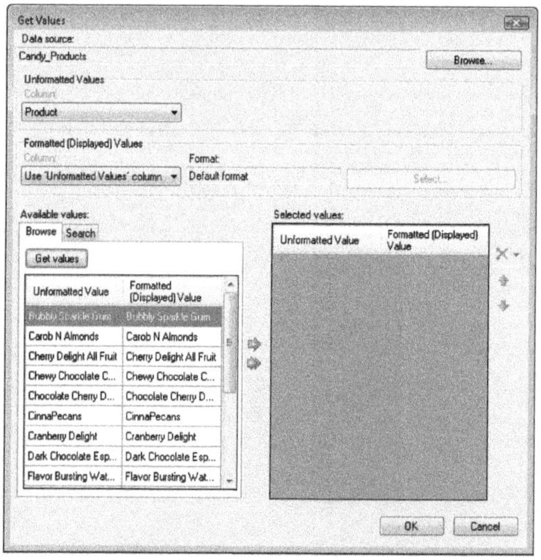

Figure 5-15: The Get Values dialog box with the updated values.

10. **Click the double arrow (in the center) to move all the values to the Selected Values section, and then click OK.**

    The Add New Prompt dialog box now has all the product values in its List of Values.

11. **Click OK to close the Add New Prompt dialog box, and then click Close to close the Prompt Manager dialog box.**

    Whew! Now that the prompt is defined, it's time to make use of it in a filter.

12. **Click the Filter Data tab, and then drag the Product column to the Filter Data area.**

    The New Filter dialog box appears.

13. **Click the drop-down arrow beside the Value box.**

14. **Click the Prompts tab, select &Product, and then click OK.**

15. **Click Finish to complete the filter definition.**

16. **From the main query dialog box, click Run.**

    The Specify Values for Project Prompts dialog box appears, prompting you to select a product.

17. **Select the desired product to filter the query for this run and then click Run.**

    The Prompts dialog box looks like Figure 5-16. We selected Chewy Chocolate Cheetahs for this example. When you click Run, the filtered output data table appears.

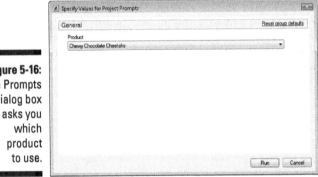

Figure 5-16:
The Prompts dialog box asks you which product to use.

This is the end of part two of this example. You can go have some milk and cookies (or Chewy Chocolate Cheetahs, if you've got some) and revel in the filtered data, or you can continue with part three.

Query example: Part three

In part III, you use the Bar Chart Wizard to create a graphical summary of net sales by region. You'll pick up where you left off in the preceding part. You should be viewing the output table that you created from the query step with prompts:

1. **Choose Tasks⇨Graph⇨Bar Chart Wizard.**

2. **When the Bar Chart Wizard appears, click Next.**

    Note that the Bars role is already set to Region.

3. **On Step 2 (of 4) of the wizard, change the Bar Height role to Net_Sales, and then click Next.**

4. **Change the Color Bars By box from All Bars the Same to Bar Category (this colors each bar a separate color). Then click Next.**

5. **On screen 4 of the wizard, change the Graph title by typing** Net Sales by Region for &Product.

   Make sure you use an ampersand before the word *Product*.

   The &Product in the graph title is a *macro variable*. This value was set at runtime based on the user selection from the Product prompt used in the query task. Macro variables can be very useful for creating meaningful titles and footnotes throughout SAS Enterprise Guide. If you didn't include the ampersand, just the word *Product* would be displayed.

   You can find out more about SAS macro variables and other programming concepts in Chapter 16.

6. **Click Finish.**

   A graph resembling Figure 5-17 is generated after a few seconds. You might find that instead of a meaningful product name in the graph title, the report shows *&Product* instead. This can happen when SAS Enterprise Guide clears the macro variable (prompt value) before the task runs. Follow Step 7 to ensure that your prompt value is retained for the Bar Chart task.

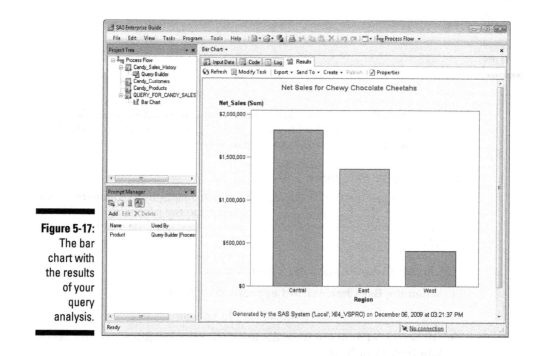

Figure 5-17: The bar chart with the results of your query analysis.

7. **Add the Products project prompt to the Bar Chart task:**

    a. **Right-click the Bar Chart item in the Project Tree and choose Properties.**

    The Properties dialog box appears.

    b. **Choose the Prompts item from the list on the left to see the list of project prompts used.**

    It will be an empty list, for now.

    c. **Click Add, and then select Product from the list of additional prompts.**

    d. **Click OK from the Select Prompts window and then OK from the Properties dialog box.**

    e. **In the Project Tree, right-click the Process Flow node and then select Run Process Flow.**

    The query and bar chart run again, prompting you for a product to use. This time, the prompt is used both in the query step (to filter the data) and in the bar chart report (in the title).

If you've been working along with this example, your work is finished! You've brought together sales data from several data tables with the Query Builder task, created a new Net Sales computed column, filtered the results to only Chewy Chocolate Cheetahs, and created a nice summary graph of the results. Good work!

Editing, Sorting, Ranking, Transposing, and Other Data Contortions

In addition to the power of the Query Builder task, many other data management capabilities are available in SAS Enterprise Guide, such as

- ✔ Editing data tables
- ✔ Sorting data
- ✔ Ranking data values
- ✔ Transposing columns and rows
- ✔ Sampling large data tables for analysis and graphs
- ✔ Comparing new versions of data tables with the previous version

The following sections give you a quick look at the many data management capabilities available in SAS Enterprise Guide.

Editing data table values

SAS Enterprise Guide provides interactive data grid access to your data table and offers basic cell-editing capabilities. You access the editing feature by choosing Edit⟹Protect Data (which toggles the data view to edit mode). Changes you type in the data grid are applied to the table immediately. You have the option of printing the data grid.

There is no Undo functionality, so be sure you edit a *copy* of any critical data source. Before overriding the original data table with the edited one, you can compare the two tables with the Compare Data task (explained a little later in the "Comparing data" section).

Appending tables

You can use the Append Table task (choose Tasks⟹Data⟹Append Table) to combine multiple tables into one output table. All rows and variables are used from every table, and the tables are combined (or figuratively stacked) one on top of the other.

An example of when you might want to append tables is to combine a sales table that was kept separately for each of the past four quarters (for example, Sales_Q1, Sales_Q2, Sales_Q3, and Sales_Q4). If you want one table with all records from the four quarters, the Append Table task makes this simple!

Sorting data

You can use the Sort Data task to sort data from your data source by columns. For example, you can drop unneeded columns or remove duplicate rows. The default behavior is the option to output a data set. You access the Sort Data task by choosing Tasks⟹Data⟹Sort Data.

If your input data source and output data location are on the same relational database, use the Filter and Sort task or Query Builder task instead.

Creating a format

The Create Format task allows you to create format *masks* to change how you show data values in your reports. When you use the Create Format task, your SAS format catalog is updated. Formats are a SAS system capability that allows you to store data one way (for example, gender as F and M) and display it another way when used in a report (gender appears as Female or Male when you use the $Gender format). Formats can apply to numeric or character columns and are frequently used to minimize the space your data needs for storage (storing a million rows of F or M is much more efficient than the full words.) The SAS format catalog needs the translation information only once, so the words *Female* and *Male* are saved in only one location. For some columns that use formats, the value translation may change over time. It's easy to quickly modify the value in just one place — the format catalog. A good example of a value translation that might change is a column that tracks customer numbers by purchase amount in the past month (high, medium, or low).

Some other examples of when you might want to use a format include converting numeric or text variables to meaningful text values and specifying ways to present them. For example, you could display the numeric value 419184523 as a Social Security number (419-18-4523) or 9192449876 as a phone number (919-244-9876).

Transposing data

By using the Transpose Data task, you can turn data "sideways," with rows transposed to columns. You can group by identifier columns so that one row per unique identifier value appears in the output table. For example, suppose that you have a table with one row per quarter for a sales year. To make the four rows (with values for Q1, Q2, Q3, and Q4) into just one row with one column per quarter (columns Q1_Sales, Q2_Sales, Q3_Sales, and Q4_Sales), choose Tasks⇨Data⇨Transpose Data.

Splitting columns

The Split Columns task is a special case of the Transpose Data task. A simple example of when you might use this task is to transpose a table that has four rows and two columns (for example, Quarter and Sales) to one row and four columns (one column for each unique quarter).

Stacking columns

The Stack Columns task produces the reverse of Split Columns. Data from many columns is collapsed into one column, with the new number of rows the same as the number of input columns. If you take the data set created in the Split Columns example (one row of data with a variable for each quarter of sales) and use the Stacked Columns task, you would go back to four rows and two columns, with the quarter value in one column and the sales amount in the other column.

Selecting a random sample of data

You use the Random Sample task to select a random sample of data when analyzing the full data source is too time consuming. This task is useful when developing a project that uses large data sources. By default, the task creates an output data set. A print report option is also available, so you can print a summary of how the sample was performed.

You can sample the following:

- ✔ As a percent of all rows or a fixed number of rows
- ✔ The same amount for each unique or distinct value of a variable

Use the Random Sample task for designing your project with smaller data volumes and performing statistical analysis. Be careful, however, not to use this task when you are reporting actual numbers, such as quarterly sales reports where every row is required to achieve accurate results!

Ranking variables

Rank is a specialized task for creating output data sets that rank a variable with one of the methods for further analysis, reporting, or graphing. Records rank can be determined in twelve ways. Commonly used methods are smallest to largest (1, 2, 3, . . . n), percentile ranks (1%, 2%, and so on), deciles (first 10%, second 10%, and so on), ntiles (determined by how many groups the data is subdivided into; five groups is called *quintiles*), and normal scores using the statistical normal distribution (see the next section for more information on normal distribution). From the sales example, you could rank the four rows of sales to see which quarter had the greatest sales (smallest to largest rank of 1) to which quarter had the least sales (rank of 4).

Standardizing data

Many common statistical techniques assume an underlying normal distribution. A *normal distribution* is the most commonly used distribution in statistical analysis; it is often referred to as a bell-shaped curve. If your data doesn't meet this assumption, you can transform it to a normal distribution with the Standardize Data task. (See Chapters 8 and 9 to find out how SAS provides the statistics to show whether your selected analysis meets the normal distribution standard.)

Summarizing data set attributes

With the Data Set Attributes task, you can create a detailed report or data set that summarizes the details of a selected data set or table. Information available with this task includes column names, column labels, column type (numeric or character), column format, and various table attributes, such as date created, date modified, and data set label. You might want to use this task to create a printed report of data used in your important analysis, such as an analysis that may be audited later by government officials.

Comparing data

The Compare Data task enables you to compare changes between an old version and a new version of a data set. Data differences, such as missing variables, added variables, changes in formats, changes in data values, and added or deleted records, are reported in a concise manner.

Trying out the data management tasks

In the next example, we once again use the sample data table included with SAS Enterprise Guide: Candy_Sales_Summary. This example illustrates some of the most commonly used data management tasks. In this example, you

1. Reduce the data size used by taking a random sample.
2. Collapse the resulting table further by

    - Summarizing sales (using the Retail_Price variable) by product and year per row.

    - Transposing the summary table so that each product has only one row per product with a column for each year, and then using the Rank task to find the most sold to least sold product by year.

3. Create a report summarizing the products ranked by sales in each year.

In this example, you won't use all the tasks previewed in this chapter. But keep in mind that every task in SAS Enterprise Guide has detailed help to assist you.

Reducing the volume of data

First, use the Random Sample task to reduce the volume of data used in later steps:

1. **Choose File⇨Open⇨Data.**

    The Open Data window appears.

2. **Navigate to the sample data directory, select Candy_Sales_Summary, and then click Open.**

   Remember, the sample data can be found in `C:\Program Files\SAS\ EnterpriseGuide\4.2\Sample\Data`. The table opens in the data view.

3. **Choose Tasks⇨Data⇨Random Sample.**

   The Random Sample dialog box appears. Like the filter capabilities of the Query Builder task, the Random Sample task reduces the number of rows in your output data. The main difference is that with random sampling, you specify how you want the data *sampled* rather than how you want the data *filtered*.

4. **In the Data pane, select the Product, Fiscal_Year, and Retail_Price variables and drag them to the Output Variables role.**

   You use these variables later in the example.

5. **Click Options in the list on the left.**

6. **Change the Sample Size to read 25 Percent of Rows, which is a reasonable percentage to sample for your initial assessment.**

7. **Click Run.**

   The random sample report appears in a few moments, summarizing the sampling performed and rows output.

In real-world data sizes, these options would trim a 50,000,000-row table to 12,500,000 rows, which greatly reduces processing time for subsequent tasks. This is an easy way to accelerate your processing time while prototyping your project.

When you finish with the development stage of this example, you can easily change the sample size to 100 percent of the rows or simply delete the task from the project and use the original data as input in your process flow.

Transposing the data

In the next part of the data management example, you transpose the data to change from many records per product (one per year) to just one record per product (one column for each year). Then you use the Rank task to find the most successful product for each year:

1. **Transpose the data from the random sample task.**

   The Transpose task expects one row per unique data combination. To achieve this, use the Query Builder task:

   a. **In Query Builder, add all three variables (Product, Fiscal_Year, and Retail_Price) to the Select Data area.**

      To review how to use Query Builder, see the section on queries near the beginning of this chapter.

b. **In the Summary column of the Select Data area, click the drop-down arrow for Retail_Price and select the SUM function.**

Because you want just one record per year, you will sum all the rows with sales data for the given product in a given year. The data will automatically be collapsed (grouped) across Product and Fiscal_Year.

Summarization doesn't always mean using the SUM function to add values. Query Builder offers a big list of functions to summarize (or aggregate) your data, including by sum, average, frequency counts, and minimum and maximum values.

c. **Click Run.**

A data table similar to Figure 5-18 appears, with one row per unique combination of Product and Fiscal_Year. The values for SUM_OF_Retail_Price in your data will probably be different than what you see in Figure 5-18 because the sum is based on a random sample of observations from the data.

2. **Choose Tasks⇨Data⇨Transpose.**

The Transpose dialog box appears.

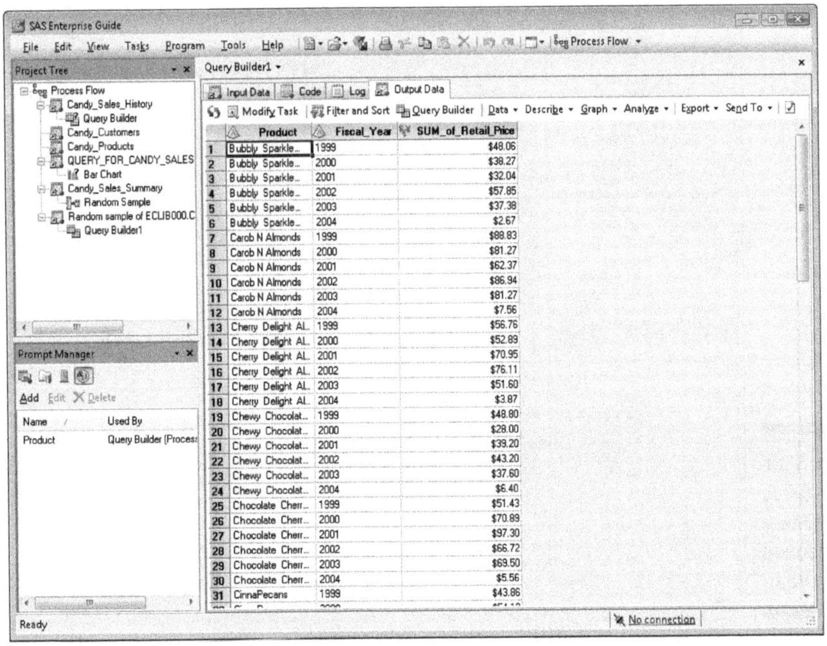

Figure 5-18: The summarized table output from the query task.

3. **Add the following:**

   a. **SUM_OF_Retail_Price to the Transpose variable role**

   b. **Product to the Group Analysis By role**

   c. **Fiscal_Year to the New Column Names role**

4. **Click Options in the list, deselect the Use Prefix check box, and then click Run.**

   You use the Use Prefix check box when you want to use another column to specify the new column name. You are using the actual year values, so you can deselect this option. A data table similar to Figure 5-19 appears, with one column per year and one row per product.

   The Transpose task is useful for reporting in a columnar manner data that has many records over time. It is also used for certain statistical analyses that require data in a converted data form.

5. **Choose Tasks⇨Data⇨Rank.**

   The Rank dialog box appears.

6. **Add columns named 1999 through 2004 to the Columns to Rank role.**

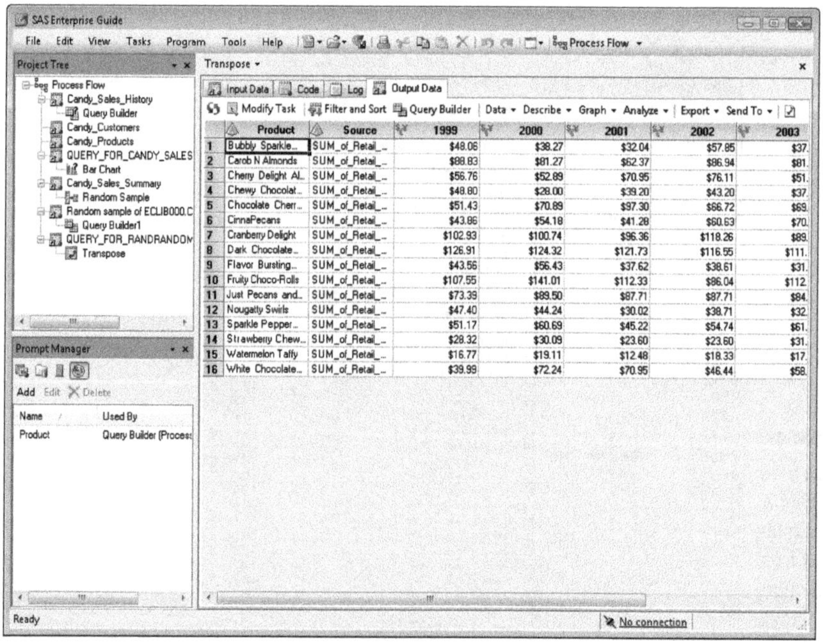

Figure 5-19: Sales summary transposed by year.

7. **Deselect the Include Ranking Values check box (on the right side).**

   You don't want the ranked values to appear in the original variable columns because they would use the current formatting for those columns. That would be a currency format rather than a standard numeric format.

8. **Click Run.**

   A data table similar to Figure 5-20 appears, with one column per year and one row per product.

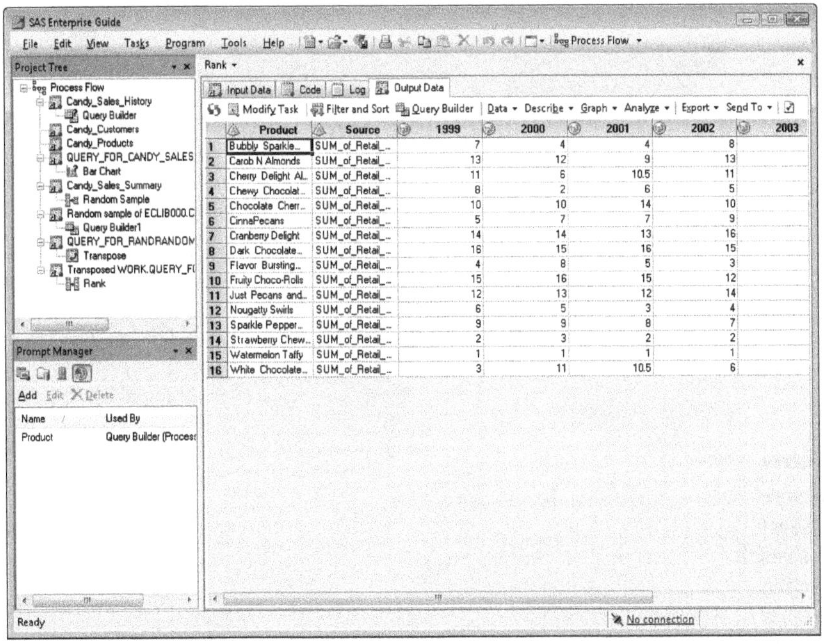

Figure 5-20: Sales summary ranked by year across the products.

The Rank task has many other ranking options: percentile ranks, deciles, quartiles, ntiles, percents, normal scores, and exponential distribution scores.

Creating a summary report

Finally, for the last part of this data management example, you create a report that summarizes the products ranked by sales in each year.

1. **Choose Describe⇨List Data.**

   The List Data dialog box appears.

2. **Add Product and columns 1999 through 2004 to the List Variables role.**

3. **Select the Options pane and deselect the Print the Row Number check box and the Use Variable Labels as Column Headings check box.**

4. **Click Titles, click Report Titles, deselect the Use Default Text check box, and change the report title to** Product Sales Ranking by Year.

5. **Click Run.**

A report similar to Figure 5-21 appears.

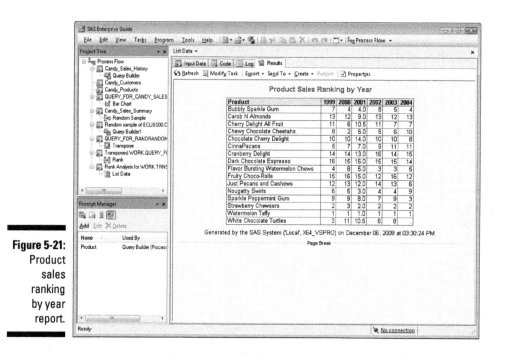

Figure 5-21: Product sales ranking by year report.

Chapter 6

Show Me a Report in Less Than a Minute

In This Chapter

▶ Using the various output types

▶ Creating simple listings and data summary reports

▶ Fine-tuning your formatting

*W*hen you mention *data reporting* to your colleagues, the phrase will likely invoke ideas ranging from simple listings of data tables to sophisticated combinations of graphs, data aggregations, complex data formatting, and even statistical analysis in one report. With SAS, you can create a wide range of reports, from simple to complex.

That said, how you create a report with SAS is somewhat different than in most other reporting applications. In SAS Enterprise Guide, a report can comprise a combination of output objects that you create in your project. For example, you can include a summary table of sales by quarter, a bar chart of new customers by quarter, and a line chart of sales by region over time on one page. You create each item in a report by using the various tasks and wizards in Enterprise Guide, and then you use these pieces to create your report.

This chapter focuses on the tasks in SAS Enterprise Guide that allow you to generate data listings, data summaries, and summary tables (or cross-tabular reports). After you understand the building blocks of reports, you can combine the results of your labor into complex reports to meet most any need.

Discovering Your Reporting Options

Tasks that you run in SAS Enterprise Guide typically create a *report*, which is a type of textual or graphical output that you can view, print, or save as a file. You can set the preferred output file type generated by tasks by choosing Tools⇨Options⇨Results General. Following are the output file types available:

- ✔ **Plain text:** No formatting available — just simple text. Harks to the days of mainframe computers and green-screen terminals.

- ✔ **PDF:** The Adobe Acrobat Portable Document File format.

- ✔ **RTF (Rich Text Format):** An export format used by Microsoft Word and other word-processing programs.

- ✔ **HTML:** Formatting is possible, but printing often truncates important information. HTML is useful for export to a Web server.

- ✔ **SAS Report:** The SAS open standard report format. Formatting and printing with proper formatting are possible, and your interactive point-and-click format changes can be preserved if you rerun your project. Reports created in this format can easily be shared between SAS Enterprise Guide and the SAS Add-In for Microsoft Office and SAS Web Report Studio.

Although the preferred task output type is specified in Tools⇨Options⇨Results General, you can easily override this on a task-by-task basis. To force a task to generate different output than normal (say, if your colleague in Europe wants a PDF of the sales report), do the following:

1. **In the Process Flow or Project Tree, right-click the task for which you want to specify a special type and then click Properties to open the Properties dialog box.**

   You can also open the Properties dialog box from any open task dialog box; just go to the Properties view for the open task.

2. **Click the Results tab.**

3. **Select the Override the Preferences check box.**

4. **Select the PDF file type, shown in Figure 6-1 (you could select more than one type if desired).**

Note that you can select more than one output type; but be warned that for every output type you select, the task runs another time to generate it. For example, a task that takes one minute to create a long sales report in HTML takes about two minutes to generate the graph in both HTML and PDF formats. It's to your advantage to request only the types of output needed for your audience.

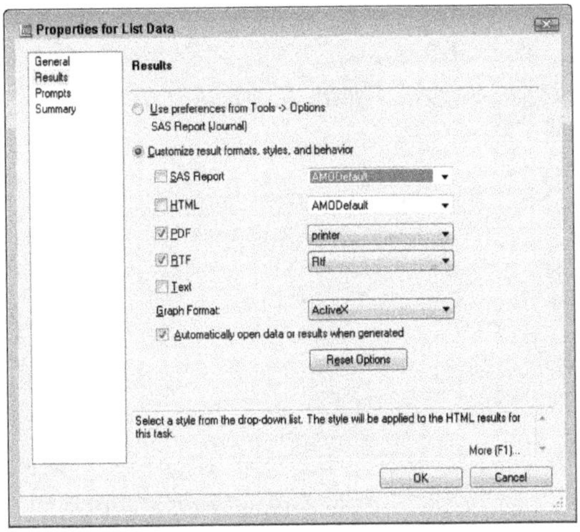

Figure 6-1:
Change the
file output
type for
a listing
report.

Plain text reports

The least robust but simplest form of output that you can select is the plain text file. This format is the lowest quality but typically has the smallest file size and is the fastest to open. These files are much like the simple text files you can create in Windows Notepad: They have the same limitations, including no character formatting, little paragraph alignment control, and poor pagination when printed. Additionally, graphs in this format show up as low-resolution, character-based graphs — or the graphs don't show up at all, depending on how the graph code is generated by SAS Enterprise Guide.

To view text files, you use a text viewer provided by SAS in SAS Enterprise Guide. You can also view text files externally in Notepad or WordPad after exporting the output. Text files aren't useful in many situations, unless you have a need to obtain reports in an unformatted manner or you want the smallest possible file size. Try to avoid this output type because of its many shortcomings. Figure 6-2 shows a sample text report generated by using the Characterize Data task with the Candy_Sales_Summary data set.

Adobe Acrobat (PDF) reports

SAS can also generate Adobe Acrobat files (PDFs). PDF is one of the most widely used file formats in the world because of Adobe's free Acrobat Reader program, which is preloaded on most PCs. If you use this format for a report that is being sent to a wide audience of unknown people (say, you want to put the sales report on your company's Web site), you can be reasonably sure that everyone will be able view it.

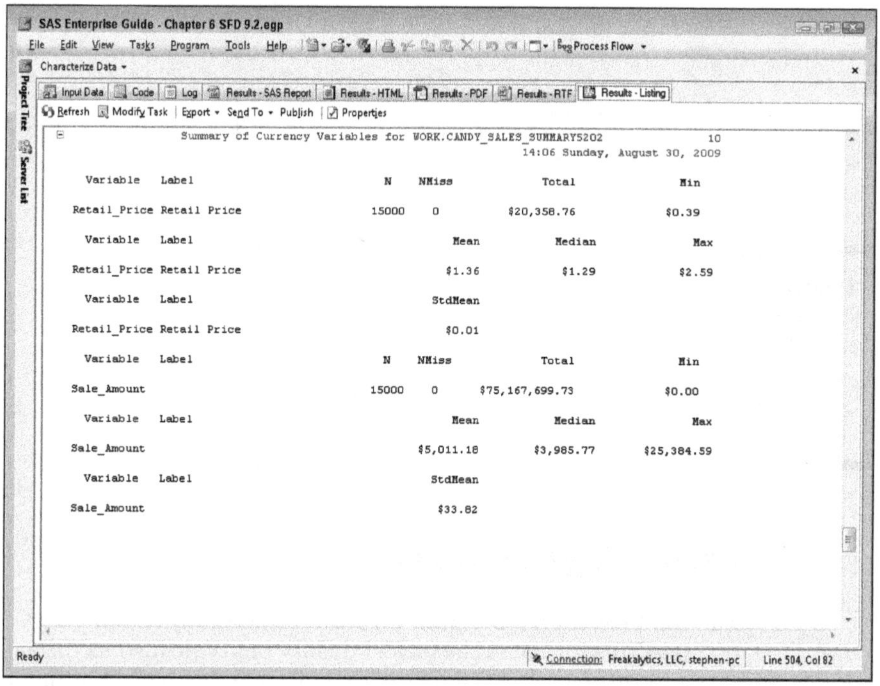

Figure 6-2:
Text output
offers a
small file
size but
poor layout
and no
formatting.

Unlike plain text (which is also very portable), the PDF format has many formatting and layout advantages, including character formatting, paragraph alignment control, and pagination when printing. Additionally, graphs in PDF format show up in high resolution, and bookmarks are automatically created to quickly find sections of your output in a large report.

A key limitation in using PDF reports is the inability to combine PDF output from more than one task. Several workarounds exist for this:

- ✔ **Use Adobe Acrobat:** This full-featured editing and authoring product from Adobe lets you combine the exported output files.

- ✔ **Manually combine the SAS code for the various tasks into one SAS program that you can run:** However, this option treads into the realm of SAS programming. See Chapters 16 and 17 for more information.

Adobe Acrobat Reader is used inside SAS Enterprise Guide to view PDF files. You can also view PDF output externally in Adobe Acrobat Reader after exporting the output (or right-clicking that output and choosing Open with Adobe Reader). Figure 6-3 shows a sample PDF report generated by using the Characterize Data task with the Candy_Sales_Summary data set. In this example, the Statistical style is used instead of the default Printer style (intended for black-and-white printing) so that the graphs appear in color. (Chapter 10 contains more tips for how to control your output appearance.)

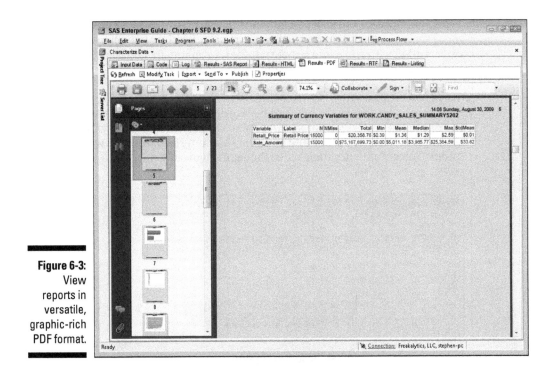

Rich Text Format (RTF) reports

SAS is also capable of generating *Rich Text Format* (RTF) files as output, which is a standard but older format for Microsoft Word. RTF is a flexible, but lesser-known, file format than PDF. When you use this format for a report that is being sent to a wide audience of unknown people (say, e-mailing a sales report to some of your investors), you can be reasonably sure that everyone will be able view it in Word or the less-functional (but free with Windows) WordPad.

WordPad is very limited. Sophisticated reports, especially those containing graphs, might not appear correctly in WordPad.

Like PDF output, using RTF has many formatting and layout advantages. Character formatting, paragraph alignment control, and pagination when printing are all available with RTF. Additionally, graphs in RTF format show up in high resolution and can be interactively modified with ActiveX graph controls. (Just right-click the graph to see the available editing capabilities, such as the capability to change the color scheme.) Unlike in a PDF, however, the RTF format doesn't automatically create bookmarks to quickly find your output in a large report.

A key limitation of the RTF format is the inability to combine output from more than one task. Several workarounds exist for this: Use Microsoft Word or WordPad with the exported output files, or manually combine the SAS code for the various tasks into one SAS program to run.

To view RTF files, Word opens inside SAS Enterprise Guide. You can also view these files externally in Word or WordPad after exporting the output (or right-clicking the output and choosing Open with Microsoft Office Word). A sample RTF report generated with the Characterize Data task with the Candy_Sales_Summary data set is shown in Figure 6-4.

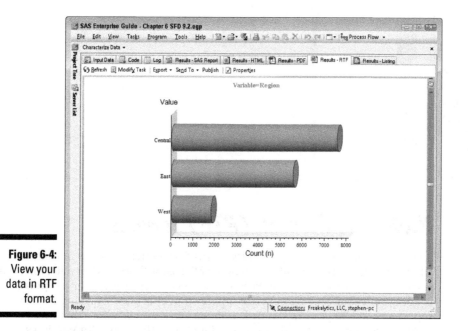

Figure 6-4:
View your
data in RTF
format.

HTML format reports

SAS can generate HTML (HyperText Markup Language) files as output. HTML, the standard format for Web pages, is a moderately flexible format. If you use this format for a report that's being sent to a wide audience of unknown people (for example, you want to place the sales report on your Web site), you can be reasonably sure that your viewers will be able see it in their standard Web browser.

Unfortunately, when you export HTML format, SAS usually creates multiple files (the HTML file and companion images). Therefore, e-mailing the output in this format can result in a poor experience for the recipient.

HTML has some of the formatting and layout advantages of PDF and RTF, including character formatting and paragraph alignment control. Additionally, graphs in HTML format show up in high resolution and can be interactively modified by using the ActiveX graph controls (right-click the graph to see the available editing capabilities). Unlike PDF, however, bookmarks aren't automatically created to quickly find your output in a large report. And unlike PDF and RTF, pagination when printing is poor — for example, a big table may split in an ugly manner across printed pages.

Unlike when using PDF and RTF, you can combine HTML output from more than one task. To access this capability, create at least one HTML output and then choose Tools⇨Create HTML Document. HTML Document Builder lets you select entire HTML outputs or sections of output from HTML outputs in your project. It simply appends one HTML file to another, creating one long report.

To view HTML files, Microsoft Internet Explorer (IE) opens inside SAS Enterprise Guide. You can view EG-created HTML files externally in IE or with other browsers, such as Mozilla Firefox. Figure 6-5 shows a sample HTML report generated by using the Characterize Data task with the Candy_Sales_ Summary data set.

SAS Output - Mozilla Firefox

File   Edit   View   History   Bookmarks   Tools   Help

Summary of Numeric Variables for WORK.CANDY_SALES_SUMMARY5202

Variable	Label	N	NMiss	Total	Min	Mean	Median	Max	StdMean
Customer	Customer	15000	0	67456	1	4.50	5.0	8	0.0187
Fiscal_Month_Num	Fiscal Month Number	15000	0	97608	1	6.51	7.0	12	0.0282
OrderID	OrderID	15000	0	112507500	1	7500.50	7500.5	15000	35.3565
ProdID	ProdID	15000	0	127792	1	8.52	9.0	16	0.0374
Units	Units	15000	0	73674000	0	4911.60	4900.0	10000	23.4604

Generated by the SAS System ('SASApp', X64_VSHOME) on August 30, 2009 at 02:06:38 PM

Summary of Currency Variables for WORK.CANDY_SALES_SUMMARY5202

Variable	Label	N	NMiss	Total	Min	Mean	Median	Max	StdMean
Retail_Price	Retail Price	15000	0	$20,358.76	$0.39	$1.36	$1.29	$2.59	$0.01
Sale_Amount		15000	0	$75,167,699.73	$0.00	$5,011.18	$3,985.77	$25,384.59	$33.82

Generated by the SAS System ('SASApp', X64_VSHOME) on August 30, 2009 at 02:06:38 PM

Summary of Date Variables for WORK.CANDY_SALES_SUMMARY5202

Variable	Label	N	NMiss	Min	Mean	Median	Max
Date	Date	15000	0	01/01/99	06/25/01	06/30/01	12/30/03

Done

Figure 6-5: View HTML output external to SAS Enterprise Guide in Mozilla Firefox.

SAS Report (SRX) format reports

Starting with SAS 9, SAS added SAS Report format as a standard report file format. This output type is also referred to as *SAS Report Files* and is the standard format for SAS Business Intelligence (BI). This is a very flexible format combining many of the advantages of RTF, PDF, and HTML. If you use this format for a report that is being sent to users of SAS Business Intelligence (for example, you want to place the sales report on your company's SAS BI Server for SAS Add-In for Microsoft Office users or SAS Web Report Studio users), you can be certain that everyone will be able to view, print, and modify it from their standard Web browser.

Unfortunately, when you export SAS Report format, SAS usually creates multiple files (a file with an SRX extension, plus any companion graph images). Therefore, e-mailing it to someone can result in a confusing experience for the recipient.

SAS Report format has all the formatting and layout advantages of PDF and RTF, including character formatting and paragraph alignment control. Additionally, graphs in SAS Report format show up in high resolution and can be interactively modified by using ActiveX graph controls. (Right-click the graph to see the available editing capabilities.) Further, if you interactively modify these graphs, the changes are remembered when you rerun the task. *Note:* This is an important capability because none of the other formats have the ability to retain format changes.

Bookmarks are automatically created so that you can quickly find your output in a large report, and pagination when printing is excellent. Finally, you can format the output with standard text formatting (bold, italics, different fonts, and so on), and the formatting changes are retained if you rerun the analysis.

As with HTML, you can combine SAS Report output from more than one task. Going beyond HTML, though, the results of SAS Report can be laid out side-by-side as well as above or below each other, allowing you to create cool dashboard-like displays that can print on a single page (see the report shown in Figure 6-6).

To access this dashboard-type capability, follow these steps:

1. **Create at least one SAS Report output.**

2. **Right-click one of the report outputs.**

3. **Choose Create Report.**

   You can also begin this process while viewing the report output. Choose Create⇨Create Report

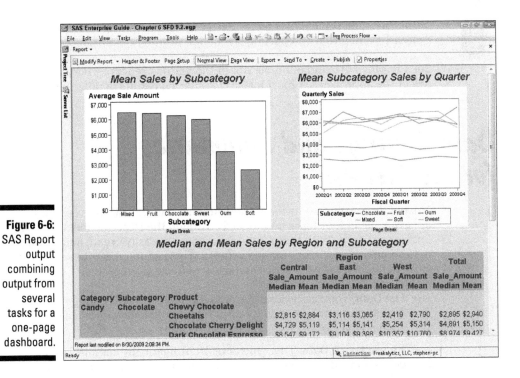

Figure 6-6:
SAS Report output combining output from several tasks for a one-page dashboard.

The SAS Report Editor appears, allowing you to add entire SAS Report outputs or sections of output from SAS Report outputs in your project.

The possibilities in the Report Editor are many and varied — from adding content using the Edit Report Contents dialog box (as shown in Figure 6-7) to selecting text and formatting it or interacting with the graphs in the report.

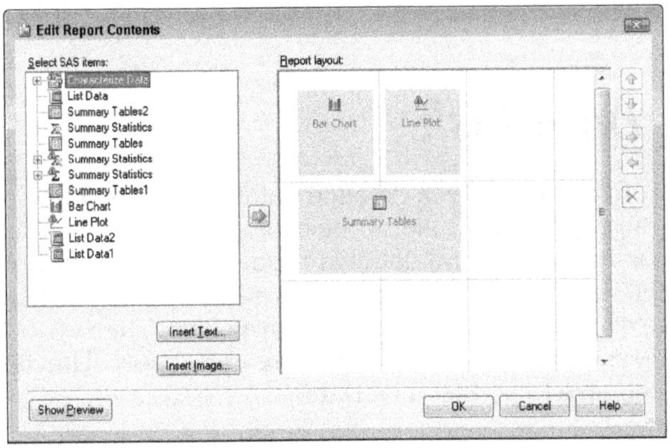

Figure 6-7:
The Edit Report Contents dialog box in the Report Editor.

In this book, most examples use SAS Report format. It is the most flexible output type in terms of reporting layout and printing reliability.

See Chapter 11 to find out more about the various report formats and how to select the appropriate report format for sharing results in different ways.

Data Listings and Summaries for the Listless

Most of the common data-listing and summarization tasks for reporting are available in four tasks and wizards through the Describe menu in SAS Enterprise Guide. With these four tasks, you can easily create data listings, data summaries, or cross-tabular reports. This section describes each task in more detail. A handy reference summary of these tasks follows:

- ✔ **List Data:** This task is a sales transaction detail report listing. Transactions are grouped by sales region with sales subtotals for each region.

- ✔ **Characterize Data:** This type of task automatically summarizes every column in a data table. See Chapter 3 for an example of this task in action.

- ✔ **Summary Statistics:** This task is a quick and easy way to summarize sales by subcategory. Results are presented in tabular and graphical form in histograms as well as in box and whisker plots. Histograms show frequency of sales by sales amount. Box and whisker plots show average sales, the main range of sales amounts, and any extreme sales amounts.

- ✔ **Summary Tables:** This task is also referred to as a *cross-tab*. It presents a tabular summary of mean sales by region and subcategory in a compact cross-tabular layout.

The List Data task

The simplest form of a report is a detailed data listing. The List Data task makes data listings quick and easy. Some examples of common reports that you can create with this task are detailed reports such as warehouse inventory listings, detailed listings of cash register sales by item, or a detailed patient adverse event listing from a clinical drug trial. The key to this task is that it prints every record in your data source as a report. This task is available when you choose Describe➪List Data.

The new List Report Wizard has been added to Enterprise Guide 4.2. It is an advanced form of the List Data task, with a wide range of report layout capabilities. The wizard is based on the powerful SAS PROC REPORT procedure.

When you assign variables to List Variables using the List Data task, the data columns are set to display in detail. If you want to sort the listing by certain variables, you add the variables to the Group Analysis by Variable role. Subtotals are linked to the group variables; adding a column to the Subtotal role enables subtotals at each change in the group variables. A grand total appears at the end of the entire data listing for each variable, designated as a Total role.

Figure 6-8 shows a sample sales report listing. The following sections walk you through creating and fine-tuning a sales report.

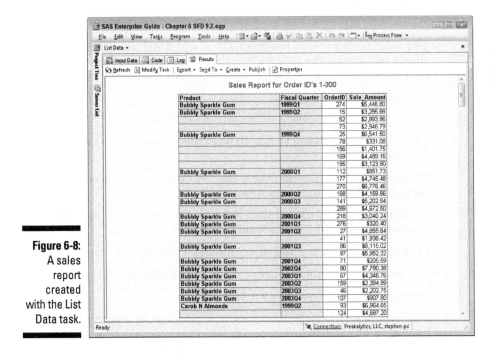

Figure 6-8:
A sales report created with the List Data task.

Creating a sales report

To help you better understand the List Data task, in this section you use the task to create a sales report. For this example, the finance department is being audited and has asked you to provide a listing of orders for Bubbly Sparkle Gum placed in 2003. You should include the sale amount, the quarter when the product was sold, and how many customers placed orders.

Because the auditor asked for the report to be organized by customer and quarter, you should sort it by these variables. To prepare the data first, you can use Query Builder, a tool described in Chapter 2. Here are the overall steps:

1. **Open the sample table Candy_Sales_Summary.**

   Because you need to filter the data for just Bubbly Sparkle Gum and Fiscal Year sold for 2003, use Query Builder first.

2. **Click the Query Builder button and select the Order_ID, Customer, Fiscal_Quarter, and Sale_Amount columns.**

3. **Filter on the Product for Bubbly Sparkle Gum column and the Fiscal_Year 2003 column.**

4. **Sort the data by this sequence: Customer, Fiscal_Quarter, and Order_ID; then run the query.**

   When subsetting your data, select only the variables needed for your next tasks. This reduces processing time and the storage needed for your work. Sorting the data by the variables in sequence ensures that the records are grouped correctly for the following tasks.

5. **Choose Describe⇨List Data.**

   The List Data task appears, displaying the Data pane.

6. **The detail variables are Order_ID and Sale_Amount; add them to List Variables.**

7. **Because you want to group the listing by Customer and Fiscal_Quarter, add them to Group Analysis By.**

8. **To make this report useful, total Sale_Amount at the end of each group and then add Sale_Amount to Total Of.**

9. **Click the Options pane and select the Print Number of Rows option.**

   This displays the total number of rows in each group section.

10. **Deselect the Print Row Number option.**

    You don't need this default because you are turning on the Print Number of Rows option.

11. **Click the Titles pane and deselect Use Default Text.**

12. **In the titles text area, type** Sales Report for Bubbly Sparkle Gum in 2003 **and then click Run.**

    The sales report appears, similar to Figure 6-9. As you can see, you can quickly find any customer, any quarter, and the number and total amount of orders in each section.

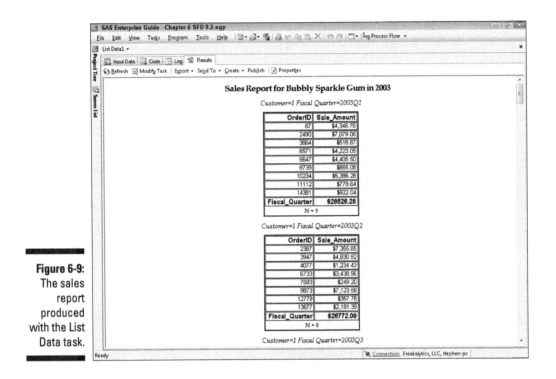

Figure 6-9:
The sales
report
produced
with the List
Data task.

Fine-tuning your sales report formatting

Look closely at Figure 6-9, and you might notice one problem: Namely, the quarterly totals aren't formatting exactly as expected. The first value reads $28526.28 but *should* read $28,526.28 — the placeholder comma is missing. If you go to the last page, you'll see that the grand total is even missing the $ sign. What's up with that?

If you look at the source table for this task, you can see that the format for Sales_Amount is DOLLAR9.2. This format dictates that one space is used by the dollar sign; one space is used for each comma separator for thousands, millions, and so on; three spaces are used for the decimal point and the cents; and the rest of the spaces are used for the dollar number characters. If the values of the dollar amount add up to something larger than $9,999.99, the DOLLAR9.2 format starts removing spaces for commas and other information you might like to see. This is a common problem when data is comprised of small values but adds up to a large value when summarized. (For example, you may not want cents shown, but that format is turned on in the default source variable.)

To correct this, change the format used by that variable in the query task or in the task where you are using it:

1. **Reopen the List Data task by clicking Modify Task while viewing the report listing.**

2. **Right-click Sale_Amount in the Total Of role and choose Properties.**

3. **In the Sale_Amount Properties dialog box that appears, click the Change button.**

   The format dialog box appears, displaying the current format DOLLARw.d, with Overall Width (w) set to 9 and Decimal Places set to 2.

4. **Change the Overall Width to 15 and then click OK.**

5. **Click OK again to dismiss the Sale_Amount Properties dialog box and then click Run.**

   The updated sales report appears. Scroll to the bottom of the report, which looks like Figure 6-10. Much better!

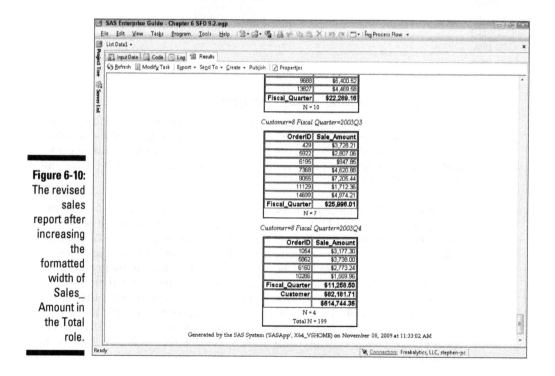

Figure 6-10:
The revised sales report after increasing the formatted width of Sales_Amount in the Total role.

The Characterize Data task: What did that guy in Accounting just give me?

If you receive some unfamiliar data to analyze and want a broad summary of every variable in a concise format, the quickest way to obtain a simplified summary report is to use the Characterize Data task. You could use a combination of other tasks to summarize different variable types (character, numeric, date, and so on), but the Characterize Data task uses a simplified approach to summarize all data types. This task automatically groups the variables in your data source by type (for example, character, numeric, currency, and date) and provides compact listings of a simple summary of each variable.

The Characterize Data task is useful as a first glance at unfamiliar data to look for unusual, incorrect, or "dirty" data values (for example, if the gender variable has 50 males, 56 females, and 2 mails; or the minimum sales amount was –$9,012.46 and the maximum was $12,349.81 for a candy stand). You have very few options to think about in this wizard. On the first page of the wizard, you can select one or many data tables to analyze. On the second page, you can select whether you want a report, graphs, or output data sets of the summaries. All columns in each table are summarized by using frequency tables or summary statistics (n, n missing, total, min, mean, median, max, or standard mean). You access the Characterize Data task by choosing Describe⇨Characterize Data. Refer to Figure 6-4 to see a sample Characterize Data report.

The Summary Statistics task: Get to the point!

Where are the statistics? This section shows how to get simple statistics for numeric variables. If you would like to analyze some sales data across product categories, you can start with the Summary Statistics task or Wizard. With this task, you can analyze numeric columns in your data for a variety of statistics.

The statistics available include mean, median, standard deviation, number of observations, min, max, 25th percentile, 75th percentile, confidence limits of the mean, t statistic, and 15 other univariate statistics.

You can optionally request data summaries graphically with histograms (shows distribution of a variable by frequency) or a box and whisker plot (shows median, 25th, and 75th percentiles, min, max, and outlier values shown as points). You can access this functionality by choosing Describe⇨Summary Statistics or Describe⇨Wizards⇨Summary Statistics. The wizard has most of the functionality of the task; it just walks you through the steps in a controlled order and hides a few advanced options. If you need access to those advanced options, you can convert your use of a wizard to the full-on task. The method for doing that is discussed in the next section.

To summarize by product category, add Sale Amount to the Analysis Variables role and Subcategory to the Classification Variables role. The histogram shows that Soft Candy sale amounts tended to be lower and more densely clustered around the mean amount than Sweet Candy sales. Figure 6-11 shows a sample sales box and whisker plot by product category. Output options also include histogram plots, which provide a more conventional way to view data distributions across categories.

The Summary Tables (cross-tabs) task: Easier than crosswords!

The Summary Statistics task is useful for analyzing numeric variables. However, if you want to add several category variables to analyze the data, these reports can become very long because there is one row per combination of category and analysis variables. If you want to analyze numeric data by several category variables, use the Summary Tables task or Wizard to use a minimum of space in a compact, cross-tabular format.

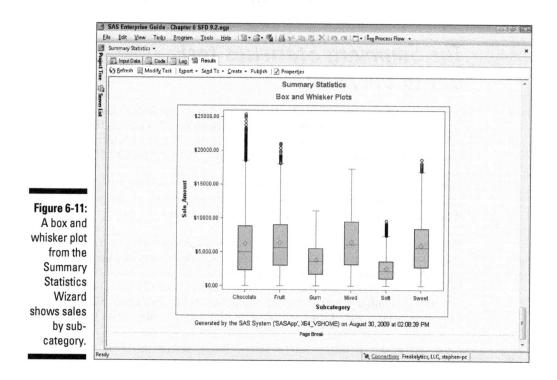

Figure 6-11:
A box and whisker plot from the Summary Statistics Wizard shows sales by sub-category.

Summary tables are similar to pivot tables in Excel or cross-tabulations that you have likely seen in various college courses or corporate financial statements. Suppose you want to analyze median and mean sales by region, product category, and subcategory. The Summary Tables task makes it possible to present this in a concise form, as shown in Figure 6-12. Note that you can easily compare across regions or products as well as compare overall regional and product performance via the Total columns. Likewise, you can compare median and mean sales for each product and region. Comparing median and mean can quickly let you know whether sales are skewed to the left or right of the mean, which is a key indicator of a few large sales skewing the mean up or down. (And all this from a compact table!)

Figure 6-12:
A Summary Table analyzing sales by region, category, and subcategory.

Median and Mean Sales by Region and Subcategory

Category	Subcategory	Product	Central Sale_Amount Median	Central Sale_Amount Mean	East Sale_Amount Median	East Sale_Amount Mean	West Sale_Amount Median	West Sale_Amount Mean	Total Sale_Amount Median	Total Sale_Amount Mean
Candy	Chocolate	Chewy Chocolate Cheetahs	$2,815	$2,864	$3,116	$3,065	$2,419	$2,790	$2,895	$2,940
		Chocolate Cherry Delight	$4,729	$5,119	$5,114	$5,141	$5,254	$5,314	$4,891	$5,150
		Dark Chocolate Espresso	$8,547	$9,172	$9,104	$9,398	$10,362	$10,760	$8,974	$9,427
		Fruity Choco-Rolls	$8,727	$8,876	$8,413	$8,752	$7,194	$9,089	$8,537	$8,857
		White Chocolate Turtles	$4,296	$4,561	$4,807	$4,844	$4,396	$4,436	$4,464	$4,665
	Gum	Bubbly Sparkle Gum	$3,054	$3,231	$3,309	$3,411	$2,773	$3,078	$3,071	$3,279
		Sparkle Peppermint Gum	$4,226	$4,311	$3,943	$4,234	$4,612	$4,824	$4,140	$4,346
	Soft	Flavor Bursting Watermelon Chews	$3,568	$3,670	$3,444	$3,690	$3,428	$3,717	$3,503	$3,684
		Nougatty Swirls	$2,780	$2,885	$2,927	$2,999	$2,602	$2,876	$2,814	$2,926
		Strawberry Chewsers	$2,207	$2,218	$2,018	$2,190	$1,907	$2,030	$2,106	$2,186
		Watermelon Taffy	$1,479	$1,569	$1,384	$1,414	$1,655	$1,569	$1,473	$1,510
Nuts	Fruit	Cherry Delight All Fruit	$4,897	$4,961	$4,785	$4,858	$3,847	$4,601	$4,702	$4,874
		Cranberry Delight	$7,450	$8,066	$7,145	$7,835	$8,585	$8,623	$7,490	$8,056
	Mixed	Just Pecans and Cashews	$5,907	$6,360	$6,841	$6,934	$4,863	$5,602	$6,086	$6,480
	Sweet	Carob N Almonds	$6,561	$6,908	$7,323	$7,384	$6,205	$6,626	$6,868	$7,035
		CinnaPecans	$4,825	$5,035	$5,211	$5,014	$3,839	$4,086	$4,853	$4,900
Total			$4,011	$4,968	$4,021	$5,066	$3,771	$5,020	$3,986	$5,011

Statistics available in the task are sum, mean, median, standard deviation, number of observations, min, max, 25th percentile, 75th percentile, confidence limits of the mean, t statistic, row or column sums, row or column percents, weighted sums, and 10 other univariate statistics. The wizard offers a commonly used subset of these statistics and limited data formatting relative to the full task, but the wizard is easier to master than the task. You access the Summary Table task or Wizard by choosing Describe⇨Summary Tables or Describe⇨Summary Tables Wizard, respectively.

Creating a summary table

The easiest way to understand summary tables is to create one. As a sample scenario, say that the sales director of your company asks you for a summary of sales data by region, category, subcategory, and product. In the summary,

she wants to see whether some regions are getting more of their sales revenue from large orders, so she has also asked that the summary show median
and mean sales amount. If the mean is much higher than the median, the data
can be said to be *skewed* by a small proportion of larger sales. An example
summary table is created in the following steps, with a summary table of
median and mean sales by product and region.

1. **Open the sample table Candy_Sales_Summary and choose Describe⇨
   Summary Tables Wizard.**

   The Summary Tables wizard appears. This Verify Data screen shows the
   server being accessed and the data in use. If desired, you can click Edit
   from this screen to apply a filter to the data in use for the wizard.

2. **Click Next.**

   The Select Analysis Variables and Statistics screen appears.

3. **Because you want to analyze median and mean sales, add the Sale_
   Amount variable to the Analysis Variables dialog box by clicking Add
   and selecting Sale_Amount.**

4. **Change the default statistic (Sum, in the drop-down box next to Sale_
   Amount) to Median.**

5. **Add Sale_Amount a second time to the Analysis Variables dialog box.**

6. **Change the second instance of Sale_Amount to Average.**

7. **Change the value of the Analysis Variables Label from In Columns to
   Hidden.**

   Hiding these labels saves space because they provide excessive detail
   for a summary table anyway. The screen looks similar to Figure 6-13.

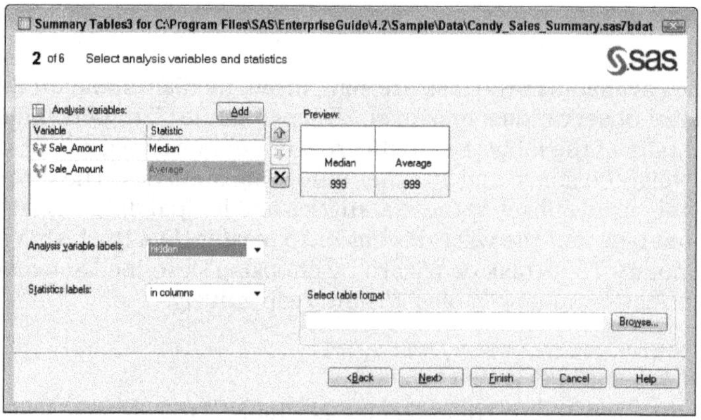

Figure 6-13:
The Select
Analysis
Variables
and
Statistics
screen.

8. **Click Next.**

The Select Classification Variables screen appears.

9. **Add Region to the Columns dialog box and Category, Subcategory, and Product to the Rows dialog box.**

A simplified preview with mock data is shown on the right side of the pane, as shown in Figure 6-14.

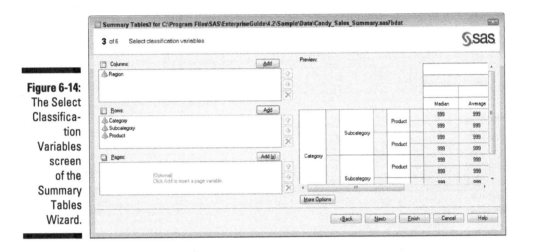

Figure 6-14: The Select Classification Variables screen of the Summary Tables Wizard.

10. **Click Next three times.**

11. **In the Provide a Title and Footnote screen, change the title to** Mean and Median Sales Summary by Category, Subcategory, and Product **and then click Finish.**

The sales summary appears, as shown in Figure 6-15. You can glean many details from this summary. The West region seems to have the most skew toward larger sales, pushing up the mean above the median. Fruity Choco-Rolls in particular seems to be the extreme case.

Enabling formatting in wizards

Wizards, unlike tasks, don't allow you to apply formats to numbers in the results. One way around this is to convert the wizard into the task form. This feature allows you to transfer the work specified in the wizard to the full-featured task version. To do this, follow these steps:

1. **Right-click the node in the project that was created using the wizard and choose Open⇨Open in Advanced View.**

The Summary Tables task appears, from which you can update the formats for the sales median and means.

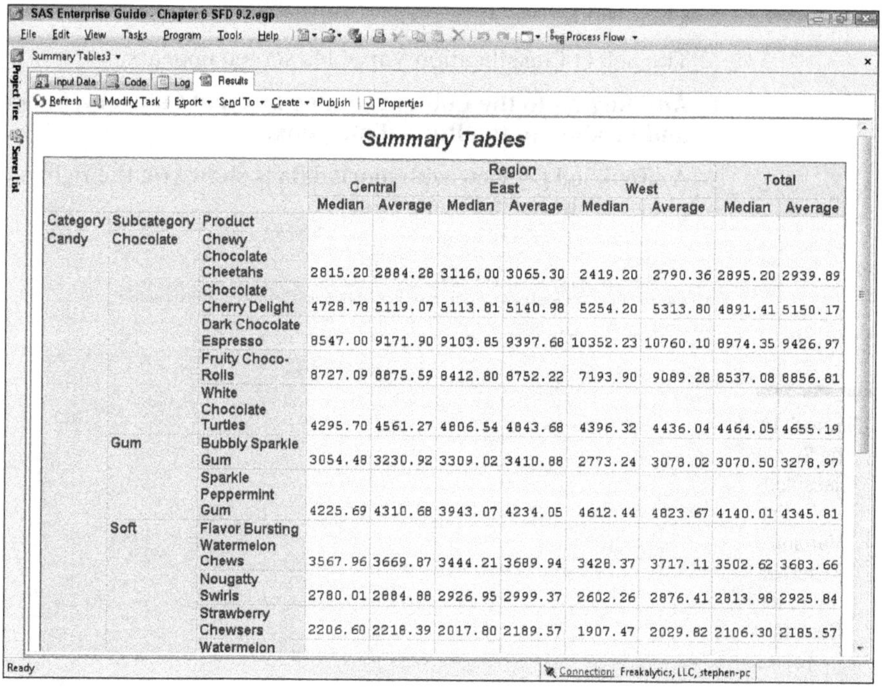

			Central		Region East		West		Total	
Category	Subcategory	Product	Median	Average	Median	Average	Median	Average	Median	Average
Candy	Chocolate	Chewy Chocolate Cheetahs	2815.20	2884.28	3116.00	3065.30	2419.20	2790.36	2895.20	2939.89
		Chocolate Cherry Delight	4728.78	5119.07	5113.81	5140.98	5254.20	5313.80	4891.41	5150.17
		Dark Chocolate Espresso	8547.00	9171.90	9103.85	9397.68	10352.23	10760.10	8974.35	9426.97
		Fruity Choco-Rolls	8727.09	8875.59	8412.80	8752.22	7193.90	9089.28	8537.08	8856.81
		White Chocolate Turtles	4295.70	4561.27	4806.54	4843.68	4396.32	4436.04	4464.05	4655.19
	Gum	Bubbly Sparkle Gum	3054.48	3230.92	3309.02	3410.88	2773.24	3078.02	3070.50	3278.97
		Sparkle Peppermint Gum	4225.69	4310.68	3943.07	4234.05	4612.44	4823.67	4140.01	4345.81
	Soft	Flavor Bursting Watermelon Chews	3567.96	3669.87	3444.21	3689.94	3428.37	3717.11	3502.62	3683.66
		Nougatty Swirls	2780.01	2884.88	2926.95	2999.37	2602.26	2876.41	2813.98	2925.84
		Strawberry Chewsers Watermelon	2206.60	2218.39	2017.80	2189.57	1907.47	2029.82	2106.30	2185.57

Figure 6-15: The Summary Tables results.

2. **Select the Summary Tables pane, right-click Median and Mean in the column headers, and then choose Data Value Properties.**

   The Data Value Properties window appears.

3. **Click the Format tab, and select an appropriate number format for the results (for example, DOLLARw.d in the Currency category).**

4. **Click OK to apply the format selection.**

   After running the formatted task, your output should be similar to the screen shown earlier in Figure 6-12.

   After you open a wizard in advanced mode and save it, you can open it only in task form. Tasks cannot be converted to wizard form because some features are inaccessible in the simplified wizard view.

Chapter 7

Graphs: More Value with SAS

. . . .

In This Chapter

▶ Understanding the basics of graphing

▶ Choosing among an assortment of graphs

▶ Cooking up your own graph

. . . .

*U*sing visuals of your data — *graphs* — to tell a story is the most widely used method in business, science, and education to convey complex information quickly and with a minimum of explanation. Knowing how to create graphs that are useful, concise, and tell the story behind the data can be one of the most valuable career skills to acquire. The great news is that SAS has a full palette of graphing capabilities!

Graphing Basics

The following list includes the basics that you need to consider when you are creating a graph:

✔ **Decide the question you want to answer or the information you want to convey before deciding which graph to use.** Graphs often do a poor job of conveying a clear and compelling message — because there isn't one! When in doubt, think long and hard about what you need to say with your graph before proceeding.

✔ **Figure out what data will be the basis for your graph's story.** Sometimes, the data might need to be filtered, updated with new or calculated columns, or even transposed or rearranged to arrive at a data structure needed for your desired graph.

✔ **Be sure that a graph is the best way to convey the message.** Graphs provide your audience with the overall shape of the data or allow quick comparisons of the relationship between many data points at once. For example, you might want to compare sales by region in a line graph to show that most regions have the same seasonal sales patterns. Perhaps you select a bar chart of the relative amount of sales for each region.

Summary tables might be more useful than graphs if any of the following are your primary purpose:

✔ You are providing details for a values lookup rather than overall comparisons.

✔ Precise values of the data are a key requirement.

✔ You want to concisely present information on the same topic that uses the same unit of measurement.

Here are some examples of when to use summary tables instead of graphs:

✔ Sales summaries for accountants who require precise reconciliation for each region

✔ Presenting sales by quarter for the year in dollars, yen, units sold, and as a percent of the prior year sales amount

 When creating graphs, turn off the 3-D effects that are the default for most of these graphs because they add little value (people thought they were cool at one time) and can make it hard for people to correctly compare values in most charts.

Graphs for Every Occasion

If a graph is the best way to present your information, your next step is to decide which graph type will tell your story clearly. The following sections describe the graph types available to you in SAS Enterprise Guide, their typical applications, and additional points to consider.

Bar charts

Bar charts are useful when you want to compare the relative differences among distinct groups. A good example would be a bar chart of sales by region for the current year, as shown in Figure 7-1.

 Make sure that you keep the vertical (y) axis starting value at zero. Otherwise, you can end up with charts that deceive at first glance because the relative height of the bars is what people perceive.

You can choose between horizontally or vertically oriented bar charts. Most of the time, vertical bar charts are fine. However, if you have many bars or long descriptions for each group, a horizontal bar chart is the better choice.

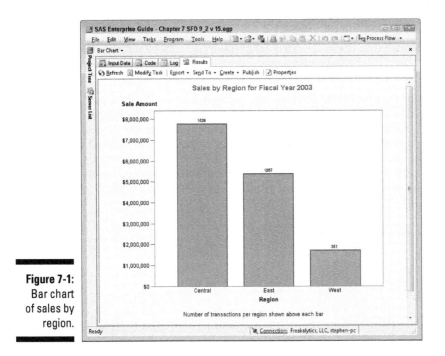

You can further expand the value of bar charts by using subgroups of bars or by stacking various subgroups in a bar. A subgroup example could be a graph of Quarter 1–4 sales by region, subgrouped on each quarter, allowing a quick comparison of regions per quarter. Likewise, you could create the same chart for each quarter instead of creating multiple subgroups on the same chart. This is particularly useful if you have many categories or many groups you want to examine, which could quickly make a single bar chart unreadable. A major downside of stacked bar charts is that most people have difficulty comparing the same stack piece across the various bars; but if only a few categories are stacked, stacked bar charts can still be useful.

Pie charts

Pie charts are one of the most popular types of charts among business users. Unfortunately, many graph experts are strongly opposed to pie charts because of the difficulties people have understanding the information and making effective decisions. A bar chart is usually superior at conveying the same information as a pie chart, from a comparison of individual values to a comparison of multiple values. That said, if you still want to use pie charts because everyone at your company or your audience just loves them, here are a few points to consider:

✔ Avoid creating pie charts with more than six to eight values.

✔ Ensure that there are fairly large differences between the values.

✔ Use high-contrast colors to make viewing easier.

Pie charts are available in standard, stacked, and grouped form. Standard pie charts are much like bar charts in function, charting sales by region, for example, as shown in Figure 7-2. Stacked pie charts are difficult for most people to understand but are similar in function to stacked bar charts because you can chart sales by region stacked by sales channel. Grouped pie charts are similar in function to grouped bar charts because you could chart sales by region in each pie and group the pies by product line.

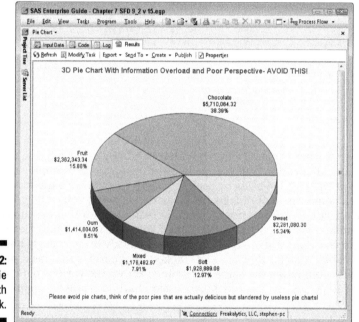

Figure 7-2:
Avoid pie charts with chart junk.

Line plots

Line plots are useful for examining trends over time. A chart showing sales over the past three years conveys the overall long-term sales trend as well as the seasonal shape of sales throughout a given year, as shown in Figure 7-3.

With SAS, you can create a variety of specialized line charts that go beyond the standard line chart. Among these are specialized forms of line charts, including splines, needles, step, regression, smoothed, standard deviations, Lagrange interpolations, and overlay plots. You can also produce line plots with multiple groups displayed on a single graph or with one graph per group.

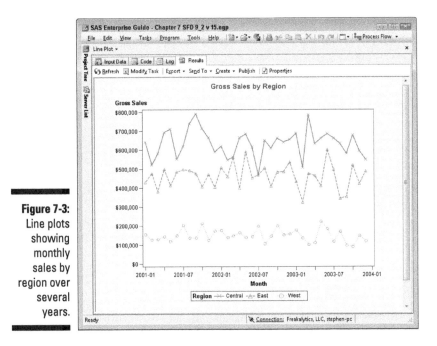

Figure 7-3:
Line plots
showing
monthly
sales by
region over
several
years.

Deciding whether to add symbols for each data point on your line plot should largely be a function of whether you want to emphasize only the overall trend (lines only) or the trend and the individual points (lines and points). Finally, you can choose to display two different vertical (y) axis variables in a line plot — one on the left side and one on the right side. These can be a different scale (say, number of units sold on left and dollars revenue on right), and each can have a separate line per measure displayed.

Beware the scaling effect! When two variables with values of a different magnitude are shown on the same chart (for example, net sales are in millions, and net returns are in thousands), the change in the variable with the large scale is perceived as much larger than the smaller scale variable. If returns double from the start to the end while sales increase 10 percent, the sales increase still appears larger at first glance. This is especially important when you compare growth rates of competing groups that start at very different values. One solution to this problem is to convert the data to the logarithmic scale, which is an option readily available in the Line Plot task, as shown in Figure 7-4. Note that the variations from month to month for the West region appear much larger in the log graph than the standard graph in Figure 7-3. Likewise, the variation from month to month for the other two regions appears much smaller because we have removed the scaling effect.

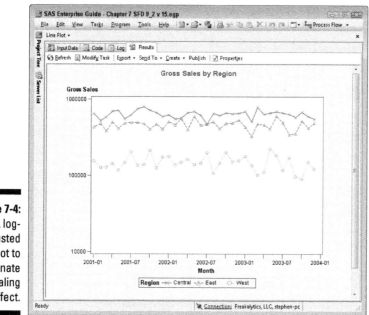

Figure 7-4:
A log-
adjusted
line plot to
eliminate
the scaling
effect.

Scatter plots

Scatter plots are great at showing the relationship between two variables of interest, which is a concept often referred to as examining the correlation of the two variables. A chart showing the relationship of the total amount of each sale with the percent discount given in each sale is an example of examining correlations.

A good rule is to place the variable that you believe influences the second variable (typically called the *independent variable,* or the *cause*) on the x axis. Place the second variable, also known as the *dependent variable,* or the *effect,* on the y axis.

Scatter plots can be further enhanced by the addition of a fitted regression line. Without getting overly technical, the *regression line* is the closest fit among the weighting of the data points. The line can be used for an approximation of the overall trend and center of the data displayed. Figure 7-5 is an example of a scatter plot with a regression line fitted to the data. An interesting observation from this plot is that larger discounts appear to yield overall smaller orders. Salespeople often argue that larger discounts lead to larger sales, but this graph contradicts that argument. More investigation might be warranted based on this simple analysis.

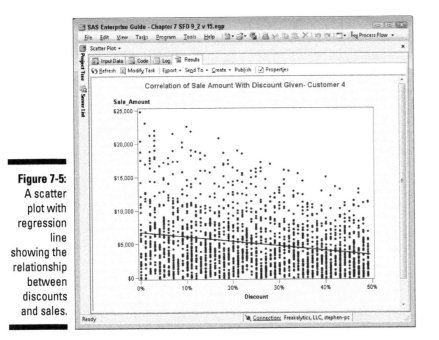

Figure 7-5:
A scatter plot with regression line showing the relationship between discounts and sales.

Area plots

Area plots are a form of the line plot with the area below the line colored to emphasize it. In general, area plots add little value over line plots. In the case of trying to display multiple groups on one plot, area plots can be difficult to read and interpret. Figure 7-6 shows the same information as Figure 7-1. Note that the Central region is much larger than the other regions and hides the other two areas. You could correct this, but why use charts that require frequent repair?

Bubble plots

Bubble plots are a specialized form of a scatter plot, using bubbles of various sizes rather than points for each data point. The bubble sizes are scaled according to a third variable displayed in the plot. Figure 7-7 is a classic example of using bubble plots to display two attributes of group data in a simple-to-read plot.

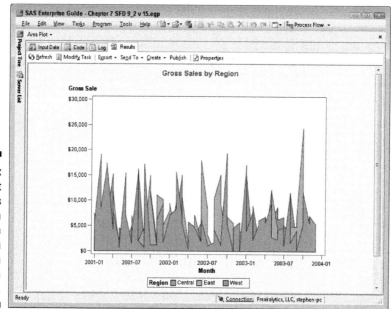

Figure 7-6:
An area plot that hides key data because one region is much larger than the others.

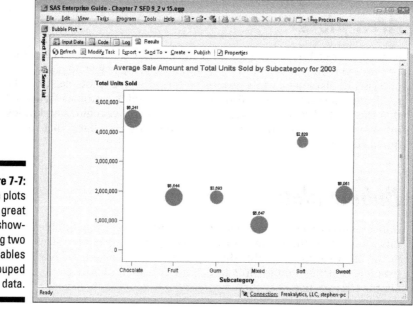

Figure 7-7:
Bubble plots are great for showing two variables for grouped data.

Box plots

Box plots are great for comparing the distribution of a variable for two or more categories or over time. A box plot displays the median and the four quartiles of the data for each category of data on the x axis:

- ✔ **Bottom line (or whisker):** The 1st–25th percentile (lower quartile)
- ✔ **Bottom part of the box:** The 25th–50th percentile (second quartile)
- ✔ **Horizontal line in the box:** The median
- ✔ **Top half of the box:** The 50th–75th percentile (third quartile)
- ✔ **Top line (or whisker):** The 75th–99th (fourth quartile)
- ✔ **Circles:** Below and above the 1st and 99th percentile

A great use of a box plot is to compare the distribution of sales by product category, as shown in Figure 7-8.

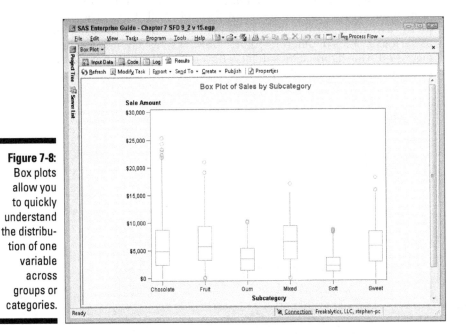

Figure 7-8: Box plots allow you to quickly understand the distribution of one variable across groups or categories.

Variations on the standard box plot include hi-lo plots, hi-lo-close plots, and box plots that use an interquartile range instead of quartiles. A hi-lo plot or a hi-lo-close plot can show the high, low, and closing price of a stock over time.

Donut charts

Donut charts are similar to pie charts except that a hole appears in the middle of a donut chart. Because they are an even more confusing form of pie chart, we don't recommend that you use them. According to multiple studies by graphing experts, accurately interpreting a donut chart is very difficult for most people.

Contour plots

Contour plots allow you to show the relationships between three numeric variables in a two-dimensional plot. Much like a map that shows elevation of land contours, a contour plot allows you to show the relationship between two variables like a scatter plot but with coloring or gradient lines highlighting the third value in your plot.

A good example of a contour plot is displaying the relationship of time of day, store number, and sales amount at a chain of retail stores. The time of day is on the x axis, the store number is on the y axis, and the sales amount appears as various shades of different colors showing sales amount, as shown in Figure 7-9. This figure shows quickly how different stores have varying times of day that might be ideal for deliveries, inventory, and restocking.

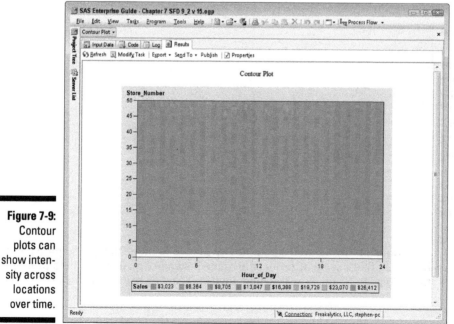

Figure 7-9:
Contour plots can show intensity across locations over time.

Contour plots can be useful for finding trends such as the time of day with the highest sales, the day of the week with the most returns by store, or the day of the month by clinical trial investigator with the most patient visits.

Radar charts

A *radar chart* allows you to present graphically the frequency or intensity in value of four to ten variables at different points in time or by using different conditions or various test subjects. Classic users of radar charts include quality control and marketing research types. On a radar chart, the values for each variable are displayed along spokes that radiate from the center of the chart and are often stacked on top of one another, thus giving this chart type the look of a radar screen.

Marketing researchers might want to show several attributes of a product and several consumer opinions of a product by each attribute, as illustrated in Figure 7-10. With one glance, you can see that only one test consumer rated the product high on all attributes and that most disliked the product on more than half the attributes deemed important to product success. Back to the drawing board!

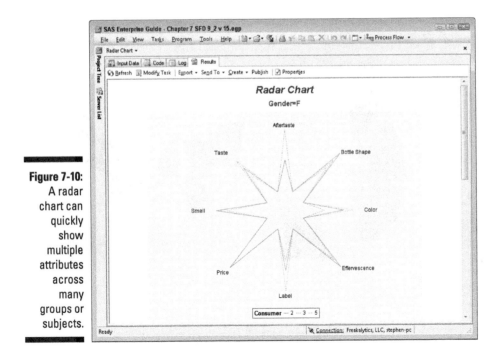

Figure 7-10: A radar chart can quickly show multiple attributes across many groups or subjects.

Map graphs

Map graphs in SAS enable you to overlay data values for a location, city, county, state, country, or continent on a map of your choice. A two-dimensional U.S. map can be used to show the states by population, as shown in Figure 7-11. In this map, population is bucketed into five groups based on population ranking. You can quickly find the most and least populous states and their proximity to one another. Variations on this include three-dimensional maps with the states rising above others based on population and two-dimensional maps with bars rising from each state, indicating population.

Tile charts

Tile charts in SAS enable you to arrange data values by categorical values (such as state, customer, and company) as variable-sized rectangles, or tiles, as part of an overall rectangle. Tile charts are also referred to as *tree maps*. The size of the tile indicates the size of the measure used in the tile chart. You can add a second measure to indicate the color intensity of the tiles and can have a second level of categorical partitioning to break up the overall rectangle into regions of relative size.

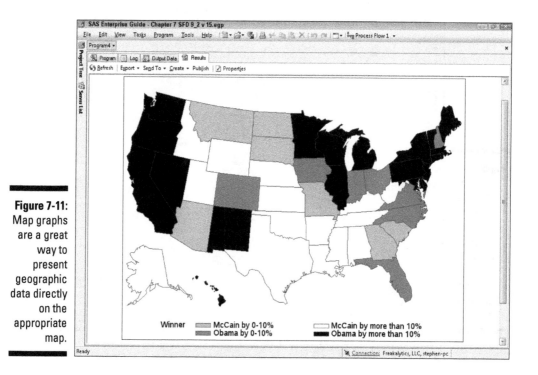

Figure 7-11:
Map graphs are a great way to present geographic data directly on the appropriate map.

A tile chart of the winners by state of the 2008 presidential race is shown in Figure 7-12. The size of each tile is based on the total popular vote of that state. You can see that Obama won approximately three-fourths of the states. A few states won by Obama and two states won by McCain were close. Still, even if McCain had won these two states instead of Obama, Obama would still have captured a clear majority of the Electoral College.

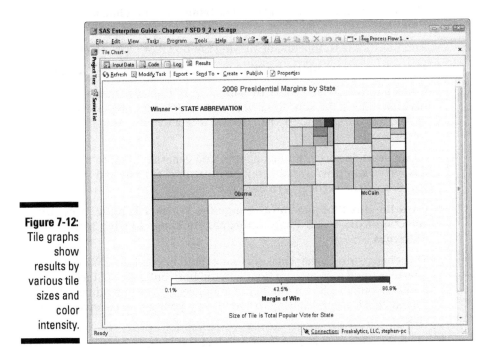

Figure 7-12: Tile graphs show results by various tile sizes and color intensity.

Creating Graphs with SAS

It's time to put some of these graphing principles to practice. This section provides examples of creating useful plots with SAS — plots that contain relevant information about your data and convey a meaningful message.

A box plot example: finding the extreme products

Large orders frequently cause the shipping department to keep people late, resulting in overtime, expedited shipping requests, and employees who are more likely to quit because of stressful deadlines. Suppose that the shipping department folks have asked you to see whether there is a way to avoid shipping so many large orders. They want you to analyze sales by category so that they can talk with the appropriate sales manager about reducing the number of large orders placed and receiving more frequently placed, manageable, and smaller orders. Follow these steps to perform this analysis:

1. **Open the sample table Candy_Sales_Summary and choose Graph⇨ Box Plot.**

   The Box Plot task appears, displaying the Box Plot type selection pane.

2. **Keep the default selection of Box Plot, and then click the Data pane.**

3. **You want to analyze orders by subcategory (because managers are divided among the subcategories) and analyze overall sale amount, so add Subcategory to the Horizontal role and Sale_Amount to the Vertical role.**

   As we mention earlier in the chapter, you generally want to place the suspected causative variable on the horizontal (x) axis and the result variable on the vertical (y) axis.

4. **Click the Box Plot pane and change the Whisker Length Percentile selection from +– 1.5 Times Interquartile Range to High/low Extremes.**

   This change forces the whiskers that extend beyond the 25% and 75% quartiles to include all data points in the horizontal group, including potential outliers. If you don't care about seeing the individual extreme values, this is a good setting to use to keep your graph clean and easy to view.

5. **Click the Titles pane, and then deselect Use Default Text.**

6. **Type the title** Box Plot of Sales by Subcategory.

7. **Change the selected section to Footnote, and then deselect Use Default Text.**

8. **Clear the default footnote text and leave it blank.**

9. **Click Run.**

   The box plot similar to Figure 7-13 appears. An interesting note is that Mixed has the highest median amount of order and Chocolate has the highest range of order value, with Fruit a close second. This could indicate more infrequent ordering of chocolate and perhaps an opportunity to work with the Chocolate sales manager and focus more on receiving smaller, more frequent orders for this product category.

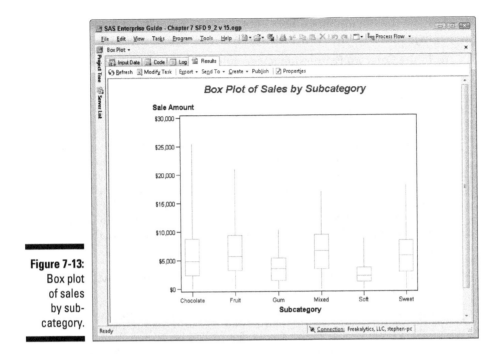

Figure 7-13:
Box plot
of sales
by sub-
category.

A line plot example: tracking regions

Suppose that the finance department has asked you to provide a chart show-ing the monthly pattern of sales by region for 2003. Understanding the rela-tionship of varying sales cycles among the regions is key for this chart.

Prepping your data

To prep your data for a line plot graph, follow these steps:

1. **Open the sample table Candy_Sales_Summary.**

2. **Open the Filter and Query task by choosing Data⇨Filter and Query.**

3. **Add the Sale_Amount and Region columns to the Select Data pane.**

4. **Select the Filter Data pane and add a filter for Date between '01JAN2003'd and '31DEC2003'd (use the entire value, including the single quotation marks).**

SAS dates are always stored as numbers, so unless you know the inter-nal number used by SAS to represent these dates, you need to use a special quoted version of the date as shown here. The day, three-letter month, and four-digit year enclosed in single quotation marks and appended by a lowercase *d* tells SAS that you want this text string con-verted to a SAS date value.

5. **Click the Computed Columns button, and then choose New⇨Build Expression.**

6. **In the Enter an Expression space, add the following expression and then click Next:**

```
INPUT( PUT( YEAR(Candy_Sales_Summary.Date )*10000
            + MONTH(Candy_Sales_Summary.Date ) *100 +
            1,8.0),YYMMDD8.)
```

This formula uses the YEAR and MONTH function to extract the year and month values as numbers and add them to form a number representation of the year and month with the day always equal to 01 (for example, 20030301). The number is then converted to text so that it can be read in as a date value, with the day from every record converted to the 1st. Note that you could have used the Recode feature instead of Expression Builder to accomplish the date range remapping to the first of each month.

7. **Change both the column name and the alias to Month.**

8. **At the bottom of the pane, change the format for this newly created column to YYMMD7.0.**

9. **Click Finish, click Close, and then click Run to execute your query.**

A data table similar to the one in Figure 7-14 is created. You now have the data needed to create a great line plot of monthly sales by region!

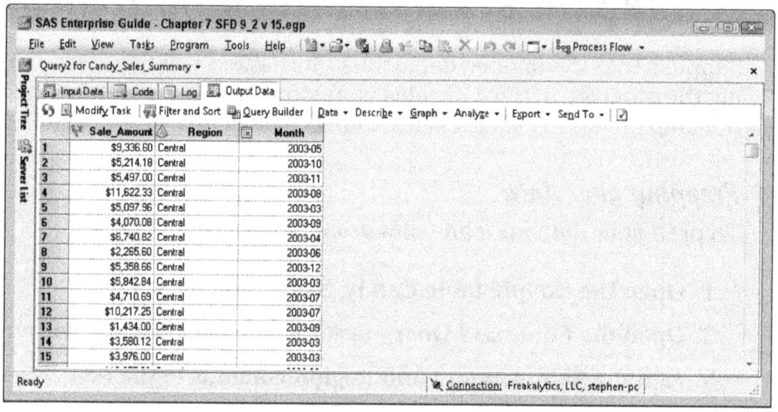

Figure 7-14: Data prepped for your line plot analysis of sales.

Creating your line plot graph

From prefiltered data, you can create a line plot graph by following these steps:

1. **Continue from the last step in the preceding section. With the filtered version of the Candy_Sales_Summary table on your screen, choose Graph⇨Line Plot.**

The Line Plot task appears, displaying the Line Plot type selection pane.

2. **Select the next-to-last choice: Multiple Line Plots by Group Column.**

   This allows the graphing of multiple lines on one graph based on the grouping column specified in the next step.

3. **Click the Data pane.**

4. **You want to analyze sales by month, grouped by region, so add Month to Horizontal, Sale_Amount to Vertical, and Region to Group.**

5. **Click Sale_Amount and select Sum from the Summarize for Each Distinct Horizontal Value drop-down list.**

6. **Click the Titles pane, and then deselect Use Default Text.**

7. **Type the title** 2003 Gross Sales by Region. **Change the selected section to Footnote, and then deselect Use Default Text.**

8. **Clear the default footnote text and leave it blank.**

9. **Click Run.**

   A line plot similar to Figure 7-15 appears. An interesting note is that the regions have different sales patterns, with the Central region having its biggest months early in the year and the East and West having bigger months in the middle of the year. Also, East and Central appear to have similar patterns in the last part of the year.

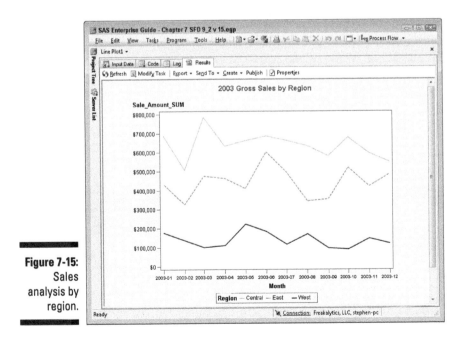

Figure 7-15:
Sales
analysis by
region.

For a different perspective, you can change the Sum value set in Step 5 to Average. Remember to update your title when you do this. Click Run. The mean sales line plot similar to Figure 7-16 appears. You see very different patterns than in the gross sales plot. The West region has the most variable average order amount, whereas the average order amounts for the Central and East regions correlate more smoothly with their total sales for each month.

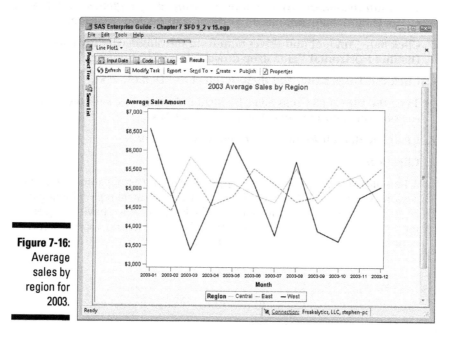

Figure 7-16:
Average
sales by
region for
2003.

Part III

Impressing Your Boss with Your SAS Business Intelligence

The 5th Wave   By Rich Tennant

"The top line represents our revenue, the middle line is our inventory, and the bottom line shows the rate of my hair loss over the same period."

In this part . . .

People spend lifetimes studying statistical methods and applied analytics, collecting PhD after PhD. In this part, we distill the entire field down to just a few chapters. Obviously, our treatment of this area cannot be considered comprehensive — and no diploma is at the back of this book.

However, we hope that our coverage is enough to raise your interest in the topic and inspire you to discover more. In the meantime, you can pick up enough lingo and concepts to recognize how SAS brings the power of analytics to almost any problem you can imagine.

Chapter 8

A Painless Introduction to Analytics

*S*tatistics and analytics are all the rage because they give people the ability to leverage past data to better understand what happened, to make better decisions about what actions should be pursued today, and to forecast future behavior and outcomes. This chapter and the next chapter provide an overview of many of the analytic methods in SAS and why you would want to use them. Note that we describe only the general concepts of each analytic method; in-depth guidance is beyond the scope of this book but is crucial to properly selecting and gaining the most from these techniques. We hope this overview provides inspiration and direction so that you can expand your perspective and pursue new areas of opportunity.

Analytic Concepts Useful for Everyone

Unfortunately, we can't make you an expert in statistics. However, we can review the principles behind many of the analytic capabilities available in SAS.

We don't cover the specialized capabilities in SAS. Because this book offers a broad review of many areas of SAS, we recommend that you pursue additional reading on the methods you're most interested in so that you can more fully understand the assumptions, the proper use, and the correct interpretation of the results from these powerful tools.

It's variable

The fundamental principle behind almost every form of statistical analysis is *variability,* which is the most important concept for understanding most results of analyses. The simplest way to illustrate variability is with a coin toss. If you repeatedly toss a fair coin (where *fair* means that the coin has an equal chance of landing heads up or tails up) ten times, you would expect the number of heads and tails to be similar (five heads and five tails). However, multiple iterations of this ten-toss scenario show that many times, the number of heads counted in ten tosses isn't five, but rather six, seven, four, or three. In fact, if you bet $1 to win $2 on five heads per ten tosses, you would quickly become poor. In Table 8-1, you can see that you would win $2 only 24.6 percent of the time, meaning an average return of just $0.492 ($2 won multiplied by 24.6 percent of the time) on each $1 bet. This example summarizes variability quite nicely.

Many early statistical methods were developed to examine gambling outcomes like the one used in this example!

Table 8-1	Chance of Various Outcomes from Tossing a Coin Ten Times	
Number of Heads	*Number of Tails*	*Chance of Seeing This Outcome*
0	10	0.1 percent (1 in 1,000)
1	9	1.0 percent (1 in 100)
2	8	4.4 percent
3	7	11.7 percent
4	6	20.5 percent
5	5	24.6 percent
6	4	20.5 percent
7	3	11.7 percent
8	2	4.4 percent
9	1	1.0 percent
10	0	0.1 percent

What is variance?

Suppose your manager asks for a report summarizing the average sale by region for your new product, Super Chocolate Toffee Bears. Also suppose that the West has a mean sales price of $1.25, and the East has a mean sales price of $1.28. These don't seem all that different, but are they?

Suppose we told you that 95 percent of all sales in the West were between $1.20 and $1.30 and that 95 percent of all sales in the East were between $1.01 and $1.61. Now do they seem similar? What does this additional information

tell us? Perhaps you could focus your marketing dollars to first penetrate the markets where the candy is selling at higher prices — and, we hope, higher margins!

The missing piece added by these confidence intervals is in the concept of variance. *Variance* is the measure of spread of values for a given measure — in this example, sales price. Variance is central to all statistical analysis and is the key to calculating confidence intervals in this example.

p-values

If you understand the concept of variability, you have one of the key concepts required to understand p-values frequently cited by various studies, journals, and newspapers. A *p-value* is often used to explain how rarely an outcome would occur by chance, given certain assumptions from the analysis used. Suppose that you want to ask whether a coin in question was indeed fair and not rigged to force more tails than normal. (See the preceding section for a definition of *fair*.) If a coin is indeed fair, you expect a 50 percent chance of a head or a tail if you conduct enough tosses.

Suppose you come across a questionable coin and doubt that it is fair, believing it to be rigged to land on tails more than 50 percent of the time, which would obviously provide an advantage to someone in a game of chance. If you flip that coin ten times and see zero heads turn up, you would likely believe that the coin was fixed. You could assign a p-value of 0.001 (0.1 percent) to this outcome because a fair coin would exhibit this behavior in just 1 out of 1,000 ten-toss tries! Sure, it *could* be a fair coin, but most people would likely insist on using a new coin because 1 head in 1,000 tosses seems like a pretty good indication that the coin is fixed.

In many fields of study, a p-value less than 0.05 (1 in 20) is usually considered *statistically significant*. Be sure not to confuse this type of statistical significance (for example, drug A is more effective than drug B based on one measure of success) with practical or real-world significance (for example, drug A is 5 percent faster than drug B at relieving bunion pain but costs 10 times more — not something of practical value to most people).

How confident are you?

The third foundation concept to help you understand analytics is *confidence intervals,* which are ranges of values that attempt to contain the true value being estimated. For example, suppose you create a sales forecast for the next month based on the last three years of sales. Offering a single number to your boss — say, $10,000,000 — seems simplistic and even dangerous! It's an estimate of the next month that doesn't seem to take into account the variability of prior months, unless they were always $10,000,000. The greater the prior months' variability, the wider the confidence interval needs to be. If the variability of prior sales were low, you would expect a smaller confidence interval range. You might offer your boss a 95 percent confidence interval of $7,200,000 to $15,000,000, with an expected value of $10,000,000, as a more informative sales estimate.

Most people new to statistics think that a 95 percent confidence interval means there is a 95 percent chance that the interval contains the true value of the statistic. But that's not how it works! A 95 percent confidence interval actually means that if the overall data for the subject at hand were collected 100 times, 95 of the 100 confidence intervals would contain the true value. Approximately 5 of those times, it would not contain the true value.

What did your mother say about making assumptions?

Every statistical method and technique has a variety of assumptions that must be met for the results to be useful and meaningful. You need to check these assumptions before using the statistical technique by using the diagnostic checks frequently available with the analysis output. If your data doesn't meet the standard assumptions for a given statistical technique, perhaps another technique has broader or different assumptions that would make analyzing your data possible. Likewise, you might be able to transform your data to make it meet the assumptions that your selected statistical technique requires.

Suppose, for example, that you use an analysis that assumes your data is normally distributed. If the data isn't normally distributed, the assumptions haven't been met, and the results and interpretations could lead to incorrect conclusions. Using some of the data management tasks in SAS Enterprise Guide, you could transform the data to a normal distribution to meet the needed assumptions. It is important to check the assumptions required by your analysis technique to make sure that you use the right method and make the proper conclusions!

Describing Your Data with Distribution Analysis

A common question asked about data is the type of distribution that it mimics or originates from. Most people who are familiar with statistics have heard of a *normal distribution*, which is the assumed distribution for analyses, such as simple correlation, analysis of variance (ANOVA), and linear regression. Knowing the distribution that your data originates from is important in selecting the proper transformation (if needed) and appropriate analytic technique.

The Distribution Analysis task (available by choosing Describe⟹Distribution Analysis) enables you to examine your data for conformance to a variety of distributions, including the normal, lognormal, exponential, Weibull, beta, gamma, and kernel distributions. Tabular summaries, fit statistics, and a variety of graphical presentation including histograms, probability plots, quantile plots (you may have heard of them as percentile, decile, or quartile plots), and box plots are also readily available.

Figure 8-1 shows a sample histogram from the Candy_Sales_Summary data provided with SAS Enterprise Guide. In this plot, the lognormal distribution is overlaid on the frequency counts of the Sale_Amount data. Visually, this appears to be a very good fit to the lognormal distribution. You can also examine the actual goodness-of-fit statistics to see whether the data conforms to the lognormal distribution. Other output from this task can help test the value of the mean and the standard deviation. Also handy from the standard summary tables are the confidence intervals for the mean, standard deviation, and variance of the data.

Figure 8-1:
Lognormal curve overlaid on the sales amount to examine whether the data is lognormally distributed.

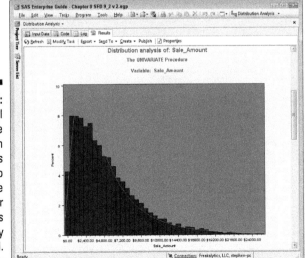

Analyzing Counts and Frequencies

In customer demographic and health care research, collecting responses for one or more categorical variables is common. Examples of categorical variables include a favorite car type, ethnic background, gender, disease progression status, a grade received in a course, marital status, home ownership status, citizenship status, credit grade, and employment status. Some categorical variables have inherent order, and others are just categories with no implicit order. Gender is a good example of a *nominal variable,* a variable with no explicit order to the values male and female. There is no reason to place female before male except for the alphabetic order of the name of the category. Disease progression status is a good example of an *ordinal variable* because Stage I of a disease occurs before Stage II, and so on. Ordinal variables simply have an order of the categories. They have no exact ratio of difference among the categories: That is, Stage I is not necessarily half as advanced as Stage II.

An example of a *two-way contingency table* is shown in Figure 8-2. This is a table of chocolate preference by gender generated with the Table Analysis task (available by choosing Describe➪Table Analysis). This type of table is also referred to as a *contingency table* or a *cross-tabular summary.* The Table Analysis task can produce contingency tables based on many variables, but practical experience shows that no more than three or four variables can be examined easily. The Table Analysis task adds more value than the Summary Tables task (covered in Chapter 6) because of the availability of many statistical methods to determine whether the differences among the various categories are statistically significant.

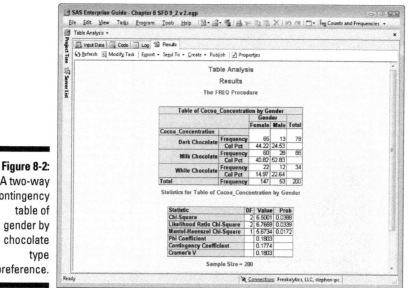

Figure 8-2:
A two-way contingency table of gender by chocolate type preference.

Examining Figure 8-2, you might wonder whether the overall taste preference profile of males and females would be the same in the general population as in this 200-person sample. Various statistical tests, such as the Chi-square test and the Mantel-Haenszel Chi-square test, can be applied with the Table Analysis task to determine whether a true taste preference difference exists among a potential customer base or whether chance differences exist between men and women in this sample.

After examining the statistics in Figure 8-2, a significant difference likely exists between males and females in the general population in their taste preferences between dark, milk, and white chocolate. This is valuable information when designing marketing campaigns, packaging, and so forth.

A wide array of statistics is available from the Table Analysis task, as outlined in Figure 8-2. The table breaks down the tests and measures into the following categories:

- **Association:** Examines whether two or more variables are related, or *correlated*. This is the most commonly used statistical test for contingency tables.

  Correlation does *not* imply that one variable causes another variable's outcome. Correlation does indicate that the two variables have a tendency to move together in a certain manner.

- **Agreement:** Used only with *dichotomous* variables (yes/no or positive/ negative).

- **Differences:** Tests for differences among classes for an ordinal variable.

- **Trend:** Examines the outcome of a two-level variable against an ordinal variable.

Other ways of addressing categorical data analysis are available; some of these are covered in the following sections. Additional methods that can be useful for analyzing categorical data include regression, analysis of variance (ANOVA), logistic regression (heavily used in marketing research), generalized linear models (GLM), and generalized estimating equation.

Transforming Your Data for Further Use

Before or after analyzing your data, you might realize that certain assumptions of your selected method aren't met. For example, perhaps your analysis requires the data to be normally distributed but the data isn't. You can either select another analytic method with different or broader assumptions or transform your data to meet the assumptions of your selected analysis.

The Standardize Data task in SAS Enterprise Guide (available by choosing Describe⊅Table Analysis) allows you to transform data from a variety of distributions (uniform, lognormal, and so on) to a standard normal distribution. You can easily convert data with percentiles (uniformly distributed) into standardized scores by using the Standardize Data task.

You can also use tasks we cover in previous chapters for transforming your data. The Rank Data task can convert data to percentiles, numeric ranks, normalized scores, or exponential scores. The Query task also has various functions for calculated columns that can also be useful in transforming your data (for example, LOG, EXP, and LOG10).

Analyzing Basic Data with Correlation Techniques

Correlation analysis is useful for examining whether two or more variables share a relationship. Simply stated, you're examining whether one variable increases, decreases, or stays the same while the other variable increases. Note that a strong relationship does *not* imply causality. That is, correlated variables are not necessarily causing each other to vary.

A simple example of correlated variables that aren't causal is measuring the body temperature of a dog and a person who have been in a steam bath for more than 15 minutes. Both temperatures would rise over the 15-minute period (positive correlation: as one rises, so does the other), but the actual cause is the steam bath temperature and exposure time to the steam bath, not each other's temperatures. Often, these hidden, unmeasured variables can be critical to a good understanding of the nature of a correlation.

With any statistical analysis, presuming causality simply because there is a significant p-value or a described relationship is dangerous! Unless you design a controlled study in which all other variables can be controlled or adjusted for, do not assume causality.

That said, correlation or positive p-values *could* be indicative of causality, especially when combined with practical contextual experience with the process at hand. Still, scientists should reject the notion of finding causality unless they verify the results with a controlled experiment. A *controlled experiment* implies that you can keep all other conditions constant or that you have a known way of adjusting for the conditions you can't control. This way, you can control and focus on just the potential causal variables and see the resulting change in the outcome of interest.

The Correlation task (available by choosing Analyze⇨Multivariate⇨Correlations) enables you to examine the relationship between one or more variables. The default technique for this task, Pearson correlation, assumes that your data in both variables is from normal distributions. Other techniques available with this task — Hoeffding, Kendall, and Spearman — have fewer assumptions about the data distribution being used to obtain the strength of correlation.

Most laypeople refer to Pearson correlation when they talk about correlation. This task generates p-values that measure the probability that the correlation seen with your selected data could happen by chance or whether the selected data was not correlated at all. In addition, this task provides you with the correlation coefficient, which is either positive or negative, depending on whether the two variables increase together (positive) or whether one decreases as the other increases (negative). Scatter plots showing the relationship of each variable with the other can also be displayed with your analysis.

An example of a Pearson correlation table and scatter plot is shown in Table 8-2 and Figure 8-3. The data used in this example is in the data set Corn, which is available in the sample data provided with SAS Enterprise Guide. This data set is a historic record of corn yield over 33 years and various environmental variables that could influence the corn yield. Note that only three of the eight selected variables exhibit a p-value less than 0.05: July_Rain, July_Temp, and August_Temp. Rainfall appears to be positively correlated (more rain likely results in better yield, adding a subjective assessment to the result), and a higher temperature generally results in a lower yield — a negative correlation. To definitively state causality, a controlled experiment would be needed. Note that in this case, it is highly unlikely that corn yield is influencing the weather!

Table 8-2   Pearson Correlation Table Examining Corn Yield Data

Variable Correlated to Corn Yield	Pearson Correlation Coefficient
Pre_seasonPrecip	0.15116
	0.4011
May_Temp	−0.11893
	0.5098
June_Rain	−0.13907
	0.4402
June_Temp	−0.14536
	0.4196
July_Rain	0.57407
	0.0005
July_Temp	−0.57884
	0.0004
Aug_Rain	0.20946
	0.242
Aug_Temp	−0.34749
	0.0475

One final observation based on experience is that temperatures in July and August are likely correlated and that the rainfall in July is likely correlated with the temperature in July. This is often referred to as *interaction,* where one predictive variable influences not just the outcome of interest but also the other predictive variables. Therefore, to find the true strength of various variables on the outcome, controlled experiments in which only one of these variables is allowed to vary would be useful. More sophisticated statistical techniques are also available that can help you separate this interaction, or covariance, of predictors.

Figure 8-3: A scatter plot showing the negative relationship between corn yield and mean July temperature.

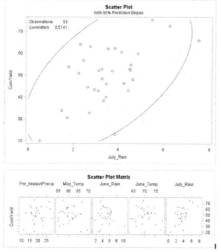

Canonical correlation (available by choosing Analyze⇨Multivariate⇨ Canonical Correlation) is often used in marketing analysis to compare multiple variables grouped against another variable. The Canonical Correlation task is similar to the Correlation task in concept except that you can group several related variables, such as July and August temperatures, and correlate them with one or more outcome variables, such as corn yield.

Understanding ANOVA and Regression: No PhD Required!

Analysis of variance (ANOVA) and regression analysis are two forms of statistical analysis frequently used in a wide range of applications to describe the relationship between two or more variables. These two forms of analysis are related and can even be combined into one analysis approach with more advanced SAS capabilities, such as Mixed Models.

Analysis of variance lets you examine the strength of the relationship between a discrete predictor variable (for example, a car type) and a continuous, predicted variable (for example, a car price.) The primary purpose of ANOVA is to allow you to determine whether a categorical variable has differing averages across the various groups.

Regression analysis is similar to correlation analysis in that both the predictor and the predicted variable must be continuous (for example, horsepower and car price). Regression provides you with an equation for the line (the y-axis intercept and the slope of the regression line) that best describes the relationship between the predictor and predicted variable. Regression analysis also provides you with the statistical strength of the regression line for predicting other values that you can obtain in the future.

Several types of analytic techniques are grouped under the ANOVA submenu in SAS Enterprise Guide (available by choosing Analyze⇨ANOVA):

- ✔ **t Tests:** These techniques examine the effect of a treatment with two categories (for example, aspirin versus a placebo) on one continuous measure (for example, blood pressure).

- ✔ **One way and nonparametric ANOVA:** With this technique, you examine the effect of a categorical variable with many levels (for example, aspirin versus placebo versus acetaminophen versus naproxen) on a continuous measure (for example, blood pressure). The nonparametric form has no underlying distribution assumption about the continuous measure.

- ✔ **Linear models and mixed models:** These are the most generalized forms of ANOVA and combine concepts from ANOVA and regression analysis. They are also the most complex form of this type of analysis to use and interpret. Linear models let you relate one or many continuous or discrete predictor variables to one or many continuous predicted variables. Mixed models further generalize on linear models in that the various predictors can be correlated and can exhibit nonconstant variability across the range of predicted values.

An example of a one-way ANOVA is shown in Figure 8-4 using the SAS Enterprise Guide sample data set CARS_1993. This example explores the relationship between car type and car price. The box plot shows the mean and range of the price across the categories in the box plot. Note a few possible surprises here: Midsize cars have some of the highest prices and compact cars can rival large car prices.

The table above the box plot shows the R-square and the p-value for this model. *R-square* is a measure of how much of the variance in mean price is explained by the model; in this case, about 42 percent of the variance is explained in the model. The p-value, less than 0.0001, indicates that there is less than a 1 in 10,000 chance that the mean is equal among the car groups. You can conclude that car type is a good predictor of car price, explaining about 42 percent of the variability in car price.

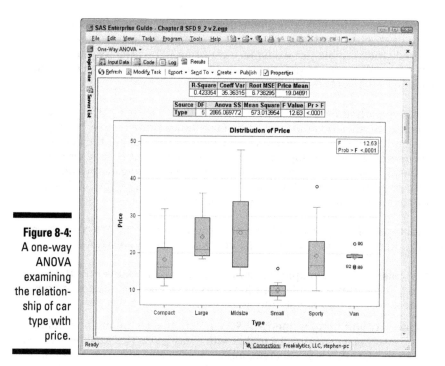

Figure 8-4:
A one-way ANOVA examining the relationship of car type with price.

The following types of analytic techniques are grouped under the Regression submenu in SAS Enterprise Guide (available by choosing Analyze⇨Regression):

- ✔ **Linear regression:** Attempts to fit a line to your data. An example is a model car price based on horsepower.

- ✔ **Nonlinear regression:** Extends the concept of linear regression where you must specify the general form of the model to fit your data. An example is a cubic relationship between horsepower and price.

- ✔ **Logistic regression:** Allows you to add binary variables (for example, yes, no) and categorical variables (such as low, medium, and high income) to the linear regression model as both predictors and predicted values. This technique is widely used in marketing research and is one of many data mining techniques.

- ✔ **Generalized linear models:** Enables you to add data not normally distributed, such as counts or proportion measurements. This technique is an extension of linear regression.

Figure 8-5 shows an example of linear regression, specifically, the predicted linear relationship and prediction limits between horsepower and car price. The graph shows the positive relationship between horsepower and car price, along with prediction bands, between which 95 percent of all data points should lie.

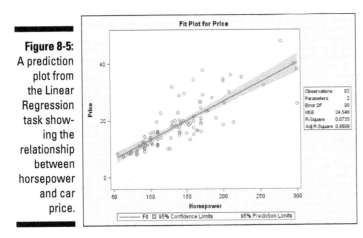

Figure 8-5:
A prediction
plot from
the Linear
Regression
task show-
ing the
relationship
between
horsepower
and car
price.

Figure 8-6 shows a variety of common diagnostic graphs for linear regression. For example, examining the center graph, you can see how the predicted price varies against the actual price for the car. The model appears to do a better job at predicting price with lower-priced cars than with the higher-priced models.

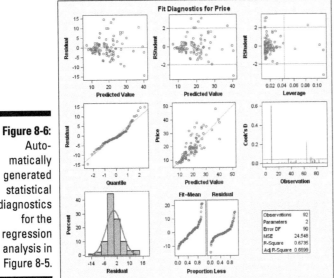

Figure 8-6:
Auto-
matically
generated
statistical
diagnostics
for the
regression
analysis in
Figure 8-5.

Chapter 9

More Analytics to Enlighten and Entertain

As you might expect, one chapter (Chapter 8) isn't enough to cover the analytics available with SAS. In this chapter, we review some of the more modern and advanced analytic techniques available with SAS, including the following:

✓ **Survival analysis:** Enables you to compare the lifespan of similar products, for example, or to determine whether one treatment decreases the time to the occurrence of an illness or death versus another treatment.

✓ **Quality control methods:** Provide a broad range of tools to understand and optimize your manufacturing or customer service process.

✓ **Forecasting:** Enables you to make simple or sophisticated models that can help project business outcomes for the coming week, month, quarter, or year.

✓ **Multivariate analysis:** Lets you examine and link vast numbers of predictor and predicted variables related to your business; this effectively reduces complex data in your business.

Staying Alive with Survival Analysis

Survival analysis might sound morbid, but death doesn't have to overshadow this area of statistical analysis. Although survival analysis can indeed be used to model time until death for people or products (light bulbs are a classic example of the latter), you can substitute other outcomes (besides death and failure) in this technique. Think of *yes* or *no* types of outcomes, for example: Yes, he defaulted after 678 days on his loan; no, she didn't default as of 893 days as a loan customer.

When comparing two drugs that prevent the onset of a new stage of a disease, the arrival of symptoms is sometimes used as the endpoint outcome for survival analysis. The amount of time until a customer cancels or closes his account is another example of an event of interest to model.

The principle behind survival analysis revolves around determining the failure rate of various groups (called *strata*) relative to an outcome of interest (such as death, product failure, or a customer canceling his account). Examples of strata include patient lifestyle categories, drug treatments, light bulb filament types, or differing promotional programs offered to new customers at time of recruitment.

Figure 9-1 shows a classic example of time to relapse or death for cancer patients. The control group (the bottom line in the graph) received no preventive therapy after their cancer was in remission. The maintenance therapy group received a drug being tested for the prevention of cancer recurrence. If relapse occurred, the patient was counted as a failure. (Patients unable to be contacted for follow-up are considered *censored* at their last visit and are treated differently than failures by the analysis.)

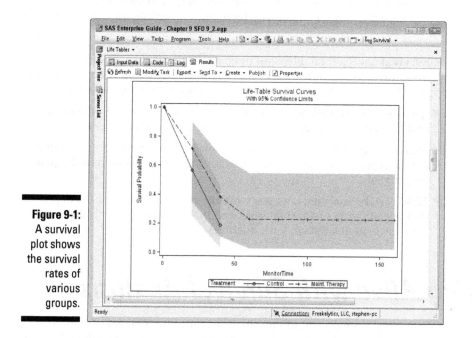

Figure 9-1:
A survival plot shows the survival rates of various groups.

As you can see, the maintenance therapy group appears to have better survival rates. (That is, at 40 months, about 38 percent in the maintenance group are still in remission from their cancer versus about 18 percent in the control group.)

Two types of survival analysis techniques — Life Tables and Proportional Hazards — are grouped under the Survival Analysis submenu in SAS Enterprise Guide (available by choosing Tools⇨Analyze⇨Survival Analysis):

- **Life Tables:** The Life Tables task estimates the survival distribution of each group. Usually, you want to compare survival curves to determine whether two groups differ significantly. The Life Tables task computes rank tests and a likelihood ratio test to test for differences across the groups in survival times.

- **Proportional Hazards:** The Proportional Hazards task uses regression analysis principles for survival data. *Proportional hazards* are widely used in the analysis of survival data to incorporate the effects of additional explanatory variables (beyond strata) on survival times. An example is expanding the previously mentioned cancer survival study and adding the number of cigarettes smoked per day by each patient during the trial. This could have a significant effect on cancer recurrence rates that might be incorrectly attributed to the treatments. The Proportional Hazards task enables you to separate out extraneous factors that could influence survival rates.

Providing Quality Control

Most organizations want to provide quality products and services. SAS can help you monitor and improve the quality of your products and services based on quality standards you and your organization set. Equally important, increasing quality often results in considerable time and cost savings — from efficiency to customer satisfaction to lower rates of returns and cancellations.

A variety of quality control techniques are available, ranging from control chart methods to specialized tools that can help improve products, maintain high quality, and increase levels of customer satisfaction. These techniques can help you

- Identify key issues that contribute to low quality
- Examine historic product quality to help set future standards
- Determine the quality of products or services in near real-time as they are produced or delivered to minimize waste

The following sections introduce you to the wide range of quality control tasks available in SAS Enterprise Guide.

Histograms

One of the simpler, yet powerful, quality-control techniques you can use is a histogram. *Histograms* show the counts or percent of observed values across a range of values for a selected variable. You use a histogram to compare the results of a user-selected process with user-defined specification limits. With a quality histogram, you can graphically see the distribution of measured values, how many items are out of specification, and how widely dispersed the outlying values are from the desired specification.

The following example uses the sample TubeAngle data set included with SAS Enterprise Guide. This data is from a bicycle manufacturing operation that creates frames for off-road bicycles. It is critical to the performance of these bikes that the tube angle is within the specification limits of 73.7 to 74.3 degrees.

You use the Histogram task by choosing Tools⇨Analyze⇨Capability Analysis⇨Histograms. The histogram in Figure 9-2 shows the counts of parts produced by angle. The specifications appear as dashed lines at each end of the chart, and out-of-range bars appear in a different color beyond the dashed lines. Overlaid on the histogram is the normal distribution for the given data based on the mean and standard deviation of the given data. You can see that the mean is slightly above the ideal 74.0-degree angle; you could probably improve this process by slightly recalibrating the equipment to achieve a smaller angle, on average.

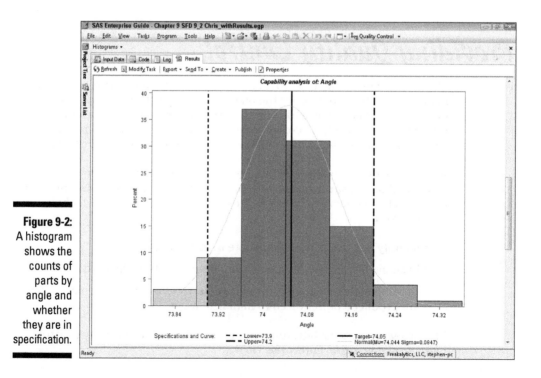

Figure 9-2:
A histogram shows the counts of parts by angle and whether they are in specification.

Q-Q plots and probability plots

Q-Q plots and *probability plots* are useful for examining the data from your process and checking whether the data is distributed according to an expected statistical distribution (such as normal, exponential, or lognormal). Q-Q plots are more useful for deriving actual distribution parameters and capability indices, and probability plots are more useful for examining actual versus expected percentiles. These tasks are available by choosing Tools⇨ Analyze⇨Capability Analysis.

Control charts

Control charts (or *Shewhart charts*) allow you to visualize product quality variation due to recurring or regular causes versus variation in results due to special or extraordinary causes. Control charts can help you identify new problems that arise from factors such as poorly trained personnel, new equipment that may not be properly calibrated, or out-of-specification products from suppliers.

Mean and range, mean and standard deviation, mean individual measurement, box, p, np, q, and c charts are useful for continuous monitoring of your process to determine whether it's in specification or possibly moving out of specification. This is helpful in monitoring any type of manufacturing process or customer service scenario to decide whether to stop the production line or add more sales representatives, respectively, at a given point in time. Determining the chart type to use depends on the type of data being collected and the type of process you're monitoring.

The mean individual measurement chart in Figure 9-3 shows two possible times that the production of bike frames should have been examined and adjusted to minimize future defects. On 3/17, a frame was made out of specification, and the moving range of the values was high enough to warrant examination. On 3/26, just the moving range was large enough to indicate a possible problem in production, but perhaps this outcome was just a result of an adjustment made to the equipment. You access these tasks by choosing Tools⇨Analyze⇨Control Charts.

Pareto charts

Pareto charts are similar to bar charts, but they are designed to identify top causes of failure so that priorities can be established to systematically reduce product failures from your process. The Pareto chart in Figure 9-4, available by choosing Tools⇨Analyze⇨Pareto Chart, shows that the majority of defects in the bike frame example are linked to just two causes: stray file marks and burrs. Eliminating or greatly reducing these two errors could cut defects by more than 50 percent!

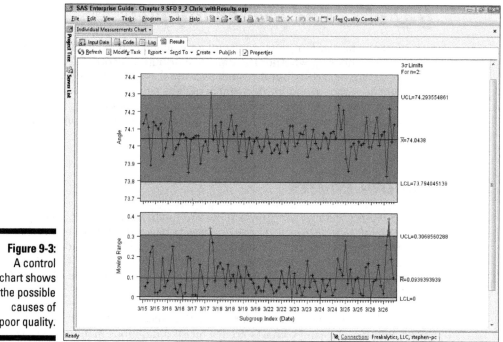

Figure 9-3:
A control chart shows the possible causes of poor quality.

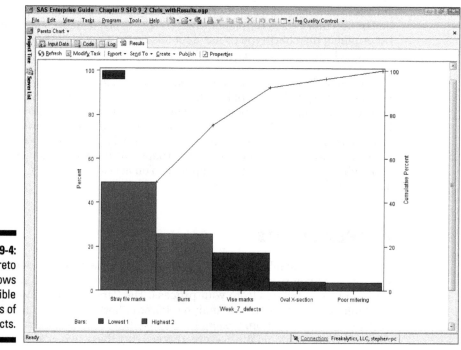

Figure 9-4:
A Pareto chart shows the possible causes of defects.

Understanding Complex Relationships with Multivariate Analysis

Multivariate analysis is a set of techniques for examining relationships among multiple variables in one analysis. One of the popular techniques available in SAS is principal component analysis. You can use principal component analysis when you're interested in collapsing many variables and discovering new relationships among the variables of interest. To find and identify logical groupings, or *clusters,* of data, you can use cluster and discriminant analysis.

Principal component analysis

The Principal Components task allows you to simplify data across multiple variables by collapsing the variables to fewer composite variables. These composite variables are reductions based on the analytic results from the Principal Components task, which identifies the relative correlation of each variable with the outcome of interest.

For example, suppose that you have the crime rates for seven categories of crimes with 12 variables that can predict crime rates in each of the 50 U.S. states. Visually examining all these variables is difficult. You can use principal component analysis to summarize the data to two or three dimensions (from seven categories) and to help you visualize and understand a simpler form of the relationship between crime rates and predictor variables.

Cluster analysis and discriminant analysis

The Cluster Analysis task and Discriminant Analysis task (available when you choose Tools⇨Analyze⇨Multivariate⇨Cluster Analysis/Discriminant Analysis) create clusters, or logical groupings of outcomes in your data. You specify how many clusters you want from your data, and the task will cluster groups of records based on the attributes you select. Both tasks can also chart the results of hierarchical clustering to produce a tree diagram (also called a *dendrogram*).

A cluster example is shown in Figure 9-5. Various ZIP codes have been clustered based on an income scale related to a crime index scale.

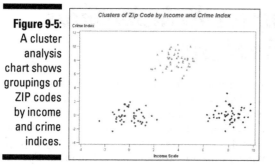

Figure 9-5:
A cluster analysis chart shows groupings of ZIP codes by income and crime indices.

Forecasting: Using the Crystal Ball

When you think of forecasting, you likely think of weather forecasts. Although it's possible to use the forecasting tasks in SAS Enterprise Guide for a similar purpose, they are more frequently used for forecasting a wide range of business and economic outcomes. Some examples of forecasting include predicting the following:

- The number of patients admitted to a hospital in the next day, week, month, quarter, or year

- The number of DVD players that will be sold next month

- How many more DVD players can be sold next year by increasing the sales staff 30 percent and tripling the marketing budget

- The number of homicides in a city next year based on the last 20 years

- The number of people who will die of various causes in the next 10 years

- How many flights will be delayed tomorrow versus the same day last year

Forecasting is concerned with collecting historical data and using it to effectively estimate future results. Various factors play into the effective analysis of data to produce forecasts, including

- **How much historical data can be gathered.** If you want to develop a forecast for the next month, for example, then thirteen months might be sufficient. However, to develop a forecast for the next two years, you would likely want at least three years of data.

- **Whether the forecasts are seasonally affected:** For example, more beer is sold in May in Miami, which is a low point for sales in Sydney.

- **Whether to break down the data being forecasted into various groups:** For example, newer beer brands might have different sales patterns than existing brands.

✔ **Examining variables that help predict the outcome:** These variables might include temperature, the number of marketing programs, and the number of stores that carry the brand.

The example shown in Figure 9-6 contrasts a forecast of beer sales based only on historic sales amounts with a forecast that also incorporates predictive variables (the number of TV ads and the effect of a specific weather forecast for the year 2006). The power of incorporating future predictive variables is likely obvious. This example demonstrates the importance of understanding your data and using predictive variables if possible when creating forecasts.

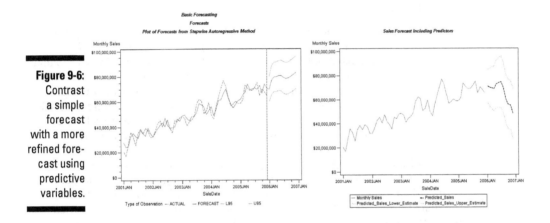

Figure 9-6: Contrast a simple forecast with a more refined forecast using predictive variables.

SAS Enterprise Guide provides two tasks to prepare your data for forecasting. Forecasting can be performed on a standard time interval of your choice, such as days, weeks, or months. These tasks enable you to prepare your historical data to be properly adjusted to conform to these time intervals.

Suppose that you have daily sales data, but you want to produce only a monthly sales analysis. With the Prepare Time Series Data task (available by choosing Tools➪Analyze➪Time Series➪Prepare Time Series Data), you can collapse the 28 to 31 daily sales records per month into one monthly record.

The Create Time Series Data task is similar to the Prepare Time Series Data task but is intended for large volumes of data or to perform more complex transformations of your existing data. This task is available by choosing Tools➪Analyze➪Time Series➪Create Time Series Data.

You can choose from five tasks to create forecasts of your data, a simple forecast based only on prior sales amounts to more sophisticated modeling techniques that allow you to add predictive variables and change the underlying assumptions about your data. These tasks are

✔ **Basic Forecasting and ARIMA Modeling and Forecasting:** The Basic Forecasting task (Tools➪Analyze➪Time Series➪Basic Forecasting) and the ARIMA Modeling and Forecasting task (Tools➪Analyze➪Time Series➪ARIMA Modeling and Forecasting) both provide a simple approach to producing forecasts based solely on the trends in your historical values. The Basic Forecasting task was used on the left side of Figure 9-6.

✔ **Regression Analysis with Autoregressive Errors:** This task (Tools➪Analyze➪Time Series➪Regression Analysis with Autoregressive Errors) allows you to add predictor variables to your forecast model; Regression Analysis with Autoregressive Errors was used on the right side of Figure 9-6.

✔ **Regression Analysis of Panel Data:** This task (Tools➪Analyze➪Time Series➪Regression Analysis of Panel Data), enables you to specify advanced details about model errors and to add cross-sectional data analysis to your time series analysis. Cross-sectional analysis is a technique that examines the correlation between various groupings of your data over time. An example of cross-sectional analysis is forecasting beer sales and potato chip sales over time and examining the correlation between these two time series: Do chip sales go up as beer sales go down?

Figure 9-7 shows an example of diagnostic plots for the forecast on the right side of Figure 9-6. It is important to understand the quality of the model fit with critical forecasts. In the bottom center of the plot, you can see that the distribution of the forecast model *residuals* — the difference between predicted and actual values in the historic data — is skewed to the right of a normal distribution. Examining the upper-center plot, you can see that the standardized residuals over the historic dates seems to skew upward, another sign that this model may be suspect.

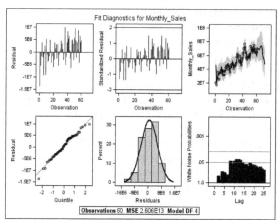

Figure 9-7:
Advanced diagnostics are available in many SAS statistical tasks.

Chapter 10

Data Mining: Making the Leap from Guesses to Smart Choices

. . . .

. . . .

*D*ata mining has been in the news and caught the attention of many aspiring executives who are anxious to improve their company's performance and gain better insights into their customers' behavior and needs. Data mining can determine the most lucrative customers, identify patients who are at the most risk for postoperative problems, and search massive data inflows for unusual patterns, such as possible fraudulent credit card transactions.

In this chapter, we review data-mining techniques available with SAS, including the following:

✔ **Sampling:** You can accelerate and even improve the building of preliminary data-mining models by taking intelligent samples of your overall data source.

✔ **Exploring:** It's generally a bad idea to start building data-mining models without first having a firm grasp of your data and the distribution of key variables.

✔ **Modifying and transforming:** Various data-mining techniques have different data assumptions and conditions. If your data does not meet these assumptions, you may be able to address this by modifying and transforming your data source.

✔ **Modeling and mining:** This step involves applying various models with different options to build the "best" model for the question at hand. Techniques include decision trees (CART/CHAID), regression, logistic regression, neural networks, and memory-based reasoning.

✔ **Assessing your models:** After you've built several models around your data and the question at hand, you can use assessment techniques to determine which model is most effective at predicting your outcome of interest.

✔ **Data scoring:** After you select the best model, you finish your project by data scoring, in which you apply the fruit of your data-mining labors to new incoming data and build estimates of how new and existing customers will behave.

Mining for Jewels in Your Data

Data mining is the art and science of leveraging your data to find informative relationships that enhance your business decisions. Specifically, data mining takes advantage of large volumes of data to find hidden patterns and features. A key difference from traditional statistics is the fact that data mining utilizes observed outcomes in situations that are not controlled experiments. Instead, data-mining data is often a reflection of an ongoing business process based on observed customer behaviors.

Data mining has become famous *and* infamous for the wide array of applications in customer behavioral insights and customer credit management. Banks use data mining to predict a customer's loan risks, to predict the likelihood that a customer will accept a marketing offer, and even to assign a lifetime profit value to a customer. Retailers such as Amazon.com use data mining to personalize your shopping experience and make recommendations for the next item you may want to add to your shopping cart. Netflix helped bring data mining to the top of the news with their Netflix Prize, which called upon data-mining experts to compete to improve Netflix's ability to find the best movies for customers based on their viewing habits and rating behavior.

Infamous examples of data mining include hotel chains leveraging past customer visit behavior (some of which was personally questionable, such as frequent daytime hotel stays within a few miles of their home) to solicit business from the spouse of this customer (whoops!). People have become increasingly concerned about large online services utilizing a combination of data from e-mail, documents stored online, Web searches, and video viewing habits to drive online consumer ads. Imagine a person receiving an ad for a wild Vegas weekend on his classroom PC during a parent-teacher meeting.

SAS provides an advanced data-mining toolset with SAS Enterprise Miner. We do not have detailed instruction on SAS Enterprise Miner usage in this book, but we do cover examples of work created with this application.

Mining for Data: The SAS Framework

We can sum the process of data mining in SAS using the SEMMA acronym, which stands for Sample, Explore, Modify, Model, and Assess. We would add one more step to the SAS Method of data mining, an S for Scoring new records.

Because data mining involves machine, or artificial intelligence, methods for building models that will fit or describe your data behavior, you must split your source data into three distinct groups to build, validate, and test your models. In SAS Enterprise Miner, the build data subset is used for training and creating your model, the validate data subset is used for validating the created model, and the test data subset is used for testing or evaluating how well the validated model performs in predicting the outcome of interest.

The training data set is typically a subset of data that the model technique uses to construct a model to fit your data for the problem at hand. You then use the validation and test data sets to validate and confirm, respectively, how well the created model will fit your data and the problem at hand. This approach is different from traditional statistical analysis, where all available records are typically used with the selected modeling technique.

Sample

Because data mining often uses large or even massive data sets with millions or even billions of historic observations or customers, it's often necessary to take a sample of the original data set to process the data in a timely manner. When the outcome of interest occurs rarely, a method called oversampling can actually improve the ability of data-mining models to successfully predict the outcome of interest.

An example of oversampling is taking a random sample of customers who did not respond to a recent credit card solicitation against the full 1% of customers who did respond to the mailing. This creates an equal-size set of customers in the responder group (the responders are "oversampled" because the sample includes them all) and nonresponder group and typically results in superior results with many data-mining techniques. Oversampling is illustrated in Figure 10-1.

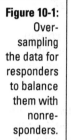

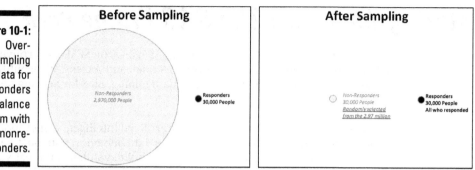

Explore

Exploring the data graphically is a key step in selecting a relevant model-ing technique, variables for your model, and model assumptions. This step includes charting your data and identifying the relevant variables for the question at hand. Figure 10-2 shows the distribution of net profit attributed to a marketing newsletter at a boutique winery. A quick glance at the histo-gram immediately tells you that any technique that assumes the target vari-able is normally distributed would likely yield poor results.

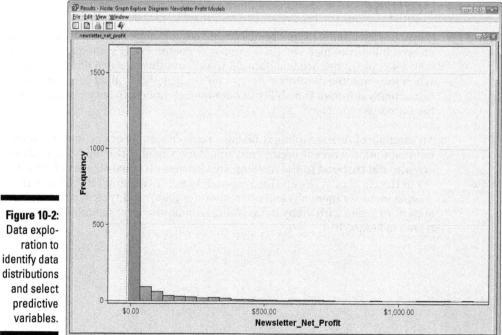

Figure 10-2:
Data explo-
ration to
identify data
distributions
and select
predictive
variables.

A key result of data exploration is the selection of variables that might be useful for predicting the outcome of interest. In the case of net profit generated by newsletters, predictive variables might include average discount on orders, whether the customer is also an e-mail subscriber, sales in the past year, and even customer wealth estimates. SAS Enterprise Guide requires you to identify variables that you want to predict, called Targets; variables that you want to use as possible predictors of the target, called Inputs; variables that are simply data record identifiers, such as customer ID number, called IDs; and variables that aren't relevant or, even worse, part of the target data profile, called Rejected variables. An example of assigning these roles to the variables in the winery data is shown in Figure 10-3.

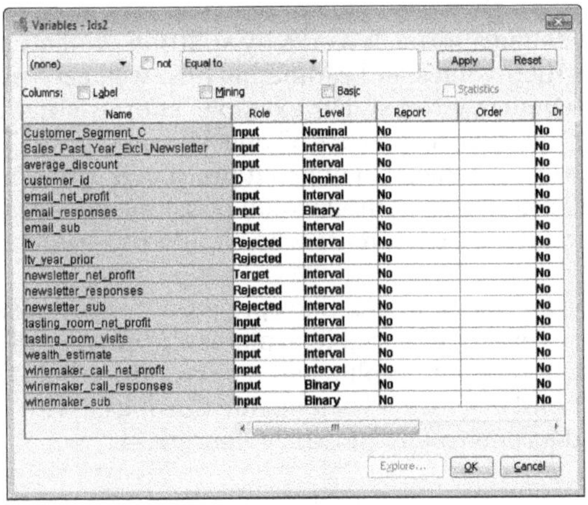

Figure 10-3: Assigning roles to variables in the boutique winery example.

After you assign roles, you need to divide the source modeling data into three separate data sets for training, validation, and testing, as discussed earlier.

Modify

Depending on your data discoveries during the exploration phase, you may need to transform your data to meet model assumptions, impute or adjust for missing data values in some of the records, create new calculated variables, and possibly filter outliers from your sample. The intent is to improve the quality of your models. Determining and applying needed transformations for your project can become time-consuming, but it is a critical step in successful data-mining efforts.

Model

Modeling is the glamorous part of data mining, but as you can see in the earlier SEMMA steps, it will produce poor results without solid preparation. Modeling typically includes the development of multiple models, each attempting to answer the same problem.

Among the many models available in SAS Enterprise Guide are decision trees, linear and logistic regression models, neural networks, and memory-based reasoning. For each model specified, the training data set is the input for building your initial model. Then the algorithms in SAS Enterprise Guide use the validation data set to refine the initial model.

The decision tree modeling approach works by splitting predictor variables into groups based on their values and estimating how well each variable helps explain the outcome of interest. For example, suppose that we split sales in the past year into two groups: $0–50 and $50 and above. This split shows very big differences in the level of profit produced with our newsletter subscriptions. The decision tree method would possibly use this split of sales to explain how best to identify customers who should receive newsletters.

Note that the decision tree node in SAS Enterprise Guide estimates how well each possible split of every Input variable explains the outcome Target variable. It then keeps the top variable splits and displays the result in a decision tree. This tree is a bit odd because it is an upside-down tree with the base at the top. An example decision tree is shown in Figure 10-4.

Reading the example in Figure 10-4, note that without any predictive work, the average profit per subscriber was about $101 in the Validation data set. Moving down one level, the first split in the tree is based on Customer Segment. The Luxury Estate segment is much more profitable than the other segments, around $280 versus an average of $25 for the other segments. Another way of putting this finding is that the Luxury Estate segment is almost 11 times more profitable than the other newsletter subscriber segments.

Going down the Luxury Estate branch one more level, you can see that the next variable used to split the data is Sales in the Past Year, with Luxury Estate customers who spent more than $50 in the past year resulting in average newsletter sales of almost $700, or seven times higher than the average customer. Of note, only 38 customers meet these split criteria in the Validation data set. This is a key limitation of letting the tree go too deep — you end up with very few customers in a "leaf." Still, if we can target new or existing customers who meet these criteria, they could be profitable additions to our newsletter subscribers!

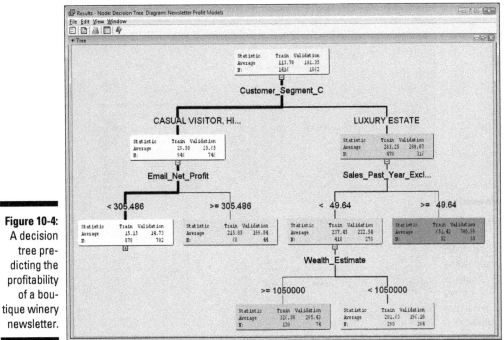

Figure 10-4: A decision tree predicting the profitability of a boutique winery newsletter.

The regression models in SAS Enterprise Guide enable you to fit both linear and logistic regression models to your data. Regression models offer many options for many different initial data assumptions, including whether the Target variable is continuous (such as net profit) or binary (for example, did you miss more than one payment in the past year?). Regression models also provide model prediction details that can be explained to your business team, as opposed to the neural network modeling approach, which is nearly impossible to explain how the model predicts your outcomes. An example of the subscriber profit model created for the winery newsletter is shown in Figure 10-5.

A quick review of the regression output shows that just a few variables can predict much of the likely newsletter net profit for a customer: wealth estimate, e-mail response, and customer segment. In fact, using only the wealth estimate, we can predict newsletter profit quite well, with an R-square of nearly 50% indicating that almost half the variability in newsletter profit can be explained with this one variable! Scrolling to the bottom, the overall model can explain about 70% of the variability in net profit with the selected variables, which is impressive.

Results - Node: Dmine Regression Diagram: Newsletter Profit Models
File Edit View Window

Output

```
The DMINE Procedure

                  Effects Chosen for Target: newsletter_net_profit

                                                                    Sum of      Error Mean
Effect                              DF    R-Square   F Value  p-Value  Squares      Square

AOV16: wealth_estimate              15    0.497925   92.561757  <.0001  26004542      18730
Group: email_responses               2    0.056729   89.040559  <.0001   2962741      16537
Group: Customer_Segment_C            1    0.054017  192.832724  <.0001   2821060      14630
AOV16: Sales_Past_Year_Excl_Newsletter 13 0.020081    5.758691  <.0001   1048771      14009
AOV16: email_net_profit             12    0.020405    6.649474  <.0001   1065647      13355
AOV16: winemaker_call_net_profit    12    0.019174    6.551999  <.0001   1001398      12737
Class: winemaker_call_responses      2    0.013896   29.692633  <.0001    725740      12221
AOV16: tasting_room_visits          10    0.009113    3.979735  <.0001    475916      11958
AOV16: tasting_room_net_profit       6    0.005889    4.350185  0.0002    307544      11783
Var:   winemaker_call_net_profit     1    0.003503   15.694826  <.0001    182926      11655
Var:   email_net_profit             1    0.001644    7.402966  0.0066     85873      11600
AOV16: average_discount             15    0.001015    0.302155  0.9953     52988      11691


The DMINE Procedure

The Final ANOVA Table for Target: newsletter_net_profit

                                     Sum of
Effect         DF     R-Square     Squares

Model          90     0.703390    36735145
Error        1325          .      15490709
Total        1415          .      52225853
```

Figure 10-5:
A regression model predicting boutique winery newsletter profitability.

Assess

In the assessment step, you compare the competing predictive models built in the preceding step. The outcome of the assessment step is the identification of the best model for explaining the outcome of interest. You may have used the same modeling technique (for example, decision trees) repeatedly to build competing models with different assumptions or model options. You may have also used several different modeling techniques.

The assessment step is critical for understanding how well your best, or *champion,* model will be with future predictions. In the assessment step, a champion model is identified and used to score the holdout test data set. These results can show you how well the champion model performs against this data relative to the actual outcomes of these customers withheld from the previous steps. For example, customer 7849 might be predicted to generate $88 of newsletter profit by the champion model, but you may see that the customer's actual newsletter profit was $139. Collectively, the assessment step examines the differences in predicted and actual profit for the test customers and uses this information to inform you of the power of the model in your future business decisions.

A famous output of this step is the lift chart, which is shown in Figure 10-6. This chart is often used to try to quantify how useful the model is by showing the average profit of randomly adding customers to your treatment group (that is, making them a newsletter subscriber) versus selectively adding the most profitable customers to your treatment group first. In other words, because mailing the winery newsletter four times per year is expensive, we don't want to mail it to all customers. Instead, we want to mail it to those who the model indicates will be most profitable, up to the budget allowed for our newsletter efforts.

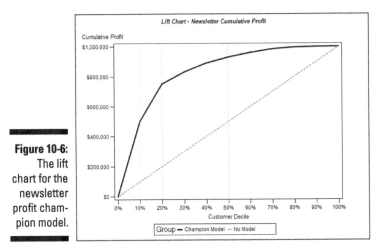

Figure 10-6:
The lift chart for the newsletter profit champion model.

Reading the lift chart, if we mailed only 10% of the customers without following the model, we would expect to generate about $100,000 in profit. However, if we use the model to select the best candidates for receiving the newsletter, we would see approximately $500,000 in profit! This amount is a lift of 500%, calculated by dividing $500,000 by $100,000. At the 20% mark, the lift is less, with a champion model profit of $750,000 versus a no-model profit of $200,000, a lift of 375%. Moving up the percent of customers, at 50% of all customers, we would see a profit of $930,000 versus a no-model profit of $500,000, a lift of 186%.

In our experience with data mining, you ideally would optimize the expected profit from mailing each customer versus the expected cost of the mailing. Marketing departments often define a minimum return on investment for an activity, often at four to six times the expected cost of the program. Assuming each additional customer receiving the newsletter costs $12 per year, we might cut off mailings at around the 50% of the champion model. This is in contrast to the no-model alternative, in which we might have previously budgeted enough money to mail only 25% of customers. In this example, we would spend an additional $30,000 on newsletter mailings for an additional $680,000 of profit.

Score

Scoring is akin to the "Goaaalllll" moment in soccer but not quite as crowd rousing. Scoring data involves using the champion model with new data to identify the likely outcome. Scoring could be as simple as assigning a probability that a prospective customer will respond to a marketing offer (Mark in Seattle has an 8% chance of responding while Sue in Austin has a 12% chance of responding and your cousin Hal in Oak Creek has a 1% chance of responding). In the scoring section, we use SAS Enterprise Guide to score new customers. Note that SAS Data Integration Studio is also available for scoring customer data. Finally, it's possible to deploy SAS Scoring to other technologies such as Java or database engines.

From SAS Enterprise Guide, you can use work developed by your data-mining team via the Model Scoring task. This task, available by choosing Analyze⇨Model Scoring, allows you to obtain the essence of the work published by your data-mining team. After the team has explored and modeled data for a particular subject, a data-mining model is available to business users to score their data.

Scoring data consists of taking some new data (such as recently acquired customers) and scoring them based on the model attributes to obtain a score. Scores are typically numeric values, such as $200 of expected net profit or an assigned response probability of 33%.

Figure 10-7 shows an example of scoring new customers with the Model Scoring task. Business users can score any set of existing or prospective customers easily and quickly.

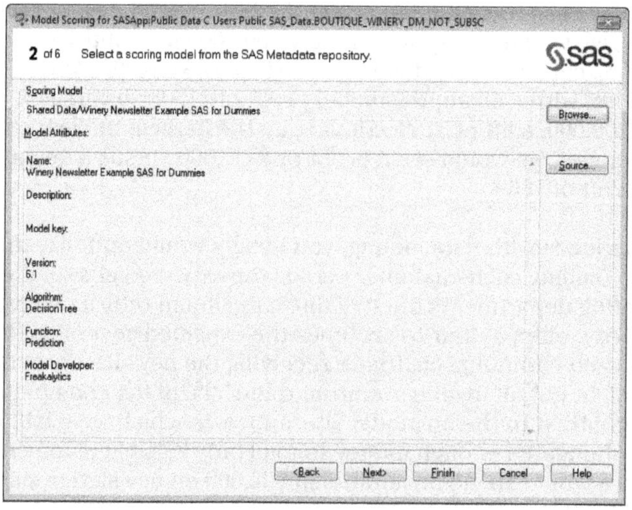

Figure 10-7: Data-mining model applied to new data and summarized as a box plot chart.

After scoring the new customers, you can use SAS Enterprise Guide to create a histogram of predicted profitability, as shown in Figure 10-8. This example was created with the Bar Chart task using the output of the Model Scoring task from the previous step.

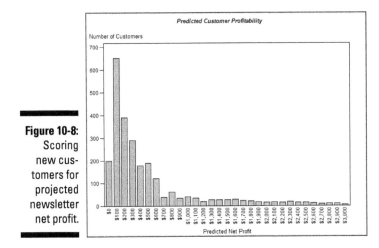

Figure 10-8:
Scoring
new cus-
tomers for
projected
newsletter
net profit.

Part IV

Enhancing and Sharing Your SAS Masterpieces

In this part . . .

This part is where the rubber meets the road. You can see how you can apply analytics and create reports in the place where you live. Do you spend all your time in Microsoft Excel? You can create SAS reports from SAS Add-In for Microsoft Office. Are you equipped only with a Web browser? SAS Web Report Studio lets you create reports with only a few clicks. Do you need to process data and create reports to give to others? See how to use SAS Enterprise Guide on your desktop to analyze, report, and distribute your results — SAS programming is optional.

Chapter 11

Leveraging Work from SAS to Those Less Fortunate

- -

- -

*I*t used to be that getting results from SAS meant getting results from SAS programmers. That is, your SAS results were only as accessible as the programmers or analysts in your organization and were often waiting in a queue with many other requests. Bribes of cookies, candy, and caffeine were commonplace.

Fortunately, SAS tools now exist that allow you to not only perform your own analyses and create your own results but also help you share those results with the world (or at least the part of the world that you care about). In this chapter, you see how to use SAS Enterprise Guide to transform your SAS reports and data into something your audience can easily access and use. You also find out about the various ways you can deliver this information to your audience.

Pulling Out Results without Pulling Teeth

Using SAS Enterprise Guide to run SAS programs ensures that all your results are retained in one convenient location, your SAS Enterprise Guide project. As you work, you might see dozens of output items in your project, including HTML, RTF, PDF, SAS Report, and SAS data sets. When you save your SAS Enterprise Guide project on your computer, however, only one file is created. This file is a SAS Enterprise Guide *project file,* which carries an .egp file extension, and contains a collection of all the work you did.

What makes temporary data temporary?

"Nothing is permanent," to quote Buddha. Still, some things are less permanent than others. In SAS, *temporary data* is data stored in a temporary location. SAS *libraries* — the folder-like structures where SAS stores data — can be defined in such a way that they exist only for the duration of your SAS session. Every SAS session has at least one temporary library named WORK. The contents of WORK are discarded when you exit the SAS application (or when you close SAS Enterprise Guide, as in our examples).

When you open the project file later, all your work is still visible in the project. You can open most of your project results, such as HTML output, without rerunning the project. However, some of your output data might be inaccessible even though a placeholder item still exists in the project because working with SAS tasks and programs sometimes results in *temporary data,* that is, data that doesn't persist across SAS Enterprise Guide sessions. Figure 11-1 shows a project flow that contains a reference to temporary data (WORK.Candy_Cust_Prod_Sales, the WORK library isn't visible until you hover the cursor over the dataset). In this example, the temporary data is a means to an end; it doesn't represent the final desired result but instead serves as a scratch pad to help on the way to achieving your final project goal.

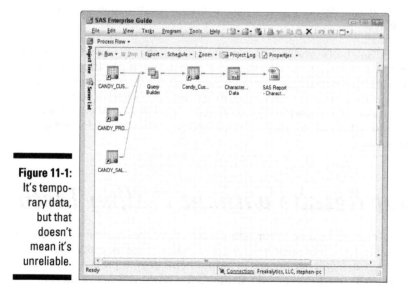

Figure 11-1: It's temporary data, but that doesn't mean it's unreliable.

Most of the time, it's okay to have some temporary data referenced in your project. After all, a project is like a recipe for cooking up interesting results, and that recipe is the valuable part of your hard work. With your project intact, showing permanent and temporary data sources, you can rerun your project — and once again, like magic, your temporary data reappears and is available for your use.

Exporting results, duty-free

When viewing your results in SAS Enterprise Guide, capturing a snapshot of the results is as simple as choosing File⇨Export. Export possibilities include HTML, PDF, RTF, SAS Reports, and even output SAS data sets.

When you export HTML results, you get an HTML file that you can view, send, or place on a Web site. Similarly, when you export PDF and RTF results, you end up with files of each respective type. However, when you export data, you have many more options:

- ✓ **Export SAS data as SAS data sets (of course).**

- ✓ **Transform data as part of the export process:** SAS Enterprise Guide can export data in a variety of formats, including Microsoft Excel; text-based formats, such as comma-separated or tab-delimited values; and even older file formats, such as dBase or Lotus 1-2-3.

The data EXPORT tax in SAS

For years, SAS has offered an EXPORT procedure so that programmers can include the export step as part of their SAS programs.

Access to the EXPORT procedure can make exporting SAS data to a text file convenient — for example, in comma-separated values (CSV) form — while running SAS programs in a batch environment. However, to use PROC EXPORT to transform SAS data to a Microsoft Excel file, an additional SAS product module must be installed on your SAS server: namely, SAS/ ACCESS Interface to PC File Formats. This product module is not part of the basic SAS package; you must license it separately.

One of the most common questions posed by SAS programmers who begin using SAS Enterprise Guide is whether they need SAS/ ACCESS Interface to PC File Formats to export SAS data to Microsoft Excel. The answer is no. Instead of using PROC EXPORT, SAS Enterprise Guide uses built-in data access components to transform the data to third-party data files.

When sharing SAS data with people who do not have access to SAS applications, Microsoft Excel is by far the most popular file format. In the following example, we use SAS Enterprise Guide to show a simple example of transforming SAS data into a spreadsheet format:

1. **Open the Candy_Sales_Summary table from the SAS Enterprise Guide sample folder.**

   The table is added to the current project and opens in the data view.

2. **Choose File⇨Export⇨Export Candy_Sales_Summary.**

   The Export window appears, as shown in Figure 11-2. This window offers a choice between

   - Local Computer: Anywhere on your computer or on your local network

   - Servers: Any SAS server that you have access to

   The choice you make here determines whether you see a file window like the ones you see in other applications when you save a file or a window specific to SAS that lets you navigate to a SAS server. Because the objective in this example is to create a spreadsheet file that we can work with on our computer, we will act locally (but keep thinking globally!).

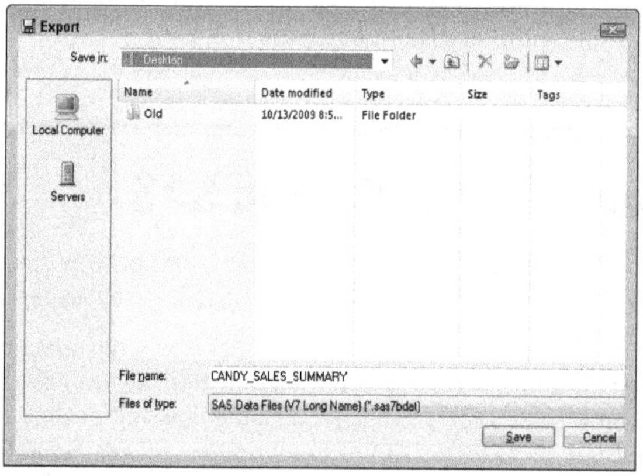

Figure 11-2:
Local
or long-
distance
export?
Choose your
PC or a SAS
Server.

3. **Select Local Computer by clicking the icon.**

   Your computer location options appear in the dialog box.

4. **From the Save as Type drop-down list, choose Microsoft Excel 97-2003 Workbooks (*.xls).**

   The list offers more than a dozen types of files.

5. **Use the Export window to navigate to the location where you want to store the file (for example, in My Documents).**

6. **(Optional) Change the name of the file in the File Name field.**

   You do not have to specify the `.xls` extension because SAS Enterprise Guide adds that for you.

7. **Click Save.**

   The window closes, and SAS Enterprise Guide saves the file as a Microsoft Excel spreadsheet file. It might take a minute or two for the export operation to complete.

These steps result in a spreadsheet file that you can share with anyone who has Microsoft Excel. Although this wasn't difficult to accomplish, repeating this process can become tedious if you frequently need to export the data. The next section looks at ways to automate the process.

Exporting as a step

Imagine that you designed a tremendous project in SAS Enterprise Guide. The project has something for everyone: a summary data report for Stan in Sales, a series of box plots by product line for Mel in Marketing, and an Excel export of output data for Alice in Accounting. You can rerun the project each week to refresh the results with the latest reports and data.

Oh, and you also have to get the information out and delivered to the people who need it. Stan prefers PDF files delivered to his mailbox whereas Mel needs HTML for his Web site. Alice needs the spreadsheet file for the data to be useful to her.

SAS Enterprise Guide has a feature that lets you specify, or "bake in," the process for saving files outside your project file and then replay those processes each time you run your project. Figure 11-3 shows an example project with these types of steps included.

Here's how to break down the work in this project:

1. The Query Builder task joins the Candy data sets.

2. Stan's Summary Table Wizard task creates a PDF result.

3. The E-mail Recipient step sends the PDF report to Stan.

4. Mel's box plot creates an HTML output file.

5. The Export step saves the box plot for Mel, saving the HTML file (and any images that it contains) to a file location on the network.

6. The Candy data set feeds into an Export step, converting the file from a SAS data set to a Microsoft Excel spreadsheet file.

7. The E-mail Recipient step e-mails the spreadsheet file to Alice.

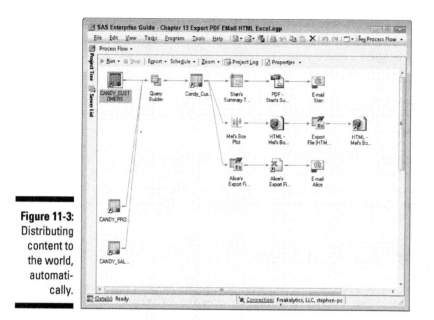

Figure 11-3:
Distributing
content to
the world,
automati-
cally.

Each time you run this project, all the steps run with it. SAS Enterprise Guide uses SAS to create the reports and then automatically distributes the output using the Export and E-mail steps.

Before you can use SAS Enterprise Guide to send e-mail on your behalf, you need to configure relevant options to teach SAS Enterprise Guide about your e-mail system. To set the options, choose Tools➪Options➪E-Mail Setting (the bottom selection of the Options window). You'll probably need help from an e-mail system administrator to determine the correct values for your e-mail server settings.

The following example shows you how to create a step to automatically e-mail a PDF report. In this example, we assume that you already have a project with a PDF result. These steps will work for any type of result, including RTF or HTML:

1. **Click the item in your project that represents the PDF result.**

   For example, in the project shown in Figure 11-3, the PDF result is the one labeled PDF — Stan's Summary Tables.

2. **Choose File➪Send To➪E-Mail Recipient as a Step in Project.**

   The Send window appears, as shown in Figure 11-4. Initially, the Send window contains a list of just the one item that you intend to send.

   You can click the Add button to select additional files to attach to the e-mail message. These additional files can come from your project, or they might be files located on your computer or on a remote SAS server.

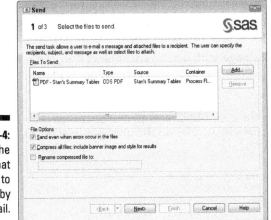

Figure 11-4:
All the
results that
are fit to
send by
mail.

Note the Compress All Files check box at the bottom of the screen. With this option selected, SAS Enterprise Guide compresses all the attached files into a Zip archive file. Your intended recipients, especially those with limited network bandwidth, will thank you for delivering big results in a smaller package.

3. **Click Next.**

   The second page of the Send window appears, as shown in Figure 11-5. This is the page where you complete the e-mail–related information.

4. **Add an e-mail address for the recipient.**

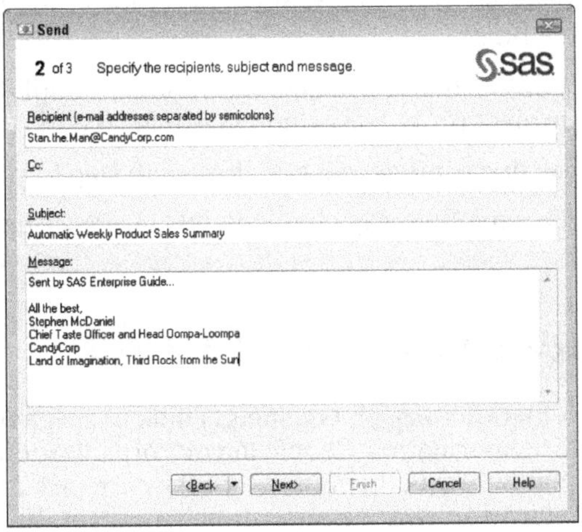

Figure 11-5:
Fill out the
address
and write
the note.
It's polite to
mention that
the e-mail is
automated.

You can specify more than one recipient by separating the e-mail addresses with semicolons. You can specify one or more e-mail addresses in the Cc field in the same way.

5. **Complete your message with a relevant subject line and a short message body.**

6. **Click Next.**

   The third page — the confirmation window — appears. This page shows a summary of the files to attach and the message to send. Figure 11-6 shows an example.

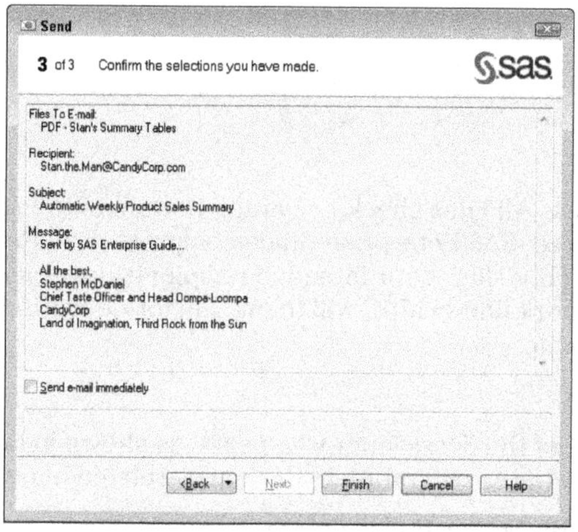

Figure 11-6:
Double-check your e-mail before you send it.

7. **If you want the message to be sent immediately, select the Send E-mail Immediately check box.**

   If you don't select this option, the e-mail won't be sent until the next time you run the project (or at least run this e-mail step).

8. **Click Finish to close this window and add the e-mail step to your project.**

9. **(Optional) Send the e-mail message immediately, as described in Step 7.**

Getting content to channel surfers

SAS can distribute information through channels. Think of a *channel* as simply a location to store information. People in your organization can subscribe to the content that interests them (and that they are permitted to see). Channel content is similar to an e-mail distribution list except that it's not limited to e-mail. Channel content can also appear within intranet portals. SAS offers one such portal: SAS Information Delivery Portal.

If your organization has a portal infrastructure with configured channels, you can use SAS Enterprise Guide to push your content out to the channel-surfing audience. The process is similar to the export and e-mail steps described earlier:

1. **Select the content you want to share.**

2. **Click the item in your project that you want to publish and then choose File⇨Publish to Channels.**

   The Publish window appears, as shown in Figure 11-7.

3. **Configure options in the Publish window to describe the package you want to publish.**

4. **Select a channel and add additional content to include.**

   The Publish step is added to your project; your updated content is republished each time you run your project.

Using Only the Good Bits: Assembling Reports in a Snap

People who grew up in the 70s and 80s may remember making mix tapes to collect all their favorite songs in one place. You could spend hours pulling the best songs from your favorite albums to make an audio cassette that contained just the songs you wanted, played in the order that you wanted to hear them.

What if you could make a "mix report" of all the best content in your project? You could take the most interesting tables and charts from work in your SAS Enterprise Guide project and assemble them into a single, concise report to share with the world.

It turns out that HTML and SAS Report formats are flexible enough to make this possible, and SAS Enterprise Guide contains tools that can help you achieve this noble goal!

Selecting your mix ingredients

When SAS creates SAS Report or HTML output, it divides that output into sections according to the SAS procedures that created it. The output from a single task can contain tables, charts, or a combination of the two. As you view the results, you see them as a single document, but SAS Enterprise Guide can break up the results into individual pieces, in much the same way that a child can break up a LEGO structure to build a new masterpiece.

With the tools in SAS Enterprise Guide, you can select the desired sections and reassemble them in multiple forms that will speak to your audience. For example, you can take portions of results from different tasks — a table here, a plot there, a chart from over there — and recombine them into a single cohesive analytic report.

After you complete this work once, your project then contains a *recipe* that points to each needed ingredient. When you rerun the tasks that make up the analytic report, the document is automatically refreshed with the latest results. You can then export or e-mail the completed document by using the techniques discussed earlier in the chapter.

Before you get started on this adventure, you have a decision to make: Will you use HTML or SAS Report format?

Use HTML when

- The report must be shared via a Web browser such as Internet Explorer or Firefox.
- You don't need precise control over the exact layout of the report.

Use SAS Report when

✓ You intend to print the report and you want great control over the page layout, sizes, and printing options.

✓ You need extra control over the report layout, including flexibility to arrange tables and charts horizontally as well as vertically.

✓ You need to resize charts to make them fit a particular page size.

✓ You intend to share this report with others who use the SAS Add-In for Microsoft Office or SAS Web Report Studio.

Stacking it up for the Web with HTML Document Builder

To get started with HTML Document Builder, create or open a SAS Enterprise Guide project with at least one task or program that creates an HTML result. Then choose Tools➪Create HTML Document to launch the Document Builder window. Figure 11-8 shows an example of the Document Builder window with some content already selected.

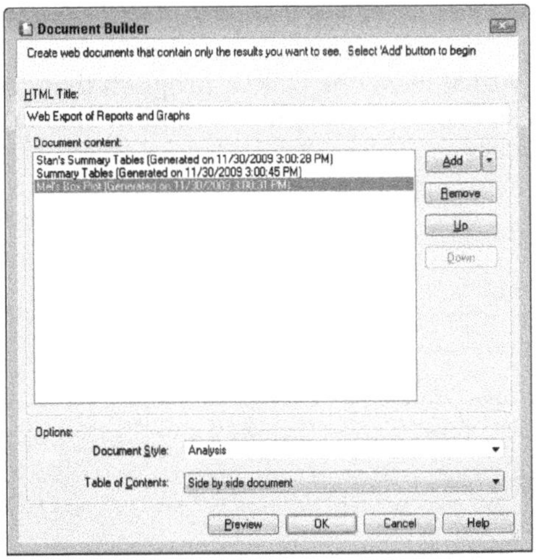

Figure 11-8: Document building; no cellophane tape required.

To select additional content for the document, click Add. You can add sections of HTML output that you have in your project. You can also add notes and links to external documents. Figure 11-9 shows the Add Results window with a list of all available HTML results in your project.

Figure 11-9:
All the
HTML
results that
are fit to
print.

Creating reports suitable for framing

SAS Enterprise Guide has always had the ability to arrange HTML; it's a capability that is both utilitarian and effective. In contrast, arranging SAS Report output in SAS Enterprise Guide can be downright fun. Why? Because you can

- Interact with your report by dragging pieces into place.
- Add and resize elements, such as charts and images.
- Add and apply formatting to titles and other text.

To build a new report with SAS Report results, create or open a SAS Enterprise Guide project with at least one task or program that creates SAS Report output. Then choose File⇨New⇨Report. A window similar to the one shown in Figure 11-10 appears.

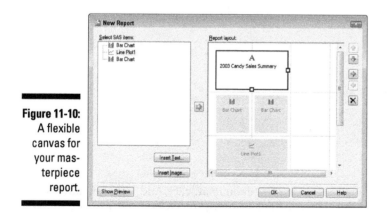

Figure 11-10:
A flexible
canvas for
your mas-
terpiece
report.

Practicing feng shui in report design

As you can see in Figure 11-10, all your available SAS Report items appear on the left side of the window in the Select SAS Items section. The right side of the window shows the report layout in a grid canvas.

To add SAS Report items to your report, simply click an item on the left and drag it over to the right, dropping it on a grid cell. (As an alternative to drag and drop, you can use the arrow buttons to move an item over and then arrange it on the grid.)

After items are on the grid, you can arrange them by dragging them. You can stack them vertically, and you can arrange them side by side (horizontally). Many SAS programmers regard side-by-side output, such as placing a chart next to a table, as the "holy grail" of SAS reporting. That is, everyone suspected it was possible but only a select few could ever achieve it. This report builder window makes single-page reporting with multiple SAS outputs a simple reality.

You can also annotate the report with additional items such as text and images. The Insert Text and Insert Image buttons provide access to windows that allow you to specify and format text or select an image file, and place the text or image in the report grid. After additional text or image items are added, you can arrange them in the same manner that you arrange other items on the grid.

Harmony is just a few clicks away

You can "stretch" an item by using the mouse to grab its handles and resize it. For example, we resized the 2003 Candy Sales Summary text title item in Figure 11-10 so that it is centered across the two Bar Chart items. Likewise, we resized the Line Plot item so that it spans the bottom portion of the report.

Figure 11-11 shows the final report. Note how the elements of the report are arranged the same as they appear in the New Report window in Figure 11-10.

When you rerun your project, the report refreshes with the most current content while retaining the specified layout.

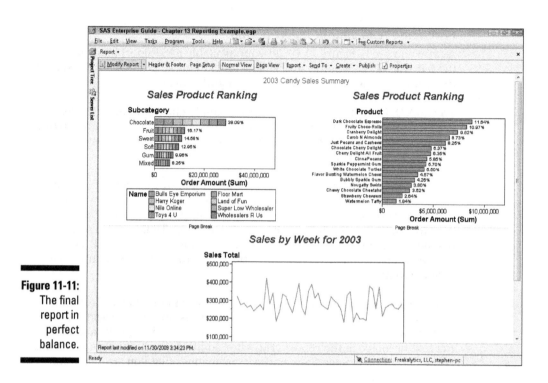

Figure 11-11:
The final
report in
perfect
balance.

Canning Your Work for Others to Use in Stored Processes

In this chapter, you've seen how to use SAS Enterprise Guide to share the fruits of your labor with the rest of the world. However, what if you work with people who want to run their own fruit harvest? A you-plant-it-and-they-pick-it type of operation.

As a person who creates SAS content for sharing with others, your goal is to equip your audience with access to relevant information, without necessarily burdening them with all the details of how you developed the information in SAS.

This is where stored processes come in! A *stored process* is fundamentally a SAS program, but it's a special SAS program because

- ✔ It's stored in a central location (on your SAS server).
- ✔ It contains information about parameters and prompts (think data filters and specifications for details), so the results can be tailored each time you run it.

✔ Access is controlled through SAS metadata, so you specify who can access and run your content.

✔ It's available from a variety of environments, including from your Web browser with SAS Web Report Studio or from Microsoft Office with SAS Enterprise Guide.

Cloning yourself — almost

A stored process is a SAS program that you can publish from SAS Enterprise Guide for others to run. Most important, people can run a stored process from the environment that makes sense for them, including the Web and Microsoft Office. Your audience doesn't need to know about SAS programming or even using SAS Enterprise Guide to benefit from your stored processes. All your viewers need to know is how to answer the prompts that you build into the stored process to customize their results.

A stored process is akin to packaging your smarts to answer your user's business questions anytime, anywhere. After you publish a stored process, it can be run at will without further intervention from you.

Distilling the complex down to the simple

Stored processes are a great way to take a process with many parts and boil it down to a single step. For example, consider the report example in the last section. The project flow from the report example is shown in Figure 11-12.

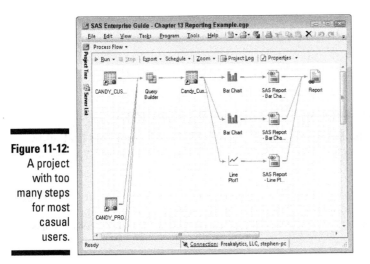

Figure 11-12:
A project with too many steps for most casual users.

You can see that it starts with several Candy data sets, which are joined through a query step. The output of the query is then used for two bar charts and a line plot. The part that you don't see is that the query contains a filter that references two parameters, which allows you to specify the sales region and product category when you run the project. It's a nice little project that offers some user flexibility at run time, which is great as long as you're willing to always run it with SAS Enterprise Guide.

To share this work with others who don't use SAS Enterprise Guide or even use SAS, you can create a stored process. To get started, follow these steps:

1. **Right-click an empty space on the process flow and choose Create Stored Process.**

   The Create New SAS Stored Process Wizard appears, as shown in Figure 11-13. Note that the title indicates that this screen is the first of six steps! Don't worry; it won't take long to take care of them all. The first page of this wizard is for general information.

Figure 11-13: The start of the Create New Stored Process Wizard.

> **Create New SAS Stored Process Wizard**
>
> **1** of 6   Name and Description   §sas
>
> Save stored process as:
> Na_me:
> SAS for Dummies Stored Process
> _Location:
> /Users/Freakalytics, LLC/My Folder   Browse...
> [Example: /BIP Tree/My Folder Name]
> Description:
> Stephen and Chris say stored processes are 'da bomb!
>
> _Keywords (comma separated):
> Sales Region Product Category Prompts
>
> More (F1)...
>
> <_Back ▾   Next>   Finish   Cancel

---

2. **Name your stored process and provide a description.**

   The optional Keywords field is useful only in environments that allow you to search for content (such as SAS Information Delivery Portal).

3. **Click Next.**

   The second page of the wizard (see Figure 11-14) displays the SAS code that will be published. This code is the heart of the stored process and describes the work developed through the tasks in SAS Enterprise

Guide. In this case, SAS Enterprise Guide generated the code within the flow, so no edits or changes are needed.

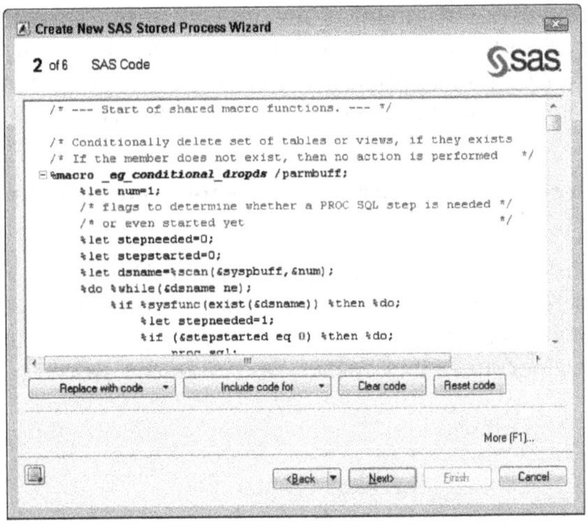

Figure 11-14: The heart of your stored process: the SAS program.

4. **(Optional) Experienced SAS programmers can use this screen to change the code to alter the behavior of the stored process.**

5. **To avoid having your eyes glaze over from staring at the SAS code, click Next.**

   Page 3 of the wizard appears, as shown in Figure 11-15.

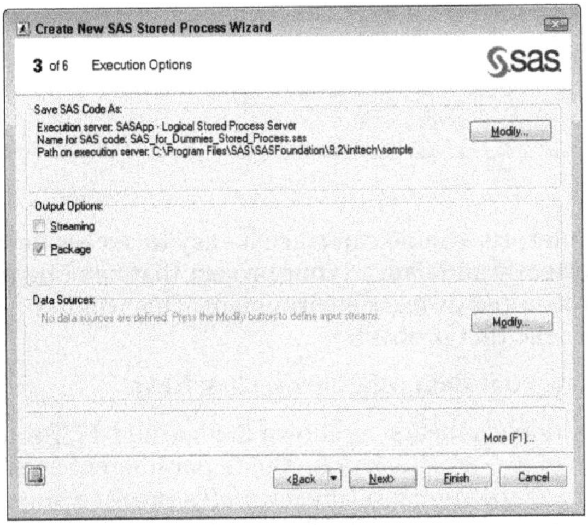

Figure 11-15: Location, location, location: Putting the *stored* in *stored process.*

6. **Specify a location for your stored process, and then click Next.**

You can specify what stored process server to use and where to store the SAS program. You can select a location from the folder structure defined in your SAS environment. Your options here depend heavily on how the SAS environment is configured in your organization. The good news is that after you make these selections for one stored process, SAS Enterprise Guide remembers these preferences for your next visit to this window.

7. **Select the data source and library options for your stored process, and then click Next.**

The Librefs window appears, as shown in Figure 11-16. This window is one of the smartest parts of this wizard. The screen shows you the data references that you use in your project flow and gives you the chance to adjust those references if necessary to run in the stored process environment.

<table>
<tr><td colspan="2">Create New SAS Stored Process Wizard</td></tr>
<tr><td>4 of 6 Librefs</td><td>§.sas</td></tr>
</table>

Library	LIBNAME statement
☑ EGSample	
☐ WORK	<SAS built-in library, no LIBNAME statement required>

☑ Include LIBNAME statement in SAS code   ☐ Use custom LIBNAME statement

Library Name: EGSample

Type: INPUT

Host name: Stephen-PC

More (F1)...

<Back ▼   Next>   Finish   Cancel

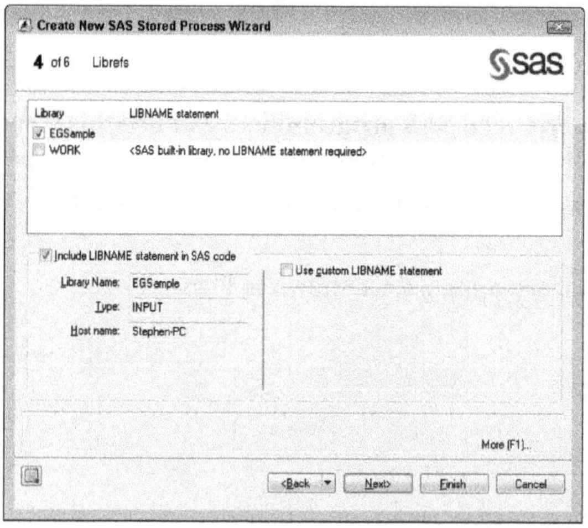

Figure 11-16: Do you know where your data comes from?

Because SAS Enterprise Guide can make it easy to access data, it's possible to inadvertently add data to your project that can't be reached from the central stored process environment. This window gives you the chance to reconcile that problem.

8. **After you review your data references, click Next.**

The Prompts window appears, as shown in Figure 11-17. Because this project contained two SAS Enterprise Guide parameters as part of the query step, the wizard automatically promotes those to stored process parameters, or user prompts that will be answered each time this stored process is run.

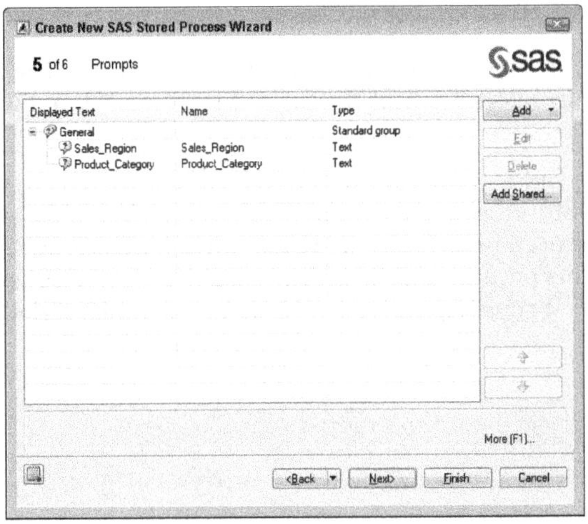

Figure 11-17:
Parameters
now,
prompted
report later.

9. **Using the controls onscreen, you can add more parameters and adjust the properties of those that are already defined.**

   Stored processes with parameters are the key to supplying your audience with *prompted reports* — reports that can be customized at run time by gathering answers to simple questions. This example has two parameters: one for the product category (Candy or Nuts), and one for the sales region (East, West, and Central). If you have a shared, reusable set of stored process prompts, you can select them here so that they're all centrally maintained across many stored processes.

10. **Click Next.**

    The last screen is a summary of all the options you specified in this wizard, as shown in Figure 11-18.

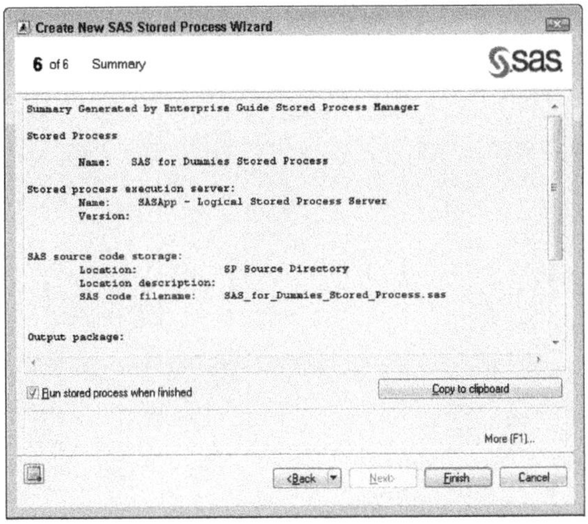

Figure 11-18:
Finally, our
masterpiece
is complete!

11. **Review the text of the Stored Process summary.**

12. **Click Finish and wait for the stored process to run the first time, unless you deselected the Run the Stored Process When Finished option.**

   SAS Enterprise Guide adds the completed stored process to your project. If the Run Stored Process When Finished check box is selected, it also runs the stored process immediately after publishing. If your stored process contains parameters, as in this example, you're presented with the prompts as it runs. Figure 11-19 shows an example of the prompt window.

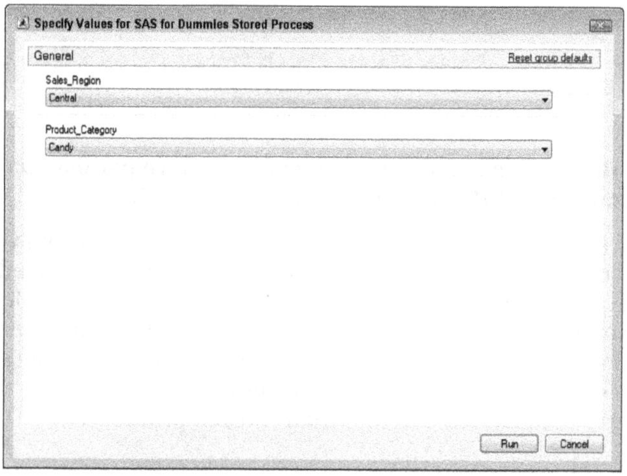

Figure 11-19:
The stored
process at
run time.

With the stored process registered for use, other people can now use it in other applications. Congratulations on making the world a better place by sharing your expertise with SAS!

Chapter 12

Use OLAP and Impress Your Coworkers

. . . .

. . . .

*D*etailed historical or transactional data is useful for reporting and statistical analysis. In the real world, this data can grow to very large sizes in companies having millions or even billions of records on just one topic, such as sales transactions or customer history. As data grows to very large sizes, even systems such as SAS can be slower than you want, especially for data exploration, where you want to ask multiple related questions of the data in quick succession.

OLAP (Online Analytic Processing) is a technology that presummarizes, stores, and accesses the data in a much more compact format than standard data tables (such as Microsoft Excel, Microsoft Access, or Oracle tables). With OLAP, a billion-row table that takes five minutes to access in a traditional manner can be accessed from an OLAP aggregated form in a matter of seconds. SAS provides a server for storing your data as OLAP data, appropriately named the SAS OLAP Server. SAS Enterprise Guide, SAS Add-In for Microsoft Office, and SAS Web Report Studio can leverage the powerful capabilities of the SAS OLAP Server in a variety of ways.

This chapter covers the basics of OLAP access and analysis with SAS Enterprise Guide.

Sweeter than Sugar Cubes?

OLAP data items are stored in one of two formats — dimensions and measures — to simplify access:

- ✔ A *dimension* is a logical grouping of data used for the same purpose. Examples of commonly used dimensions include geography, time, and customer. Geography could have multiple levels of the dimension that are available for your analysis. *Levels*, which are organized as a hierarchy of the most encompassing grouping to least encompassing grouping of the data for a given dimension, could be set as continent, country, state, and city — in that order.

- ✔ *Measures* are data attributes or facts that can be counted, added, summed, or averaged. Examples of measures include sales amount, units sold, employee compensation, or number of stores. Measures can typically have a wide range of mathematical operations performed on them, such as summing, averaging, finding the range (maximum minus the minimum), and counting the number of records as well as the number of distinct occurrences.

Similar to the way in which data stored in a standard database is called a *table*, data stored in an OLAP Server is commonly referred to as a *cube*.

You can do a wide range of amazing analysis with OLAP using just the concepts of dimensions, hierarchical levels within the dimension, measures, and operations that can be performed on the measure. Figure 12-1 shows a view of a sales OLAP cube accessed with SAS Enterprise Guide. On the left side, you can see the Product Hierarchy dimension displayed with two levels: Category and Subcategory. Values for Customers are Grocery, Retailer, and Wholesale. Across the top we have one dimension (Year, consisting of the years 1999–2003) and one measure (Measures, consisting of Average Sale_ Amount).

The SAS OLAP Server provides easy access to presummarized data that is calculated from your SAS or relational database sources. Someone in your organization would define the OLAP cubes that you need by subject area and build the definitions. On a periodic basis, the cube definitions are run so that your cube is built or refreshed or both on a regular basis.

The SAS OLAP Cube Studio application facilitates defining and building these cubes, but we don't cover this feature in this book. The manual for SAS OLAP Server covers this application.

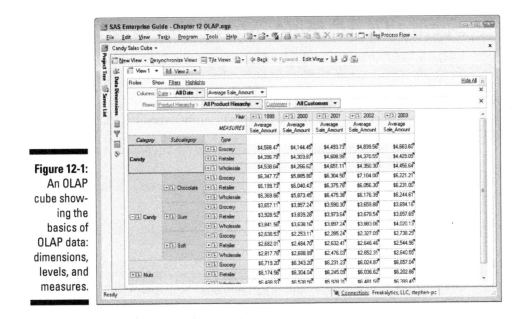

Figure 12-1:
An OLAP cube showing the basics of OLAP data: dimensions, levels, and measures.

The time your queries take with OLAP data are typically much faster than with traditional relational data. This is because the detail records are pre-summarized (instead of detailed transactions down to the individual order lines, you have sales for the day by product type and region); key information is gathered and stored very efficiently so that you can quickly analyze and explore it. The time it takes SAS to build or update a cube can take anywhere from seconds to hours; but it is rare for a user to wait more than a few seconds for each request.

Introducing OLAP Features

The great thing about working with OLAP data and the OLAP viewer provided in SAS Enterprise Guide is that you work interactively. You specify a new measure to view (for example, average sales amount) and it appears immediately in your viewer. Everyone likes immediate gratification, and OLAP delivers in this area. Drilling down and up enables you to move through the various dimensions in your table or graph (for example, you can drill down from the United States to all states or from product lines to individual products). Filtering (also called *slicing*) data allows you to subset the data you are viewing. OLAP also lets you view the data using a wide variety of charts, including bar, pie, and geographic map charts to show the data (a map of sales by region for 2005, for example). Finally, you can export data from your OLAP view to a relational table format. This is useful if you want to export a current OLAP view to SAS or Microsoft Excel for reporting or further analysis.

Seeing OLAP table interaction in action

Seeing how OLAP works is the quickest way to become proficient, so follow along with this example (with your own cube) if you have an OLAP Server. SAS OLAP Server is included with SAS Enterprise BI Server.

Note that SAS Enterprise Guide can access two other vendors' OLAP servers:

- **Analysis Services:** This is the SAS OLAP Server equivalent available from Microsoft SQL Server.
- **SAP BW:** SAP BW (*business information warehouse*) is the SAS OLAP Server equivalent from SAP.

Most of the functionality shown in this chapter is available with the OLAP servers from these other vendors.

The first step to accessing an OLAP cube is the Open dialog box. Cubes can be opened in SAS Enterprise Guide by choosing File⇨Open⇨OLAP Cube.

OLAP analysis is a highly interactive activity. You can quickly add and remove the information you want from an OLAP table, like the one shown in Figure 12-2. From Cube View Manager, shown on the left of Figure 12-2, you can add new dimensions, such as Product or Customer, to table rows or columns. You can also add new measures or existing measures (by switching to a new statistic for a measure already used in the table).

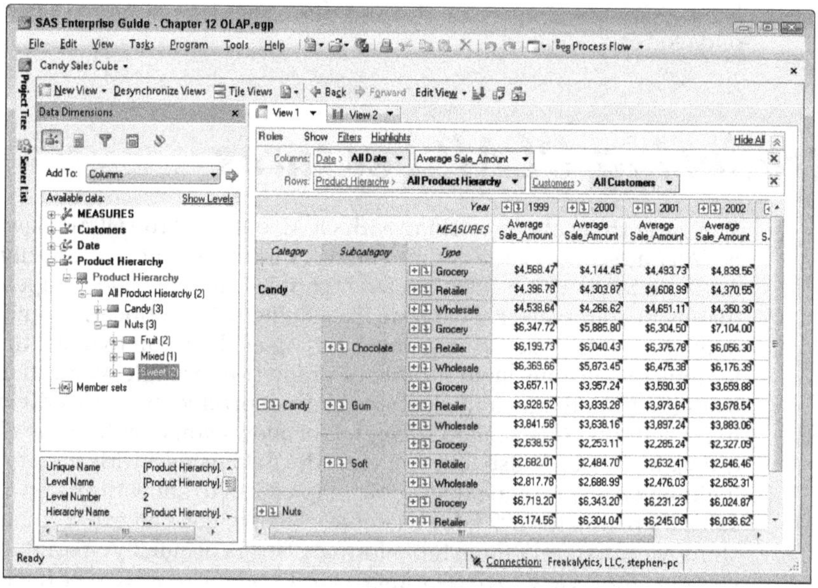

Figure 12-2:
Viewing an OLAP cube within Cube View Manager.

After you add a measure, you can easily change the statistic being applied to the measure. For example, when you add Units to a table, the default statistic for that measure might be Sum of Units Sold. After you add this, you might change the units to Average Units per Sale, Minimum Units in a Sale, or Median Units per Sale. Measure statistic types available in a cube are determined by the author of your cube.

Drilling and expanding your mind

After you select the dimensions and measures for your table from Cube View Manager, you can interact with the table directly. For example, if you drill down on the Chocolate subcategory in Figure 12-2, you see the levels below it: Chewy Chocolate Cheetahs, Chocolate Cherry Delight, and so on. (To drill down, click the down-arrow icon to the left of the level.) When you drill down, the level you were just at is no longer displayed in the table, but the values of the level below are now displayed. Therefore, drilling down on Chocolate displays Chewy Chocolate Cheetahs and Chocolate Cherry Delight but not the Chocolate subcategory. You can drill up to the previous level by right-clicking a level value and choosing Drill-Up.

Similar to drilling down and up is the concept of expanding and collapsing. Expanding a level displays the level below the current one while keeping the current level displayed in the table. This is what we did in Figure 12-2. Specifically, we expanded the Candy subcategory by clicking the plus symbol next to the word *Candy*. Conversely, click the subtraction symbol next to an expanded level to collapse it in the table.

Filtering out the weak and isolating members

Sometimes, you just want to be left alone. This is where *member isolation* can be useful. It allows you to focus on one value or several values in the level of a dimension. By right-clicking a member (such as the Chocolate subcategory of Candy) and choosing Isolate (see Figure 12-3), your table automatically goes down to the next level of the dimension. Isolating shows just the values within the selected level.

The results of isolating Chocolate are shown in Figure 12-4. (We also expanded Chocolate to the Product level.) You now see just the products within Chocolate. Also, note that the navigation information at the top of the table shows the current location within the Product Hierarchy dimension: Candy⇨Chocolate⇨Product⇨type.

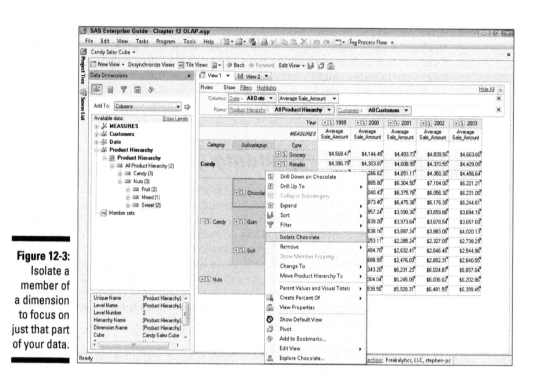

Figure 12-3:
Isolate a member of a dimension to focus on just that part of your data.

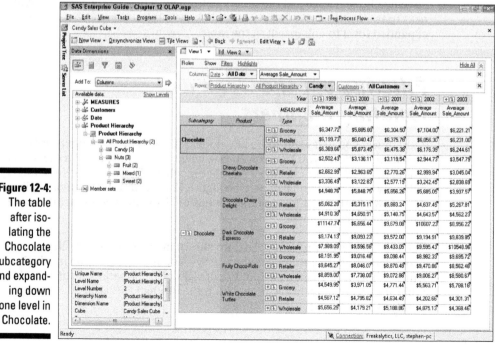

Figure 12-4:
The table after isolating the Chocolate subcategory and expanding down one level in Chocolate.

You can easily undo your actions in the table view by clicking the Back button on the toolbar, just below the Open Project toolbar item on the OLAP viewer toolbar. The Back button allows you to navigate backward in your cube actions in a manner similar to using a Back button in most Web browsers. After you start navigating backward, the Forward button becomes available.

To filter the data on a dimension not in use within the table or graph, you can use the Filter tool in the OLAP viewer.

Suppose that you want to keep the current table view and analyze only sales for Customer 1. Click the Filter link, and the Filter tool appears. Then, expand Customers in the Data Dimensions area of SAS Enterprise Guide until you see 1, as shown in Figure 12-5.

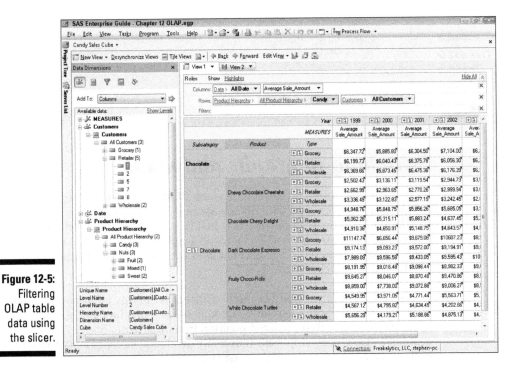

Figure 12-5: Filtering OLAP table data using the slicer.

The results of filtering for just Customer 1 appear in Figure 12-6.

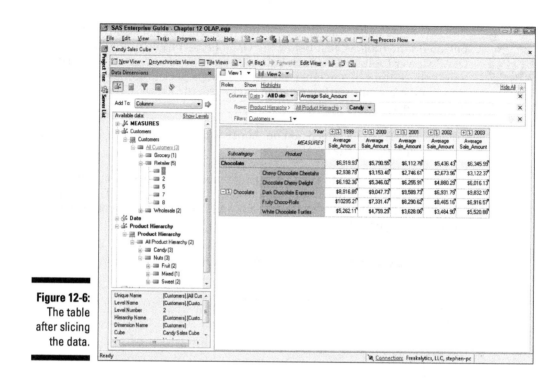

Figure 12-6:
The table after slicing the data.

Switching to graphs and maps

SAS is heavy on graphical capabilities, and OLAP Analyzer is no exception. Graphs tend to work best with one measure in use. You can remove a measure by clicking the drop-down arrow just to the right of the measure and choosing Remove from View. To view the graph, simply click the second automatically created tab, called View 2, at the top of the table just below the OLAP toolbar's Back button.

Figure 12-7 shows the Candy example from earlier in this chapter with a line chart graph. Note how the relative ranking of each product easily stands out, including products that changed position from first to second across the years. It's also readily apparent that many products, except Fruity Choco-Rolls, were on an upswing in the past year.

The great part about OLAP data is that you can explore and zoom in on an unexpected outcome that might be important to your business. Note that you can also display other chart types, such as horizontal bar, pie, plot, or area charts.

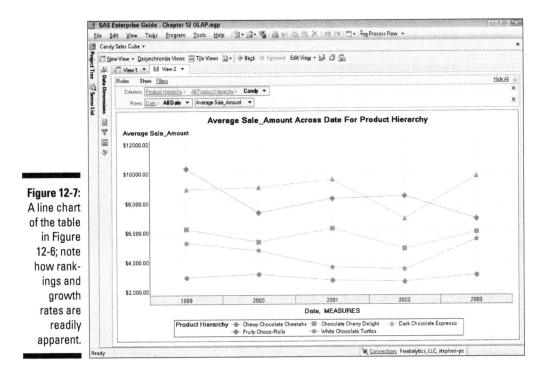

Figure 12-7:
A line chart of the table in Figure 12-6; note how rankings and growth rates are readily apparent.

Understanding the percentages: It's all relative

If you're interested in exploring the details of one dimension, especially the relative percent contribution of each value in a level, Cube Explorer is a valuable feature to use. Cube Explorer is available from the OLAP toolbar by choosing New View⇨Cube Explorer. We accessed the cube used in this chapter with the Cube Explorer and drilled all the way down into the Chocolate products, as shown in Figure 12-8.

In this example, we're examining the average sale amount across the various product levels. Starting at the top, you can see an average sale amount of $5.011.18. Going down one level, you see the average sale amount for each product category, with Candy the lowest and Nuts the highest. You also see the values as percentages of the parent level, which is all product sales in this case. Nuts are 125% (124.93%, to be precise) of the overall average sale. When you double-click any value, the interface automatically goes down one level from that starting point.

When we made this view, we double-clicked All, Candy, and Chocolate. This view offers a lot of insight in a static form. It is even more valuable interactively; try it out if you have the chance!

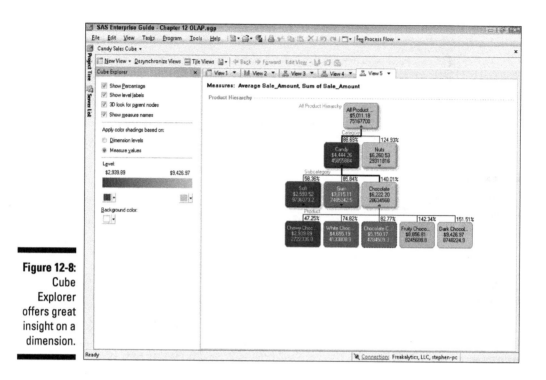

Figure 12-8:
Cube
Explorer
offers great
insight on a
dimension.

Slicing data for further analysis

What if you find something of interest in your OLAP data, but you want to use other SAS Enterprise Guide tasks, such as correlation or ranking with that data? Here's a solution: After you're at the level of OLAP data that you want to analyze, just select the task you want to run from the Tasks menu. In Figure 12-9, we ran a Box Plot task against a view of the OLAP data. The box plot shows the distribution of average sales by customer type over the five years of data. Other tasks people use with cubes include forecasting tasks and reporting tasks.

Figure 12-10 shows the data slice that was automatically created to use the Box Plot task.

Keep in mind from the analytics discussion in Chapter 8 that variance is a key to almost every type of statistical technique. OLAP, because of its summarized nature, loses data details to provide you with greater speed. Be sure to use the detail data that your OLAP cube was created from for any business-critical statistical analyses. The aggregated OLAP data is useful for a first "dirty" pass at the data, but it is not a substitute for statistical analysis with the detailed data.

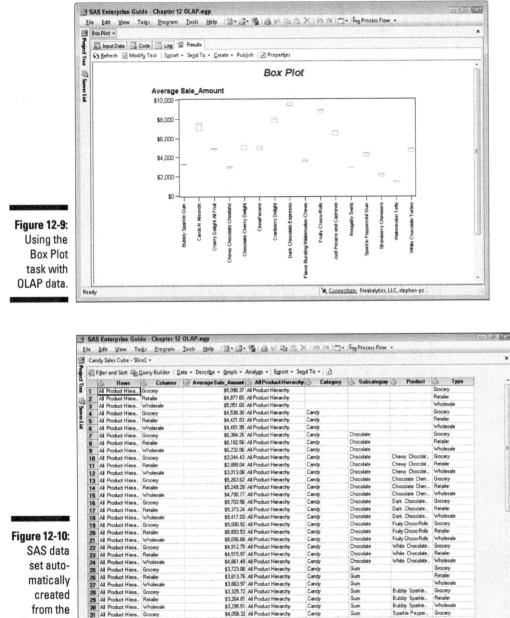

Figure 12-9:
Using the
Box Plot
task with
OLAP data.

Figure 12-10:
SAS data
set auto-
matically
created
from the
OLAP data
when a task
is run.

Discovering More OLAP Features

Maybe you thought the last section had it all; but no, the OLAP viewer has even more great features! Bookmarking allows you to save a current OLAP cube view (including layout, levels, and filters) and quickly return to it just like you do with an Internet browser bookmark. Calculated measures let you create custom measures (such as net sales) from measures available with the cube. Another great feature of OLAP is the capability to drill to the detailed transaction values behind a single number. For example, from the average sales amount for June 2006, you can drill down to all sales transactions in June 2006 with one click. Conditional formatting allows you to highlight values that are particularly good or bad so that you can quickly find anomalies, such as a net profit percent above 55% or below 10%. Finally, if you are brave and really like tweaking your results, you can use MDX Editor to send the exact query you want to the OLAP Server — going beyond what the point-and-click capabilities will let you do!

Bookmarking: Where was I?

Bookmarks allow you to save a particular view of your cube, much like favorites in your Web browser. Dimensions, drilling, expanding, isolating, measures, and slices can all be preserved in a named bookmark of your choice. To bookmark a view using the OLAP toolbar, from the OLAP pane window, select Bookmarks⇨Add Bookmark (the icon below the Desynchronize Views button), as shown in Figure 12-11. To open a bookmark, simply click the desired bookmark from the same view. Note a special bookmark always exists here to take you back to the initial cube layout, called the Initial default view.

Using calculated measures

If the measure you want doesn't exist in your cube, don't despair. If you want a measure that can be based on other measures in the cube, you can add a *calculated measure*. A simple example is net sales, based on gross sales minus returns. To create a calculated measure, click Customized Items and Sets from the OLAP pane and then choose New⇨Calculated Measure. The Calculated Measure Wizard appears, ready to walk you through many types of calculations. Here are the major categories:

✔ **Simple Calculations:** For example, Sum and Difference

✔ **Time Series Analysis:** For example, Rolling Totals, Average Over Time, and Growth

✔ **Trends and Forecasting:** For example, Correlation and Linear Regression

✔ **Count Analysis:** For example, Unique Item Count

✔ **Relative Contribution Analysis:** The contribution of a cell as a percentage of the overall total (such as sales for tennis balls in Ohio as a percentage of all sporting goods in the United States)

✔ **Custom Calculation:** Complex calculations not available with the wizard

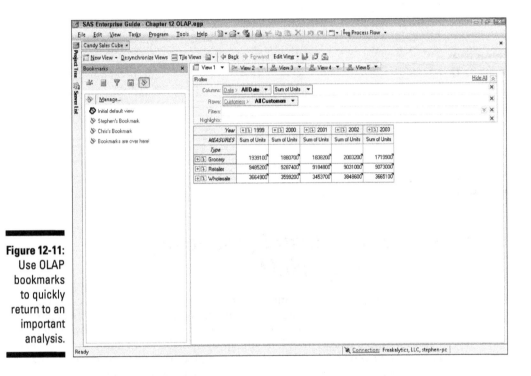

Figure 12-11:
Use OLAP bookmarks to quickly return to an important analysis.

Drilling down: Just the facts, please

When you want to investigate a value in the OLAP table, you can drill through to the detail data that was used to make the OLAP cube. For example, in Figure 12-1, you might want to see the orders for Chocolate Grocery store sales in 2002, a particularly solid year for this subcategory. To drill through to the detail, just click the cell of interest ($7,104.00), right-click, and choose Drill through Detail. A detail table opens, shown in Figure 12-12, just like any other data table accessed with SAS Enterprise Guide. Note that not all OLAP cubes have the Drill to Detail feature enabled, so ask your cube author to turn it on if it isn't enabled.

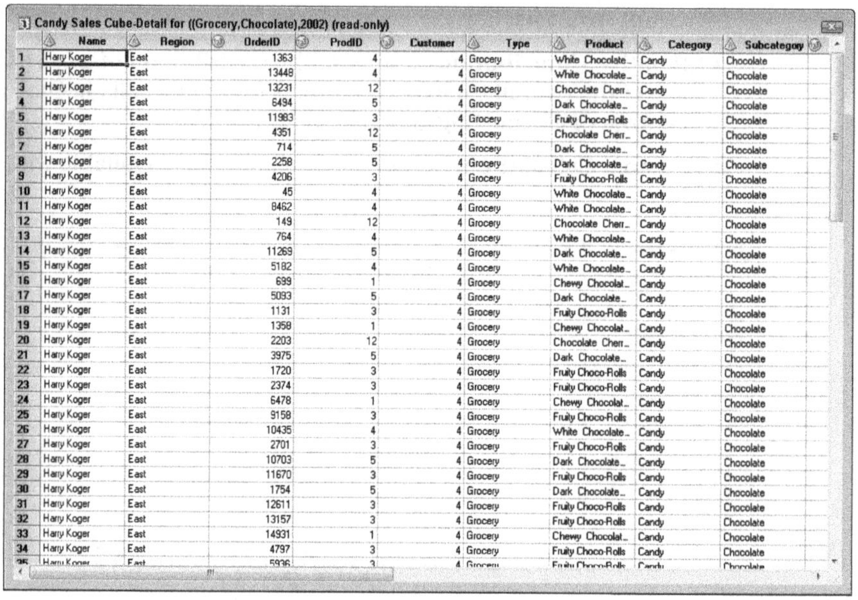

Candy Sales Cube-Detail for ((Grocery,Chocolate),2002) (read-only)

	Name	Region	OrderID	ProdID	Customer	Type	Product	Category	Subcategory
1	Harry Koger	East	1363	4	4	Grocery	White Chocolate...	Candy	Chocolate
2	Harry Koger	East	13448	4	4	Grocery	White Chocolate...	Candy	Chocolate
3	Harry Koger	East	13231	12	4	Grocery	Chocolate Cherr...	Candy	Chocolate
4	Harry Koger	East	6494	5	4	Grocery	Dark Chocolate...	Candy	Chocolate
5	Harry Koger	East	11983	3	4	Grocery	Fruity Choco-Rolls	Candy	Chocolate
6	Harry Koger	East	4351	12	4	Grocery	Chocolate Cherr...	Candy	Chocolate
7	Harry Koger	East	714	5	4	Grocery	Dark Chocolate...	Candy	Chocolate
8	Harry Koger	East	2258	5	4	Grocery	Dark Chocolate...	Candy	Chocolate
9	Harry Koger	East	4206	3	4	Grocery	Fruity Choco-Rolls	Candy	Chocolate
10	Harry Koger	East	45	4	4	Grocery	White Chocolate...	Candy	Chocolate
11	Harry Koger	East	8462	4	4	Grocery	White Chocolate...	Candy	Chocolate
12	Harry Koger	East	149	12	4	Grocery	Chocolate Cherr...	Candy	Chocolate
13	Harry Koger	East	764	4	4	Grocery	White Chocolate...	Candy	Chocolate
14	Harry Koger	East	11269	5	4	Grocery	Dark Chocolate...	Candy	Chocolate
15	Harry Koger	East	5182	4	4	Grocery	White Chocolate...	Candy	Chocolate
16	Harry Koger	East	699	1	4	Grocery	Chewy Chocolat...	Candy	Chocolate
17	Harry Koger	East	5093	5	4	Grocery	Dark Chocolate...	Candy	Chocolate
18	Harry Koger	East	1131	3	4	Grocery	Fruity Choco-Rolls	Candy	Chocolate
19	Harry Koger	East	1358	1	4	Grocery	Chewy Chocolat...	Candy	Chocolate
20	Harry Koger	East	2203	12	4	Grocery	Chocolate Cherr...	Candy	Chocolate
21	Harry Koger	East	3975	5	4	Grocery	Dark Chocolate...	Candy	Chocolate
22	Harry Koger	East	1720	3	4	Grocery	Fruity Choco-Rolls	Candy	Chocolate
23	Harry Koger	East	2374	3	4	Grocery	Fruity Choco-Rolls	Candy	Chocolate
24	Harry Koger	East	6478	1	4	Grocery	Chewy Chocolat...	Candy	Chocolate
25	Harry Koger	East	9158	3	4	Grocery	Fruity Choco-Rolls	Candy	Chocolate
26	Harry Koger	East	10435	4	4	Grocery	White Chocolate...	Candy	Chocolate
27	Harry Koger	East	2701	3	4	Grocery	Fruity Choco-Rolls	Candy	Chocolate
28	Harry Koger	East	10703	5	4	Grocery	Dark Chocolate...	Candy	Chocolate
29	Harry Koger	East	11670	3	4	Grocery	Fruity Choco-Rolls	Candy	Chocolate
30	Harry Koger	East	1754	5	4	Grocery	Dark Chocolate...	Candy	Chocolate
31	Harry Koger	East	12611	3	4	Grocery	Fruity Choco-Rolls	Candy	Chocolate
32	Harry Koger	East	13157	3	4	Grocery	Fruity Choco-Rolls	Candy	Chocolate
33	Harry Koger	East	14931	1	4	Grocery	Chewy Chocolat...	Candy	Chocolate
34	Harry Koger	East	4797	3	4	Grocery	Fruity Choco-Rolls	Candy	Chocolate
35	Harry Koger	East	5936	3	4	Grocery	Fruity Choco-Rolls	Candy	Chocolate

Figure 12-12: Use OLAP Drill to Detail to see what's behind a particular outcome.

Using conditional formatting: Isn't that special?

Some people just love to stand out, so they dye their hair blue or pierce various body parts. Creating conditional highlighting in your table can do the same for your table but with much less trouble and cost. *Conditional highlighting* is a feature that lets you apply specific font changes (say, bold), colors, and even special icons to the cell value (such as a green up arrow or a red down arrow). For example, suppose that you want sales values lower than $20 to be accompanied by a red down arrow and sales values higher than $40 to get a green up arrow (see Figure 12-13). You can do this with conditional highlighting from the OLAP toolbar Highlight menu.

Adding details about your values

Some OLAP cubes have extra data — member properties — about the values in their dimensional levels. *Member properties* provide the ability to add special details to a value, such as the population for the state of Wisconsin or the manager name for a product line. Member properties are obtained by right-clicking a member value and choosing Show Member Properties.

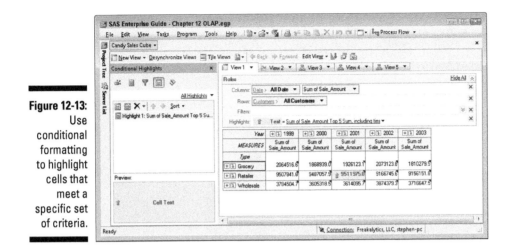

Figure 12-13:
Use
conditional
formatting
to highlight
cells that
meet a
specific set
of criteria.

Speaking MDX with the OLAP cube

Every time a new view of the OLAP data is retrieved from the OLAP Server, a special language is used to specify the data to retrieve on your behalf. This language is MultiDimensional Expression (MDX). MDX is similar to Structured Query Language (SQL), except MDX is for OLAP data, and SQL is for relational data.

If you want to use an MDX query for a given table view in another application or modify it yourself for SAS Enterprise Guide, use MDX Editor (see Figure 12-14). Just click the Edit View icon and choose Edit with MDX Editor on the OLAP toolbar. From MDX Editor, you can copy the query, modify it, or paste in your own MDX query.

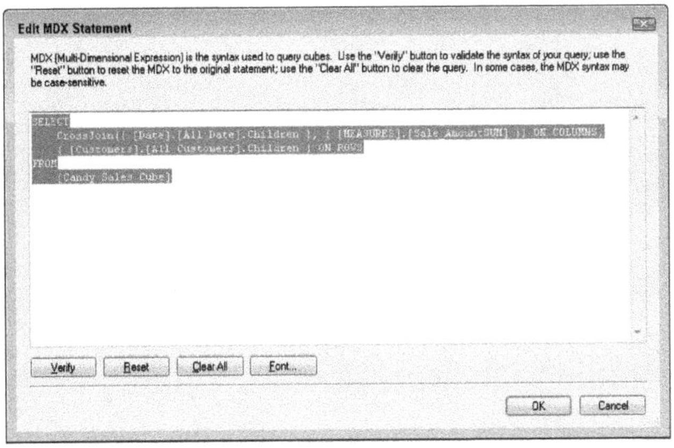

Figure 12-14:
A sample
MDX query
viewed in
MDX Editor.

Chapter 13

Supercharge Microsoft Office with SAS

. . . .

In This Chapter

▶ Merging SAS with Microsoft Office for fantastic power

▶ Diving into the SAS Add-In for Microsoft Office

▶ Checking out SAS server data from Office

▶ Viewing analysis from Office

▶ Ending spreadsheet hell

▶ Sharing your SAS and Office content

. . . .

*T*he SAS Add-In for Microsoft Office (shortened to *the add-in* in this chapter) is an application from SAS that works from inside Microsoft Office applications. It's available from the menu, toolbars, and ribbon (in Office 2007 and later) in Excel, Word, and PowerPoint. The add-in, which is part of SAS BI Server, takes advantage of the architecture in Office that allows other applications to integrate in the Microsoft Office environment, known as the Add-In model. Hence, the name! You can use all the Office formatting and layout features with the content you create using the add-in.

This chapter shows you how the add-in provides you with an easy way to access the power of your SAS servers for data access, reporting, graphics, and analytics directly from the familiar applications of Excel, Word, and PowerPoint. Your SAS server results are immediately available to format, lay out, print, analyze with Office functionality, and present just like your usual Office spreadsheets, documents, and presentations. Equally important, you can refresh your SAS content at will — whenever you need to update your analyses with the latest data or tweak your results for those last-minute revisions that managers tend to request.

Much of what you've read in the first half of this book is directly applicable to the add-in because the add-in and SAS Enterprise Guide share a large amount of functionality, especially the tasks and wizards. The add-in has a slightly different workflow than SAS Enterprise Guide and is missing some of the more powerful capabilities of SAS Enterprise Guide, but the add-in has additional functionality relevant to the Office environment. The add-in is one of the most universally loved applications from SAS because it offers easy access to the power of SAS from the familiar world of Office.

Using the Power of SAS from the Cozy World of Office

To start using this awesome combination of modern computing platforms, you need to have access to a SAS BI Server in your organization. If the add-in isn't already installed on your PC, ask to have it installed. In this chapter, we show version 4.2 of the add-in combined with Office 2007.

After installation, you'll see something similar to Figure 13-1 when you open Excel. We focus on Excel throughout the chapter because it is the most powerful general-purpose business analysis tool in Microsoft Office. On the Excel ribbon, located at the far right, is the new SAS ribbon.

The Open Data feature lets you open data from your SAS server directly into Excel worksheets or pivot tables. You can browse this data and even use it in with standard Excel functionality. The Analyze Data feature enables you to access SAS-based data management, reporting, graphics, and analytic capabilities (through SAS tasks and wizards) covered in previous chapters. Next to Analyze Data is the Reports feature, which offers you access to published reports and stored processes created in other applications such as SAS Enterprise Guide and SAS Web Report Studio.

Stored processes are referred to as *reports* in the add-in because many non-technical users are familiar with this term but would not be familiar with the term *stored process*.

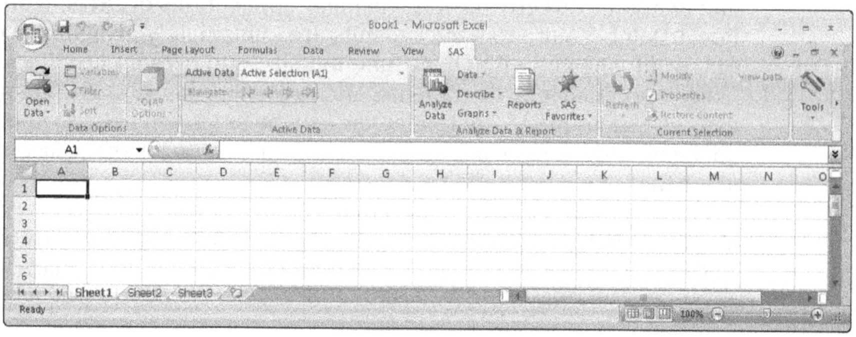

Figure 13-1:
The SAS
ribbon
viewed in
Excel 2007.

Exploring just a little bit more, you can see the items available from the SAS ribbon in Figure 13-1. Additional areas of functionality are

- ✔ **Active Data:** Allows you to navigate through the rows of your data source from the SAS server (available only in Excel)

- ✔ **SAS Favorites:** Lets you quickly access your favorite data, reports, and tasks

- ✔ **Refresh:** Enables you to update your results from SAS that are currently displayed in Office with the most current data and results

- ✔ **Modify:** Enables you to change the settings for a SAS result previously created with the add-in

- ✔ **Tools:** Lets you access a variety of utility functions, including Server Connection information

- ✔ **View SAS Contents:** Enables you to review all the SAS analyses and data sources used in the current document

- ✔ **Options:** Lets you set general add-in behavior options

- ✔ **Help:** Provides help specific to the add-in

Understanding options for SAS Add-In for Microsoft Office

SAS Add-In for Microsoft Office Options offer a variety of ways to control the add-in's behavior and are useful to review after you've used the add-in a bit. The Options dialog box is shown in Figure 13-2 and is available by clicking Options from the SAS ribbon. Note that the selections will vary depending on the Office application from which you open the Options dialog box.

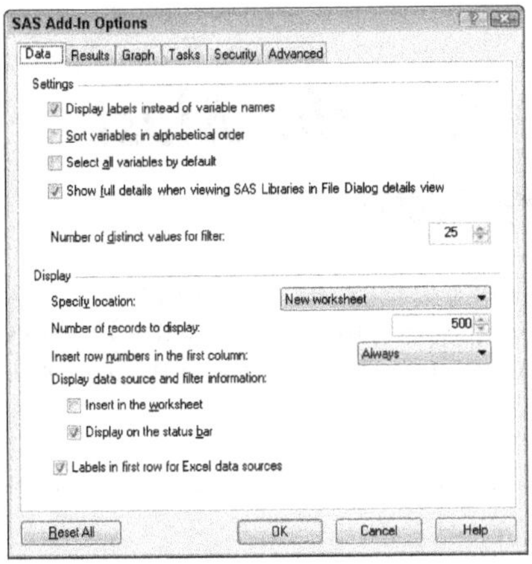

Figure 13-2:
The options for SAS Add-In for Microsoft Office.

Some of the most useful options allow you to control data browsing, results type and style, graph settings, task settings, stored process defaults, and advanced settings. Here are some of the important areas to examine:

- ✔ **The number of records to display when browsing data:** On the Data tab; the default is 500. You might want a smaller number, such as 25, for quicker data viewing.

- ✔ **Turning off the Status window:** On the Results tab; the Status window is on by default and pops up each time you run SAS requests. If you find the Status window distracting, you can turn it off by default and display it when you want by clicking the Status button on the toolbar.

- ✔ **SAS output format type:** On the Results tab; the format output type is set for each Office application. The default is SAS Report because it offers the best flexibility for formatting, but you can specify other formats such as CSV (comma-separated values), HTML, and RTF.

Just as important as Options is configuring your SAS server connections by choosing Tools⇔Connections. This command allows you to set your user name, password, server name for the SAS metadata connection, and the default SAS server on which to process your requests.

Knowing which Office applications are supported

The add-in requires Office 2000, XP, 2003, or 2007. Older Office versions are not supported. The add-in is available from Excel, Word, and PowerPoint. Excel offers access to all add-in features. Word and PowerPoint do not have a data grid amenable to browsing data similar to Excel, so they lack most of the functionality of the Active Data section of the SAS ribbon. You can still use Word and PowerPoint to select and filter data, analyze the data, and run reports.

Using the Add-In to Get the Most Out of Office Integration

The SAS Add-In for Microsoft Office brings the power of SAS into your Office application and also lets you use Excel data sources with SAS server functionality for advanced analysis. The main features of this integration include the capability to

- ✔ Access data of any size from within Excel for use with your SAS server
- ✔ Perform ad hoc analysis on this data

✔ Run predefined SAS programs or report from within the Office environment and incorporate the results into your spreadsheet, Word document, or PowerPoint slideshow presentation

After you have SAS content in your Office documents, you can easily refresh this content with the latest data and share the results across your organization.

Accessing and managing data of any size from almost anywhere

Microsoft Office applications are easy and familiar, but they're generally not very capable at analyzing large data sources or data from non-Microsoft systems (including mainframe-based data, UNIX data, Oracle databases, and DB2 databases). In particular, Excel worksheets have a limit of 1 million rows of data with no more than 16,384 columns. This is fine for simpler applications, but many times needed data is in a remote source or is large or both, with millions or even billions of rows of data commonplace in many companies.

The SAS Add-In for Microsoft Office can help you blow past this issue because SAS accesses and analyzes the data for you from the SAS server even though you can preview and browse it in Excel. The add-in achieves this by using SAS as a data-caching mechanism. The add-in shows you data in small pieces — the default is 500 rows — and allows you to easily filter and browse this data at will. Most important, the add-in allows easy access to the massive array of analysis tasks and wizards with these large data sources.

Opening data with the add-in

From Microsoft Excel, you can easily open SAS data, select the relevant columns, filter the data, and browse it at will:

1. **To access the Candy_Sales_Summary sample table, choose Open Data⇨ Into Worksheet from the SAS ribbon.**

   The Open Data Source dialog box appears, as shown in Figure 13-3.

2. **Select the Candy_Sales_Summary data set, and then click Open.**

   The Modify Data Source dialog box appears. Unlike with SAS Enterprise Guide, you are provided with further data access options before viewing the data. This dialog box has the following tabs: Variables, Filter, Sort, and Output Location.

3. **In the Available box on the Variables tab, select the following (press the Ctrl key while clicking these items): Customer, Product, Retail_ Price, and Discount. Then add them to the Selected box by clicking the right arrow button.**

   After you do this, the dialog box should look like Figure 13-4.

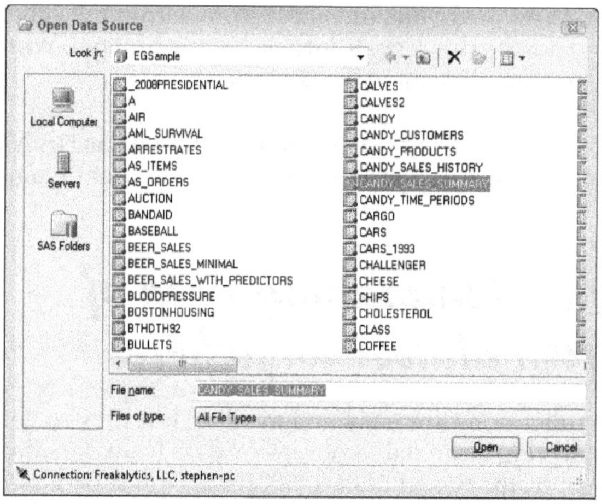

Figure 13-3:
Opening
SAS data
from Excel.

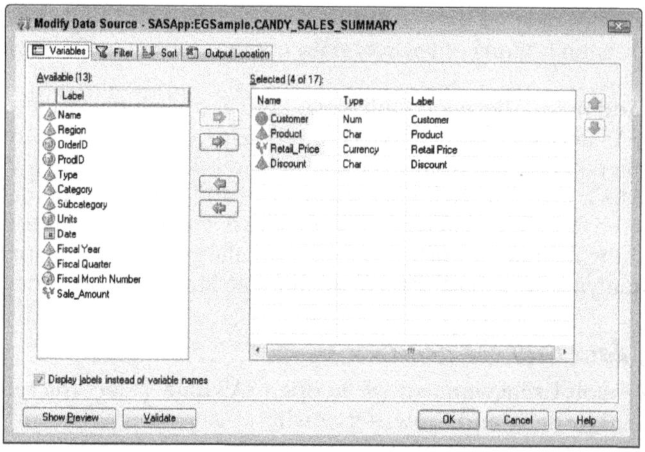

Figure 13-4:
Select
just the
variables
you want
to view in
Excel.

4. **To filter the data for the East region and the first quarter of 2004, do the following:**

   a. **Click the Filter tab.**

   b. **Choose Region from the first drop-down list.**

   c. **Choose Is Equal To from the second drop-down list.**

   d. **Click the button with the ellipse (...) in the third drop-down list, and then choose East.**

   e. **Choose AND from the fourth drop-down list.**

5. **For the second row of filter criteria, choose**

   • **Fiscal Quarter**

- **Is Equal To**

- **2004Q1**

Your dialog box should look like Figure 13-5.

6. **Click OK.**

For more sophisticated filtering, the Advanced Expression Editor is available from this dialog box by clicking Advanced Edit. The filter conditions you just defined with the standard dialog box are displayed in the Advanced Expression Editor shown in Figure 13-6.

When you click OK, the data appears in Excel, similar to Figure 13-7.

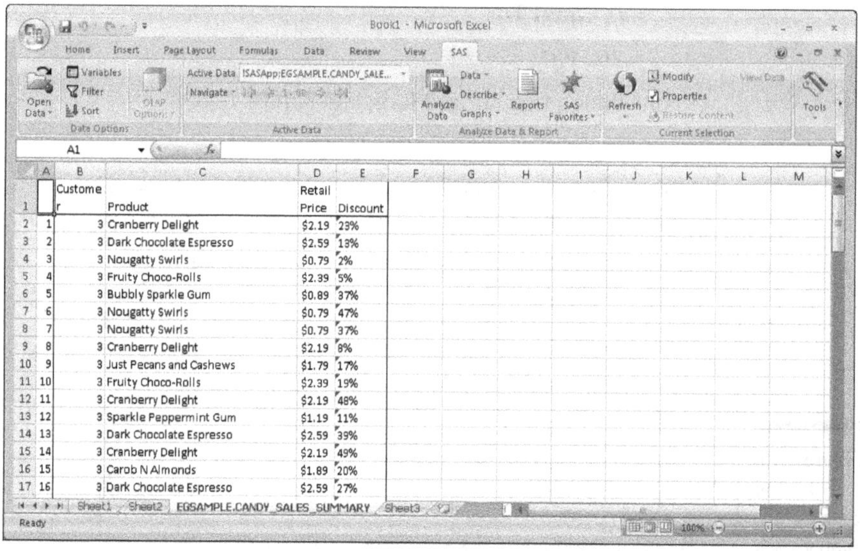

Figure 13-7:
The filtered
data in
Excel.

Note that only the variables you selected are displayed. The number of rows accessed is shown in the SAS Active Data Navigation area, in this case, rows 1–88. Just above that information is the Active Data dialog box, which shows that we opened the data set referenced from the SASApp server. (The worksheet is also named after the data you just opened.)

The arrow icons next to the row information allow you to page forward and backward through the data. These are available only if you can't bring all the data into Excel at once. You can also update the selected variables and filters by clicking the Modify icon on the Current Selection area of the ribbon.

Using the add-in to move your Excel data to SAS

The add-in not only makes it easy to access SAS data sources from Excel but also allows you to transfer Excel-based data to your SAS server for use with SAS tasks and wizards. To do so, follow these steps:

1. **Open your Excel data source.**

   See Figure 13-8 for the example from the SAS Enterprise Guide sample directory, Boards.xls.

2. **Click the Active Data drop-down icon from the Active Data part of the SAS ribbon, and choose Copy to SAS Server.**

   The Copy to SAS Server dialog box appears, as shown in Figure 13-9. Note that the WORK library is the default, with _EXCELEXPORT the default data set name. WORK is a temporary data directory specific to the current SAS server session in the open Office application. To reuse the data at a future SAS session, be sure to save it to a permanent SAS directory.

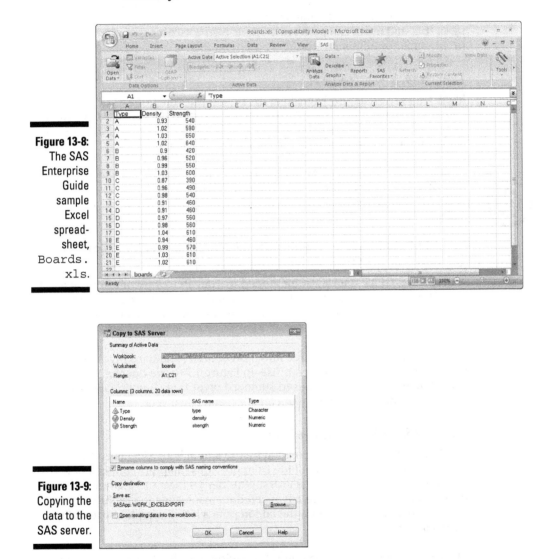

Figure 13-8:
The SAS
Enterprise
Guide
sample
Excel
spread-
sheet,
Boards.
xls.

Figure 13-9:
Copying the
data to the
SAS server.

3. Click OK to transfer the data to the SAS server.

Your data is now on the server and available for use with your SAS tasks, which we discuss in the next section.

Accessing ad hoc analysis: Awesome!

You can apply SAS power to your Excel or SAS data quickly with ad hoc analysis techniques, including pivot tables and built-in SAS tasks. These are tasks that end users can perform on their own with no support from a SAS programmer or administrator.

Turn, step, pivot (table)!

Many users of Microsoft Excel love the pivot table functionality. The add-in allows you to use the power of pivot tables with SAS data sources. If you have SAS OLAP Server or data in SAS, you can easily open these data sources into a pivot table by choosing Open Data⇨Into PivotTables.

Although you can open OLAP server data or any other SAS data source, note that OLAP data will be faster — perhaps much faster — than the same data from the original relational database table data sources. There are two reasons for this:

- ✔ **OLAP data is already summarized in a manner similar to how pivot tables present information.**

- ✔ **All non-OLAP data must be moved to your PC for pivot tables to work.** This is a limitation of Excel pivot tables. This second scenario means that data sources larger than a few million rows are unsuitable for opening into pivot tables.

After you open your data source into a pivot table, standard pivot table functionality is available for your use. In Figure 13-10, we opened the Candy_Sales_Summary data set and used standard pivot table functionality to analyze candy sales by category, subcategory, and fiscal year.

Using SAS tasks from the add-in

Combining the data access provided by the add-in with SAS tasks (the same ones in SAS Enterprise Guide from previous chapters) offers a new world of possibilities for Office users. Whether you want to analyze large volumes of data or use the more advanced data management, graphics, or statistical capabilities SAS offers, the add-in puts a lot of oomph in your Office environment.

Almost every SAS task in SAS Enterprise Guide is available, with the notable exception of the Query Builder task. The Query Builder task is replaced with the simpler Modify Data Source dialog box, which appears by default when you open data in a worksheet.

Using the board strength data from the previous section, you can follow this example to perform an analysis of variance using the add-in. In this sample scenario, your board materials supplier claims that her new Type A material is superior to your other materials, so you should pay a premium for Type A material. You will determine whether board strength is linked to the type of board material used, or the board density, or both factors. Using the 20 test boards created with the various materials and board densities, you want to see whether you should pay more for Type A material. You suspect that board density with the much cheaper Type C material will still allow you to have boards that are strong enough for your customers without the added cost:

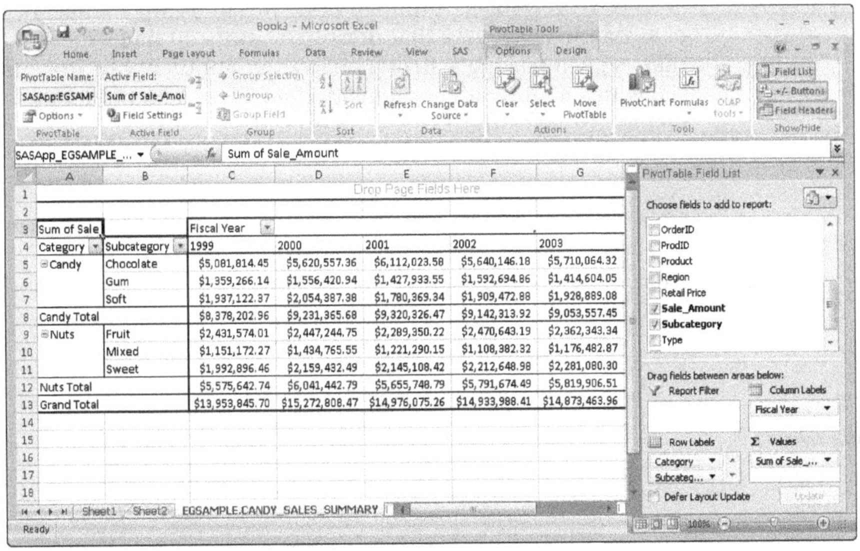

Figure 3-10:
An Excel pivot table based on a SAS data set, Candy_ Sales_ Summary.

1. **Follow the steps in the "Using the add-in to move your Excel data to SAS" section, earlier in the chapter.**

2. **Choose SAS⇨Analyze Data⇨ANOVA⇨Linear Models Task.**

   The Linear Models dialog box appears, as shown in Figure 13-11.

3. **Because Strength is the variable to predict, add it to the Dependent Variable role.**

4. **Add Density and Type to the Quantitative Variables and Classification Variables roles, respectively.**

   Density and Type are the variables used to predict board strength.

5. **Specify the model by clicking Model in the leftmost pane; select Density and Type in the Variables to Assign pane. Then click the Main button in the Model view.**

   By doing this, you are stating that there is a simple predictive relationship for Strength as a function of Density and Type. (Strength was specified as the variable to predict earlier in Step 3.)

6. **Click Run to execute the analysis.**

   The Choose Location dialog box appears, prompting you to choose a location in Excel to place the results.

7. **Select the New Worksheet option and type a useful name, as shown in Figure 13-12.**

   The analysis shows that the strength of our test boards is 95 percent explainable (see the R-square of 0.946) with just Density and Type as the predictive variables. Although both variables are significant predictors of strength, it appears that density is about 20 times more important than type in making a strong board. Put another way, the cheaper material with a slightly higher density than Type A material appears to be just as strong as the Type A material.

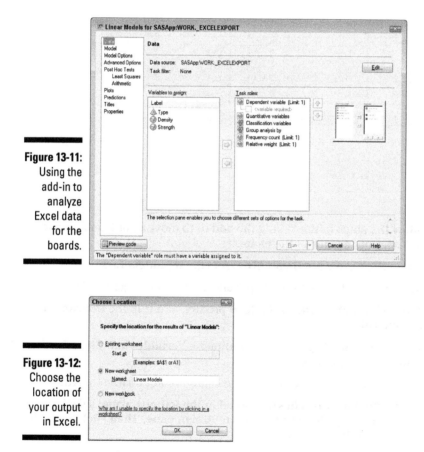

Figure 13-11: Using the add-in to analyze Excel data for the boards.

Figure 13-12: Choose the location of your output in Excel.

Based on your analysis, you tell the salesperson that you want Type A material only if it is no more than 5 percent more expensive than Type C. The statistical diagnostic and predictive plots that SAS automatically generated are shown in Figure 13-13.

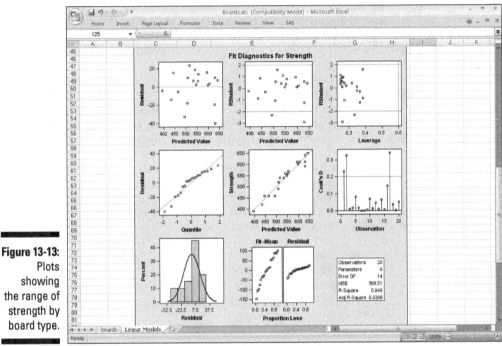

Figure 13-13: Plots showing the range of strength by board type.

Although we used Excel in this section, don't forget that the output of SAS tasks can be used directly in PowerPoint and Word! The main restriction in PowerPoint and Word is that you can only preview the data used in your task in the Open Data Source dialog box (by clicking the Show Preview button in Figure 13-4).

Ascending beyond spreadsheet hell with stored processes

As you might recall from Chapter 11, a *stored process* is a centrally stored SAS program that can have simple prompts for a user to specify details about the analysis. When you run the stored process, you are presented with the results of the program based on your specified details. Stored processes can be run from the add-in. This section gets you up to speed on why and how you access stored processes using the add-in.

Checking out an example of how not to use data

Although Excel is indeed customizable and powerful, the details of the work performed in one spreadsheet are not easy to integrate in another spreadsheet. A simple example can illustrate the problem. Peter in Sales wants to project the sales of an updated product at his company. He jumps through some hoops and finally programs a spreadsheet to create a forecast. Unknown to him, Cindy in Marketing does the same work in her Excel spreadsheet with the same historic data. They both show up at a meeting with the CEO and tell him two very different numbers! How could they avoid this scenario?

If Peter and Cindy had collaborated and created a forecasting stored process published by one of them, they could open it and refresh it at will with the latest data from Excel, Word, or PowerPoint. Because the stored process exists in only one place (on the SAS server) and has access to all their corporate data stores, it is one version of the truth for their forecasting problem.

You could also run this stored process from the Web in SAS Web Report Studio (see Chapter 14) or from SAS Enterprise Guide. If the logic for the stored process is updated next week for some new business rules, anyone who opened it before will access this new logic the very next time he or she reruns a forecast estimate. To summarize:

> Centralized data access
> Centralized data management
> Centralized analysis rules
> +   Access from the Web, Office, and SAS Enterprise Guide
> One version of the truth!

In addition, no more egg on Peter's or Cindy's face when the CEO is presented with two very different forecasts!

Remember that almost anything SAS can do is accessible from stored processes, so go ahead and use them to simplify your life! To brush up on the basics of creating stored processes, read Chapter 11.

Accessing stored processes via the add-in

Accessing stored processes from the add-in is easy: Just choose SAS⇨ Reports. A dialog box similar to Figure 13-14 appears. The Reports dialog box shows you the SAS metadata folder tree; this is the place in metadata from which content such as stored processes are available. Your view will likely be different depending on your SAS server setup.

In this example, we browsed the SAS server folders to the My Folder area and then double-clicked the 2008 Presidential Election Tile Chart by Region in the contents pane on the right. After opening the stored process, the prompting dialog box in Figure 13-15 appears.

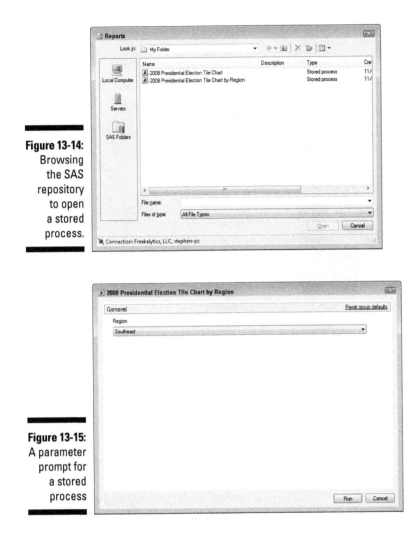

Figure 13-14: Browsing the SAS repository to open a stored process.

Figure 13-15: A parameter prompt for a stored process

This stored process has three parameters, or prompts, to specify which forecast you want to see. The drop-down selectors were used to specify a 12-month sales forecast for the United States. After clicking Run, you can see the results in Excel, as shown in Figure 13-16.

Just to show the wide availability of stored processes, we ran the same stored process from PowerPoint and then Word. The results are shown in Figures 13-17 and 13-18, respectively. Note that in both examples, the add-in separated the table from the graph by putting them on separate slides in PowerPoint and pages in the Word document. The add-in intelligently breaks up your output onto slides or pages. Also, note that in Figure 13-17, we used the standard functionality of PowerPoint to add our own title to the second slide.

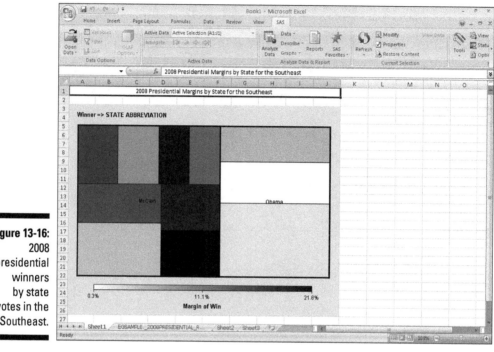

Figure 13-16:
2008
presidential
winners
by state
votes in the
Southeast.

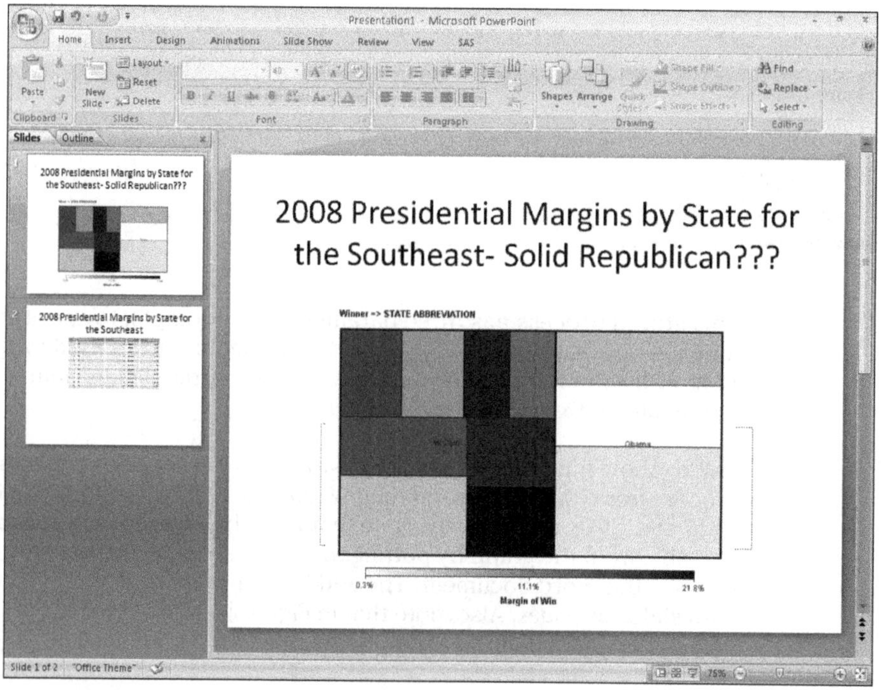

Figure 13-17:
Sales
forecast in
PowerPoint.

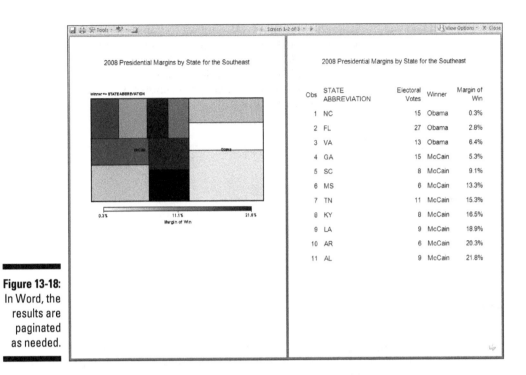

	2008 Presidential Margins by State for the Southeast			
Obs	STATE ABBREVIATION	Electoral Votes	Winner	Margin of Win
1	NC	15	Obama	0.3%
2	FL	27	Obama	2.8%
3	VA	13	Obama	6.4%
4	GA	15	McCain	5.3%
5	SC	8	McCain	9.1%
6	MS	6	McCain	13.3%
7	TN	11	McCain	15.3%
8	KY	8	McCain	16.5%
9	LA	9	McCain	18.9%
10	AR	6	McCain	20.3%
11	AL	9	McCain	21.8%

Figure 13-18: In Word, the results are paginated as needed.

Refreshing results from the add-in

You have several options after opening data, creating some output with a SAS task, or opening a stored process. All these results can be modified or refreshed. After clicking the SAS output in your Office document, you can choose SAS⇨Modify, Refresh, Refresh Multiple, or Properties.

If you choose SAS⇨Modify, you can do the following:

- ✔ **For data:** Modify allows you to update the Modify Data Source dialog box (Variables, Filter, and Sort).
- ✔ **For task output:** Modify takes you back to the task dialog box to update the options for that task.
- ✔ **For stored processes and reports:** Modify allows you to respecify the parameters selected.

The SAS⇨Refresh command reruns and opens the updated data, task output, or stored process.

Note that results do not automatically update when you reopen the Office document. You must refresh them or set the property (from the Properties dialog box) to automatically update all SAS results upon opening an Office document.

If you want to refresh some or all SAS content in your document, choose
SAS⇨Refresh Multiple, which allows you to rerun all content or selected
content, and invoke the Modify dialog boxes before rerunning if desired. See
Figure 13-19 for an example Refresh Multiple dialog box. Note that the far-
right column of the Refresh Multiple dialog box shows where the SAS content
is located, which is a useful feature.

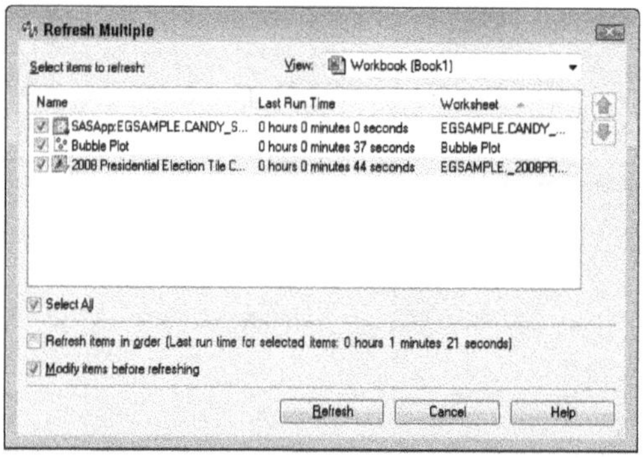

Figure 13-19:
Refresh
Multiple
SAS items
from the
add-in.

To view the properties of SAS content, choose SAS⇨Properties. The
Properties dialog box appears, as shown in Figure 13-20. Information and
options available include

✔ Date created

✔ Date modified

✔ Last run time

✔ Data used

✔ Any filters applied to the data

✔ Whether to automatically refresh the item when you open the file in Office

✔ Various appearance settings

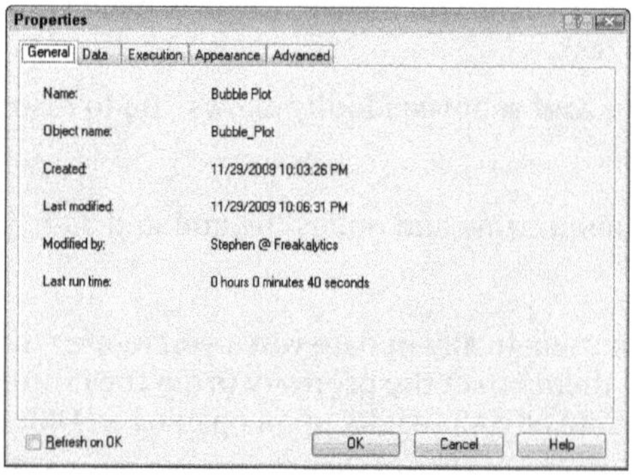

Figure 13-20:
SAS result
item
properties.

Sharing your work with others

The add-in provides a new possibility for sharing your content. Just like any other Office document, you can save your Office documents with SAS content in the same manner. In addition, if you e-mail your Office document to folks who do not have the add-in, they can still view and print the entire document just like you do; however, they can't refresh the results, view properties, and so on. The add-in provides true Office content. As a result, you can use all the formatting (bold, coloring, and font) and layout capabilities (multiple slides or one, moving SAS results at will amongst various worksheets and even across Office applications).

The SAS folders you navigated to access stored processes can also be used as a location to centrally save your Office document. To save your Office document to the SAS server, choose SAS⇨Tools⇨Publish. The Publish dialog box is shown in Figure 13-21. The two advantages to this approach are as follows:

✔ **You can centrally store your SAS and Office documents in the same folders where you access your stored processes.**

✔ **Your SAS data warehouse administrator has access to Impact Analysis data about your document.**

Impact Analysis allows your data administrator to see whether data sources are used by end users so they can understand the effect of making any significant changes or deletions to the data you use.

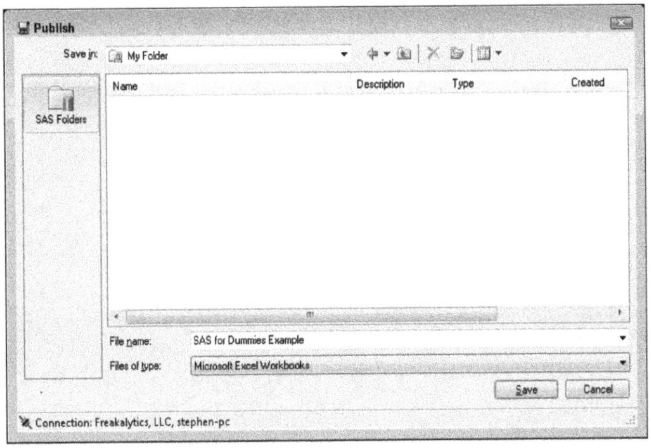

Figure 13-21: Publish to the SAS server.

You can use the Publish functionality regardless of whether SAS output is in your document. Anyone who has the add-in can open your documents from the same dialog box used to open reports and stored processes, by choosing SAS⇨Reports.

Chapter 14

Web Reporting Fever: SAS Has That Covered

In This Chapter

▶ Web-based reporting made easy yet powerful

▶ Going beyond basic Web reporting

▶ Printing, exporting, and scheduling your reports

Many people use the Web for accessing e-mail, searching for information, reading the daily news, accessing bank statements, or researching stocks and mutual funds. People love the Web because it makes getting to relevant data easy and fast. Although applications such as SAS Enterprise Guide and SAS Add-In for Microsoft Office are powerful and flexible, they require installing software and a certain amount of training before you can be productive with their many capabilities.

SAS has a great Web application to provide you with easy access to SAS reports on the Web: SAS Web Report Studio. Like other Web activities, minimal training is required to get going and no additional application is installed on your PC to use this application. Casual users of SAS, who aren't technical and don't consider learning SAS clients to be a good use of their time, are good candidates for SAS Web Report Studio.

SAS Web Report Studio makes it easy to

✔ Access reports created by others

✔ Customize and refresh reports

✔ Create new reports through reporting wizards

✔ Print reports

✔ Export results to Excel

✔ Schedule and share reports with others

This chapter covers the highlights of SAS Web Report Studio functionality as highlighted in the preceding bullets.

Self-Service Reporting for Everyone

It's great that you can use SAS Web Report Studio like most other Web sites to open content that someone else has created for you. But what if you have a fairly different question to answer than what your friendly SAS expert has provided? Never fear. SAS Web Report Studio makes it easy to create your own ad hoc reports with a mix of easy-to-create tables, powerful cross-tabulation tables, simple graphs, and easy-access to expert-generated stored process output (created in SAS Enterprise Guide).

With SAS Web Report Studio, you can create reports using only information maps and report wizards. An *information map* is a user-friendly, subject-relevant view (for example, sales, customers, and inventory) of data created by your SAS administrator. *Information maps* are useful because they greatly simplify how complex data sources are presented, using terms that are meaningful to a business user of the data instead of showing all the gory technical details.

Without information maps, you could end up seeing a table called S_R_Ref instead of an information map named Sales Returns and Refunds, or you could see a column named N_Re_010 instead of Net Returns.

The best part is that the Report Wizard walks you through the report creation process in just five simple steps, as you see in the following example. This example shows you how to use the Orion Star sample data, available from the SAS Support Web site, to create a sales report by product category, continent, and gender for the calendar year 2005:

1. **Obtain the Web address for SAS Web Report Studio at your organization (for example, http://www.mycompany.com/ SASWebReportStudio), and type the address in the address bar of your browser.**

   You see the SAS Web Report Studio login screen.

2. **Enter your user name and password.**

3. **Start the Report Wizard by clicking the New Using Report Wizard button.**

   The first step of the Report Wizard appears. This step allows you to select your information map and the items from the information map, as shown in Figure 14-1. You can click the Change Source button to select the correct information map needed for the question at hand.

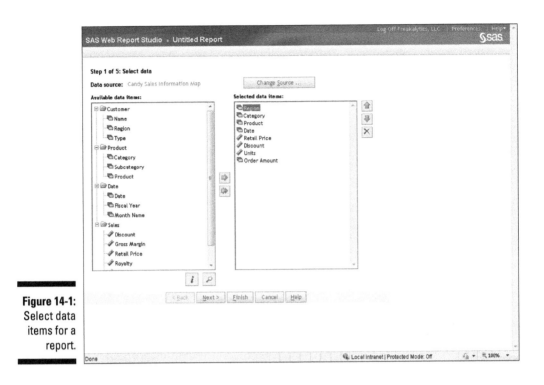

Figure 14-1:
Select data
items for a
report.

4. **Add the data items that you want to use in your report to the Selected Data Items pane by clicking each item in the Available Data Items pane and then clicking the Add Selected Data Items arrow (in the middle of the panes).**

   For this example, we added Region from the Customer folder; Category and Product from the Product folder; Date from the Date folder; and Retail Price, Discount, Units, and Order Amount from the Sales folder.

5. **Click Next.**

   Note that the Finish button could be clicked in any step. Step 2 of the Report Wizard appears, as shown in Figure 14-2. This step allows you to filter the data.

6. **For this example, click the Section filters, at the bottom of the pane.**

   The Sections Filter dialog box appears.

7. **Turn on filters for Product, as shown in Figure 14-3, and then click OK.**

   You don't select the values for the filter yet; you're simply adding the filter as a prompt to appear each time you run the report.

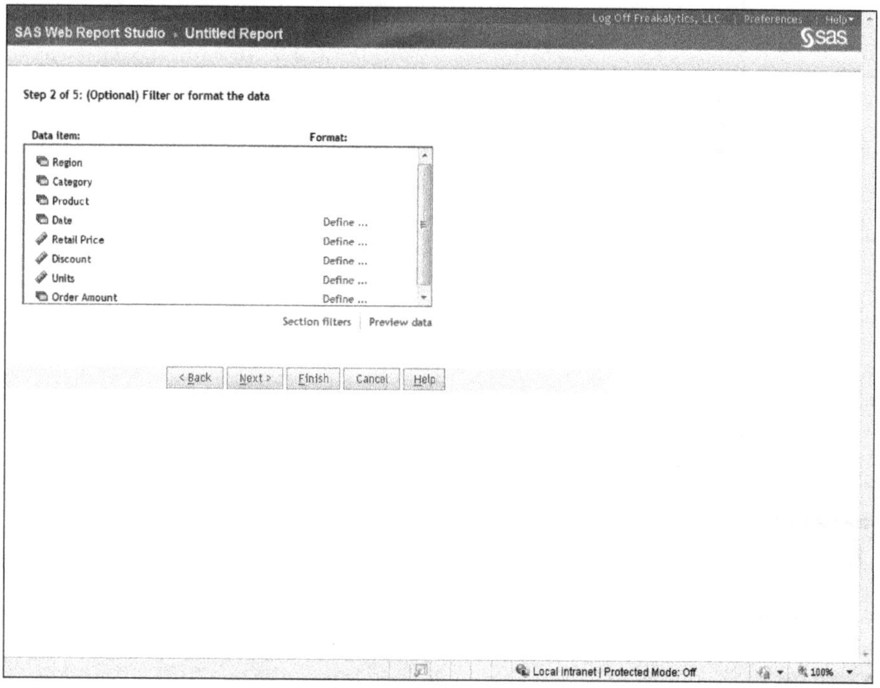

Figure 14-2:
Specify the
data filter
for your
report data.

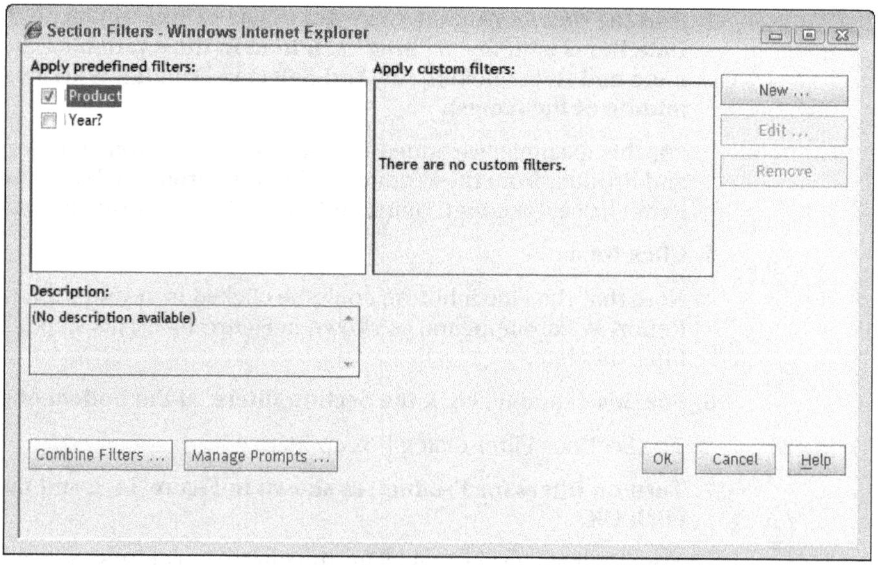

Figure 14-3:
Specify
which sec-
tion data
filters to
enable for
your report.

8. Click Next.

Step 3 of the wizard allows you to specify group breaks for your report, as shown in Figure 14-4. These breaks allow you to order the overall report by group break variables with a separate section for each unique group break.

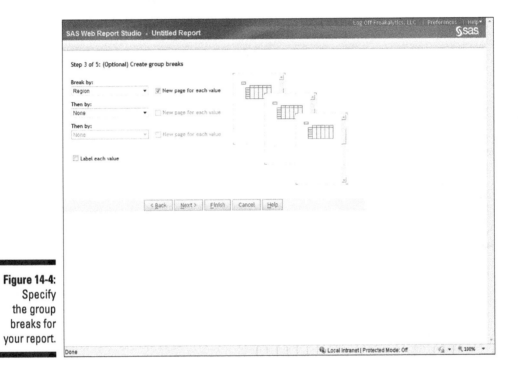

Figure 14-4: Specify the group breaks for your report.

9. For this example, click the Break By drop-down list, choose Region, and then click Next.

Step 4 of the wizard appears, as shown in Figure 14-5. This step allows you to select whether you want a table, a graph, or both. You can choose between a list table or a cross-tab table layout for the table, and you can also choose which columns to display. Additionally, you can turn on a graph, select a graph type, and select the items to use for the various parts of your graph.

10. For this example, click the Graph check box, select Units from the Bar Height drop-down list, and select Products from the Bars drop-down list. Then click Finish to generate your report.

(We skipped Step 5 of the wizard here. That step lets you specify the titles and footnotes for your report.) The full-featured Report Editor appears, as shown in Figure 14-6.

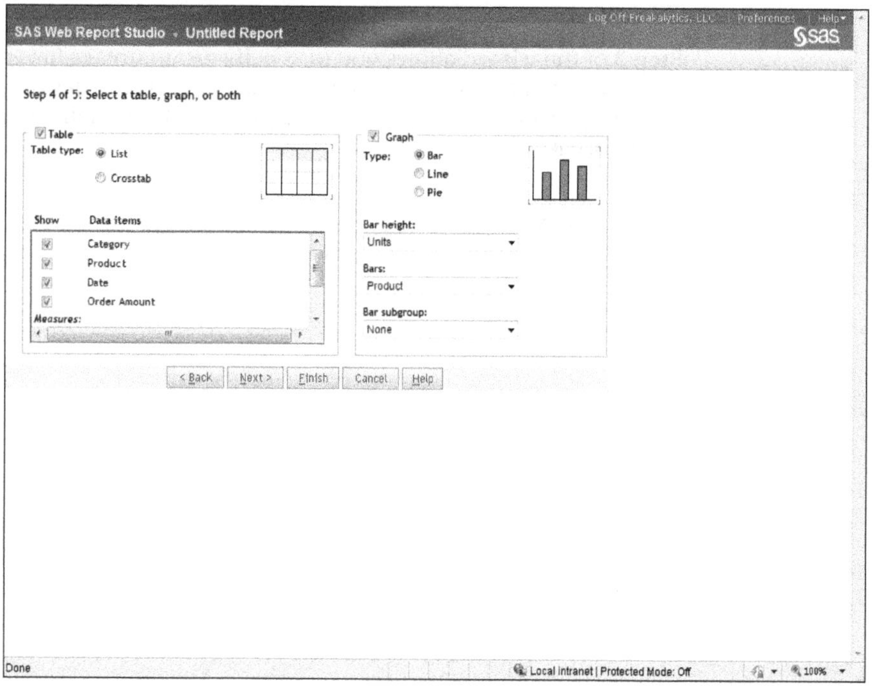

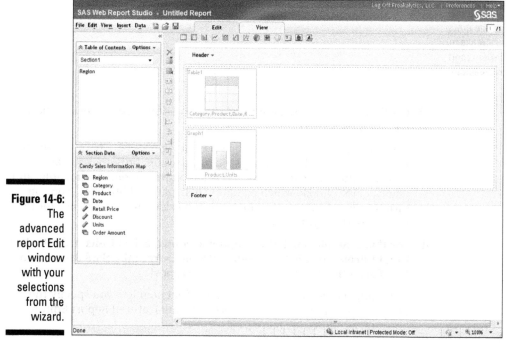

Figure 14-5:
Choose
report table
and graph
details.

Figure 14-6:
The
advanced
report Edit
window
with your
selections
from the
wizard.

11. **Click the View tab just to the right of the Edit tab.**

    The prompts for Product and Year appear for selection before the report is available, as shown in Figure 14-7.

12. **Select the various products of interest. Then click the View Report button to see the report, which is shown in Figure 14-8.**

13. **Navigate by clicking the region of interest.**

    Each region has a unique list table and bar chart for the category.

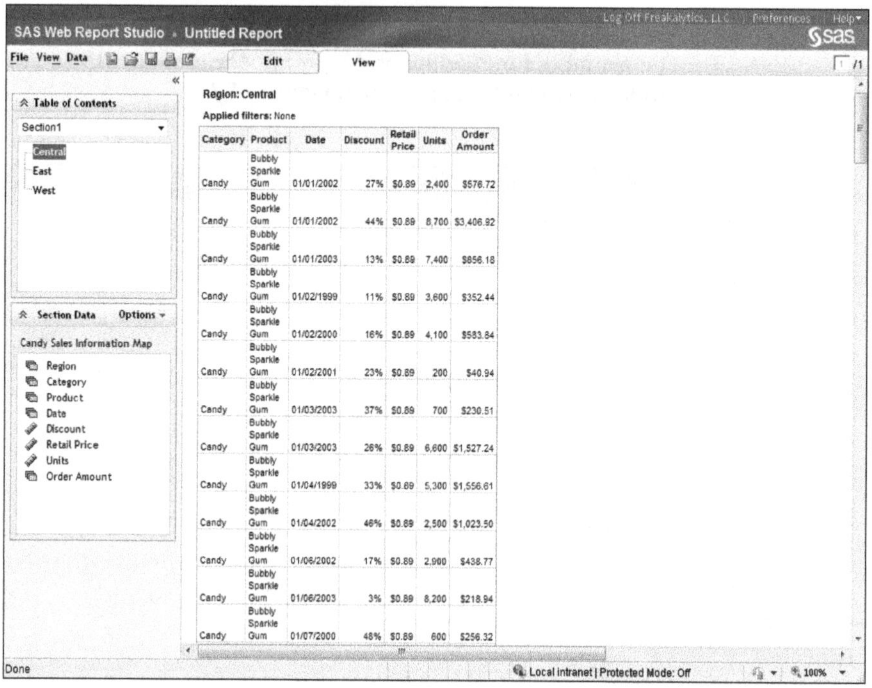

Figure 14-8:
Your
requested
report!

Going beyond Basic Reporting

As you can see in the preceding section, SAS Web Report Studio makes ad hoc reporting from the Web simple, fast, and flexible. If you desire more advanced report creation and editing capabilities, you can harness those from SAS Web Report Studio. An example of the advanced report-editing interface was shown in Figure 14-6.

Because of the extensive number of advanced report-authoring features, we present a simplified overview here:

✓ **Data**

- Use OLAP (Online Analytic Processing) or relational data in a cross-tabulation layout. Much like pivot tables in Microsoft Excel, SAS Web Report Studio allows you to view relational data sources in cross-tabular format.

- Use conditional highlighting based on data values in your tables. For example, sales greater than $1,000 are green and less than $100 are red.

- Specify whether to show detailed or summary data in list tables. The default is summary aggregations of your data.

- Modify the format of a data item in a report.

- Create new custom (calculated) data items from items in your information map.

✔ **Interaction**

- Users of your report can drill down, drill up, expand, and collapse your OLAP-based cross-tabulation tables and charts.

- You can add drill-to-detail transactional data from cross-tabulation reports.

- You can link reports so that users can drill from a high-level report (such as sales summary by continent and quarter) to a detailed report (such as sales transactions for a particular continent and a particular quarter).

- Add prompts to a report so that the data is automatically filtered whenever a user opens it.

✔ **Tables and graphs**

- Specify chart types, for example, bar, bar-line, line, pie, progressive bar, scatter, and geographic maps of your data.

- Customize table layout, including adding multiple table or chart sections to your report.

- Add rankings by a particular data item to your tables and graphs, such as sales ranked by continent.

- Turn on or off totals and subtotals in tables.

- Add the ability to synchronize multiple tables and charts with drill down, drill up, expand, and collapse functionality.

✔ **Miscellaneous**

- Leverage a stored process as a report section.

- Open a report published from SAS Enterprise Guide in SAS Web Report Studio. You can add additional content to these reports.

- Open a report published from SAS Web Report Studio in SAS Enterprise Guide or SAS Add-In for Microsoft Office.

- Save a report as a template for the creation of new reports.

- Add background images to a report, such as a big, bold, red *Confidential* image in the background of your report.

- Add text objects to the body of your report.

Getting More Details on SAS Web Report Studio

Because we describe SAS Web Report Studio in this single chapter, we can cover only the most commonly used of its estimated 200 reporting features. This section presents a few examples of the advanced features available in this product.

Securing reports

You can secure each report created and specify it as available for anyone who uses SAS Web Report Studio, for a specific subset of user groups based on SAS metadata, or as a report just for your own use.

Users of SAS Web Report Studio can also be given specific usage permissions regarding product functionality. The roles that you can assign to users range from using the full authoring capabilities to having the ability to only open and print reports.

Printing smart

If you've used the Web to print important documents, you might have observed that Web pages do not always print correctly. For example, pages might be too wide to print, pages might be missing headers or footers, and page breaks might cut tables or graphs in half. SAS Web Report Studio gets around these limitations by automatically converting the Web page you see to an Adobe Acrobat PDF document that you can print. This enables the product to provide you with intelligent pagination and headers and footers, thus avoiding the typical poor printing from most Web pages. The only requirement is that you have Adobe Reader installed. (You can download Adobe Reader for free from www.adobe.com.) If you don't have Adobe Reader, you can simply use the standard browser-based printing, which will have some of the same problems as any other Web page.

Exporting data to Microsoft Excel

If you have the Microsoft Excel spreadsheet program, you can export the entire report view or the data behind a table or graph to Excel. When exporting the entire report, a compressed or Zip file is created that contains a spreadsheet, an HTML file, and various image files. After you save the Zip file to your PC, just open the spreadsheet inside the Zip file and answer Yes to any warning prompts in Excel to view the report in Excel. Data from a table or graph can also be opened in Excel as a tab-delimited text file.

Exporting from a table has an additional option to use the report formats for the data when you open the table in Excel. This option is handy because you won't need to reformat fields such as currency or date fields.

Note that each export mechanism method listed results in a static Excel spreadsheet. To update the spreadsheet, you need to re-export the contents from SAS Web Report Studio. If dynamic content in Excel is important, use SAS Add-In for Microsoft Office (discussed in Chapter 13) to create your spreadsheet instead.

You can also distribute reports via e-mail as a PDF file or an HTML file. You can send the report to a single person or a wide audience based on your mailing lists.

Scheduling reports

When you're opening or viewing a report, you can decide to schedule it if you want it to run on a periodic basis.

It's a good idea to schedule reports that take quite a while to run, especially if the report uses large data sources or is used frequently by many people in your company.

You can also archive scheduled reports so that colleagues can easily compare today's report with last week's report.

Part V
Getting SAS Ready to Rock and Roll

The 5th Wave   By Rich Tennant

"Unless there's a corrupt cell in our spreadsheet analysis concerning the importance of trunk space, this should be a big seller next year."

In this part . . .

This part is where we quarantine most of the truly technical information. Software setup and configuration usually involves professional IT staff, but understanding how the software works is a good idea for anyone who uses it. And after your SAS software is installed, you can get to work on writing your first SAS program (or at least running one that someone else wrote for you).

And no matter how much you thought you knew about SAS programming, there's always something new to master, such as how to use SAS Enterprise Guide to do more, faster.

Chapter 15

Setting Up SAS

. . . .

In This Chapter

▶ Installing SAS Enterprise Guide and SAS for Windows locally

▶ Using server-based SAS with SAS Enterprise Guide

▶ Defining data sources once and for all

. . . .

*I*nstalling and configuring SAS software can be as simple as downloading a package to your computer and clicking a few buttons — no more difficult than loading some music on a portable music player. Or it can be more complicated, like assembling a home theater system, requiring moderate site preparation before you get started. Then again, it can be a terrific engineering and political challenge, like launching an international space station, involving months of planning and coordination among several stakeholder groups before the first button is clicked.

In this chapter, you read about the basic configuration of SAS on a personal computer, which is the easiest configuration to set up and use. You also read about some of the behind-the-scenes work required to configure SAS for use in a multimachine environment, where several people use a centralized SAS installation in an administered setting. Finally, you see what's involved in configuring your data sources so that nothing will stand in your way when you want to use SAS to access and analyze your data.

Assessing Your Situation

What makes the difference between a simple, no-fuss install process and a complicated deployment is determined by your answers to questions like the following:

✔ **What type of computer hardware will you use to host and access your SAS software?** By far, SAS for Microsoft Windows is the easiest to set up. It installs similarly to most software packages that you might use at home. However, SAS is also available for use on most operating systems employed by businesses today, including Linux, various flavors of UNIX, and the IBM z/OS on mainframe systems. Installing on these server-class machines requires personnel with system administrator experience.

✔ **How many people need access to use the software, and where are they located relative to the computer hardware?** When you have multiple people who need to access SAS on a single computer, installing SAS is only the first step. You must also install and configure the additional products and technologies that allow remote users to access SAS as a central server.

✔ **How many different SAS software products do you plan to use (and therefore configure)?** A complete SAS deployment might comprise dozens of products. Some products are simple to install and need no additional configuration. For example, you can add the SAS/OR product to the mix, which supplies you with a collection of SAS procedures to support operations research and optimization modeling.

After installation, no extra configuration is necessary. In contrast, installing a product such as SAS Forecast Server requires that you configure SAS Analytics Platform, which is a services layer that allows multiple people using the SAS Forecast Studio application to create and work with forecasting projects. SAS deployment tools attempt to make these types of additions manageable, but they can do only so much to simplify this complex process.

Keeping It Local

With SAS and SAS Enterprise Guide installed on your personal computer (running Microsoft Windows), no additional configuration is necessary. It just works. In this setup, the SAS installation is on your PC (local to your machine). You don't need SAS Metadata Server (discussed in the following section) because SAS Enterprise Guide can detect that SAS is available without having to look up where to find it. SAS support folks call this setup *local-local* because SAS is local to your machine and no intermediate layer is necessary to connect to SAS.

Figure 15-1 shows a SAS Enterprise Guide session with this simple setup. Notice that the message in the status bar on the bottom right indicates No connection, meaning that you do not need to tell SAS Enterprise Guide how to connect to SAS. And the only SAS server that appears in the server view is Local.

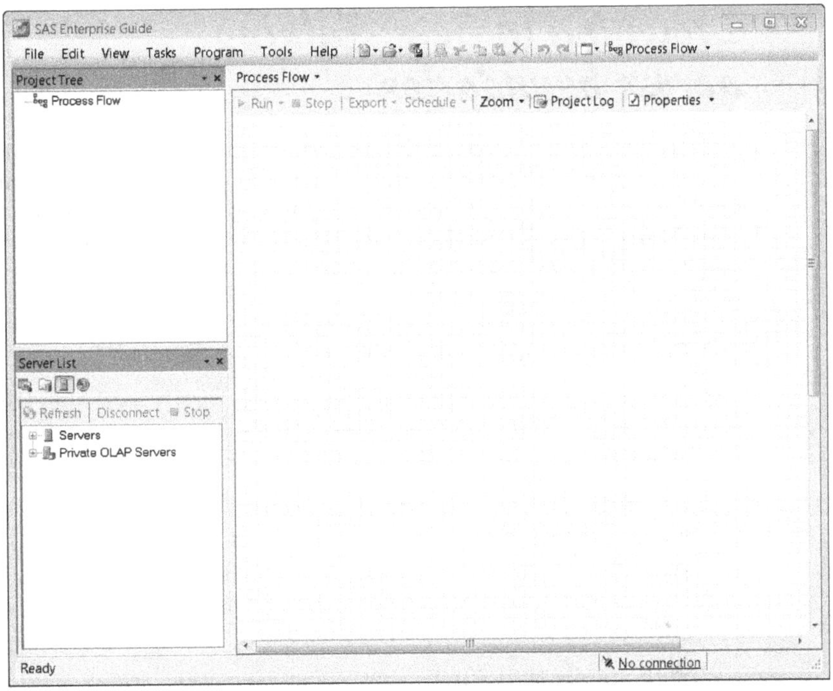

Figure 15-1:
Think
globally, but
act locally!

To tell whether you have SAS installed on your local PC (as well as what version), choose Help⇨About SAS Enterprise Guide. In the About SAS Enterprise Guide window, click Configuration Details. The first few entries in the Configuration Details window show you whether SAS 9.2 is installed.

Distributing SAS to the Masses

If you work in an environment where many people use SAS, chances are good that you make use of a centralized configuration. For example, you might have SAS Enterprise Guide on your desktop, but your SAS server is located somewhere else (in another room, another building, or even another state or country). If so, you're living the dream of *distributed computing,* made possible by powerful server machines and fast computer networks.

Now, whether you *feel* like you're living a dream depends on your perspective. Many end users prefer the good old days when their SAS installation was local. However, today's IT departments use words like *total cost of ownership* and *centralized control* to justify the distributed environment. The upside of this type of arrangement is that usually more people in the organization have access to SAS because not everyone needs a personal copy installed on their machines.

Drowning in tiers: Talking across boundaries

A distributed SAS environment can have many pieces, and they all have to be able to find and talk to each other to work smoothly. The pieces are divided into *tiers,* which are logical boundary points between the various parts. Sometimes tiers are configured on separate machines; other times they're simply logical service layers that share space on a single machine. These are the main tiers in broad terms:

- **Client tier:** Usually where you are, at your desk or PC.
- **SAS server tier:** Where your SAS session runs, processing your analysis and reports and crunching the numbers. The server can be a SAS workspace server or a stored process server.
- **Metadata tier:** SAS Metadata Server, which serves as a directory for finding everything else.
- **Data tier:** Where your data resides. The data sources can include database data such as Oracle, OLAP data from the SAS OLAP Server, or other SAS data servers such as SAS/SHARE.
- **Web middle tier:** Where your Web-based applications reside, such as SAS Web Report Studio or SAS Information Delivery Portal.

As an end user, your main interaction is with the client-tier pieces. Your client-tier applications include SAS Enterprise Guide, SAS Add-In for Microsoft Office (running in Microsoft Word or Excel, for example, as discussed in Chapter 13), and your Web browser (to access Web-based SAS applications).

Configuring metadata: The keys to the kingdom

SAS Metadata Server is the central repository that directs all the pieces of the SAS environment. It contains information about how to find the resources available at the various tiers. It also provides a central point of control for administrators to decide who can access what resources and data.

The main tool of the SAS administrator is SAS Management Console. Figure 15-2 shows an example of this SAS product. Note the types of items that you can manage here, including servers, data libraries, and stored processes.

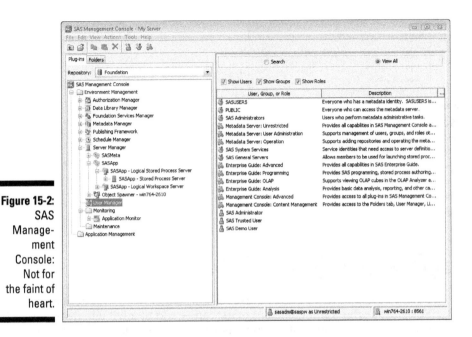

Figure 15-2:
SAS
Manage-
ment
Console:
Not for
the faint of
heart.

At the client tier, the main configuration activity required is to ensure that you are pointing to the correct metadata server. This client configuration step can be automated as part of the SAS software deployment. In many organizations with dozens or hundreds of users, a SAS administrator might have performed this step for you.

If you need to adjust this configuration, choose Tools⇨Options to display the Options window. The metadata configuration appears in a Connections box in the Administration section at the bottom of the screen.

A *metadata configuration* consists of just a few key pieces of information:

   ✔ The name (machine host address) of the metadata server

   ✔ A port (unique address on the machine)

   ✔ A user ID and password

Figure 15-3 shows an example of the metadata configuration window in SAS Enterprise Guide. The settings that you supply here will be particular for your environment and will almost certainly be prescribed by your friendly SAS administrator.

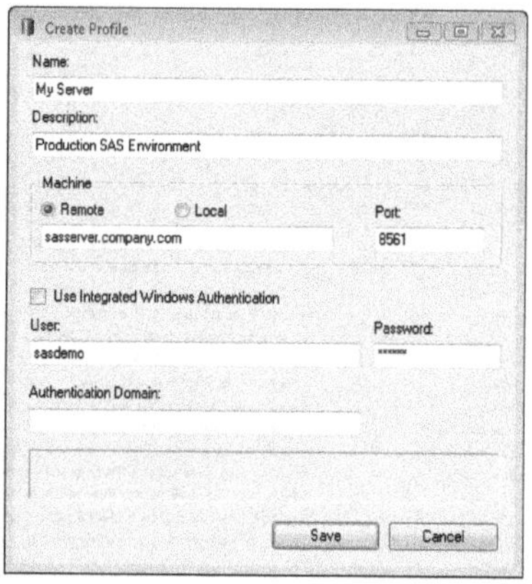

Figure 15-3:
Configure
your meta-
data to get
on the cor-
rect path.

Plunging into Your Data

Data access can be mysterious, like drawing water from the kitchen sink. You can see the water come out of the tap — and touch it and taste it, which is instantly gratifying. But do you really know where the water comes from? And do you know exactly how much water there is beyond that magical water faucet? Probably not — that's something that most of us simply take for granted.

However, when you have a problem — water doesn't flow or it flows too slowly — you really notice. And diagnosing plumbing issues is something that most people are uncomfortable with.

Data access works the same way. When your data flows freely into your SAS Enterprise Guide session, it seems as though you can do nothing wrong. You can view the data in the data grid, create queries, and run tasks. However, when data access points are not defined efficiently, that data flow can feel like you're trying to suck an elephant through a straw. Everything seems to take so much longer to accomplish.

Taking a crash course in data plumbing

Diagnosing data access issues can be easier than household plumbing chores. You simply need to answer three main questions:

✔ **Where does the data source originate?** For example, is the data source in a database system such as Oracle, or is it in a text file on your server file system?

✔ **How large is the data source?** SAS and SAS Enterprise Guide can deal with data sources that consist of millions or even billions of records. However, understanding the data size is important to understanding the tradeoffs of various data configurations.

✔ **What route does the data travel to get to your SAS session?** Because SAS needs to process your data for analysis and reporting, your data needs to travel the shortest distance possible from its point of origin to your SAS session. Even though you might use SAS Enterprise Guide to select your data source, what counts is how many hops the data must make to get to the SAS session, where the real work occurs.

All these considerations lead to the golden rule of efficient data access with SAS: **Define your data sources in terms of your SAS server.** Use SAS libraries to connect to your data sources, and route all your data access through those libraries.

Passing Niagara Falls through a garden hose

Because SAS Enterprise Guide makes it easy to get to data in many ways, you might inadvertently choose an inefficient path. For example, you can choose File⇨Open⇨ODBC and select a data source defined relative to your local PC. However, when you use that data in your project, SAS Enterprise Guide realizes that the data is not presently accessible to your SAS session, so it attempts to perform the great favor of copying the data for you.

SAS Enterprise Guide is a great tool for many things, but it can be a bottleneck in the process of copying data. Copying data from an external source to your SAS session with SAS Enterprise Guide as the go-between is very inefficient. If the data is large, this operation can take several minutes (or longer!). In technical terms, this is called "going around your elbow to get to your thumb."

Using a plumber's helper: SAS/ACCESS

Fortunately, it's easy to avoid moving all those data records through SAS Enterprise Guide: Simply define access to the external data source on the SAS server. SAS makes this easy to do by providing a set of data access products called SAS/ACCESS. A SAS/ACCESS module exists for just about every major database type in use today. For any that are missing, you can use SAS/ACCESS Interface to ODBC, which is like a universal pipe fitting to connect to any data source.

The SAS/ACCESS products allow you to define the data sources in terms of SAS libraries. And after a data source is in a SAS library, your SAS programs can access it just as if it were a native SAS data set.

SAS libraries can be defined in your environment by a SAS administrator or defined as needed in your SAS Enterprise Guide project.

Trying an example: Project meets data, just in time

It's time to create a project library. In this example, suppose that you need to access a set of data tables in a Microsoft Access database. You have a note on your desk from your database administrator that tells you the location of the data source and other important access information. With this information and the Assign Project Library task in SAS Enterprise Guide, you can define a SAS library for this data source. Just follow these steps:

1. **Choose Tools⇨Assign Project Library.**

   The Assign Project Library appears, as shown in Figure 15-4.

2. **In the Name field, type the name that you want to give to the library.**

   The name must comply with SAS naming conventions, which means it must contain only letters, numbers, and underscores and also be no longer than eight characters.

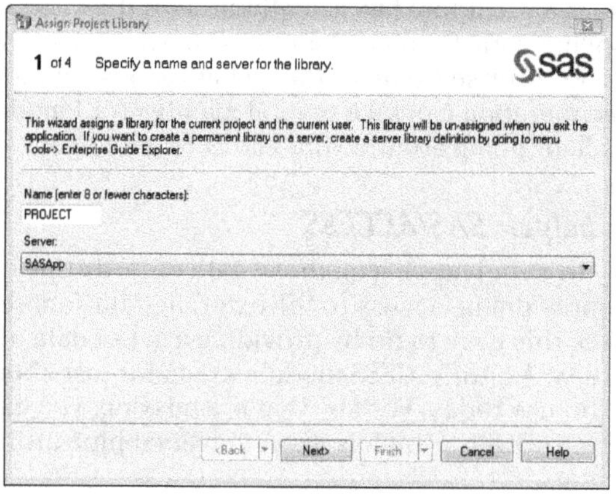

Figure 15-4:
What's in a name? No more than eight letters.

Assign Project Library

1 of 4   Specify a name and server for the library.   §sas

This wizard assigns a library for the current project and the current user. This library will be un-assigned when you exit the application. If you want to create a permanent library on a server, create a server library definition by going to menu Tools-> Enterprise Guide Explorer.

Name (enter 8 or fewer characters):
PROJECT

Server:
SASApp

‹Back   Next›   Finish   Cancel   Help

3. **Select the SAS server environment where the data resides, and then click Next.**

   In this example, the database is on the SASApp server, which the SAS administrator set up for us. The server must also have the correct SAS software installed (in this case, SAS/ACCESS Interface to PC File Formats). Some databases also require additional database connectivity software (known as *clients* or *drivers*) to be configured.

   When you click Next, the second page of the wizard appears, as shown in Figure 15-5.

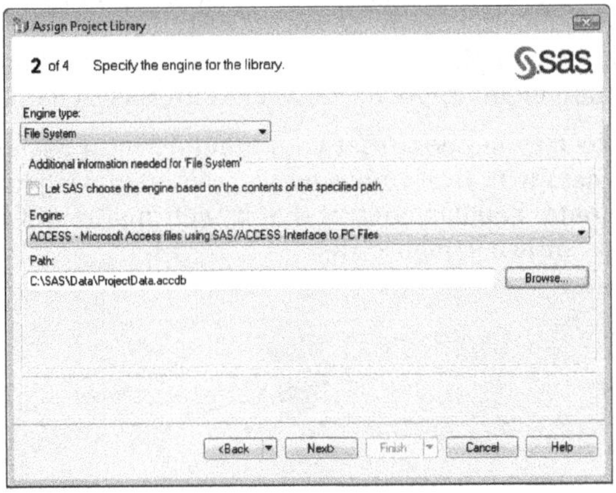

Figure 15-5: Library engines make your data go vroom!

4. **Select the type of library engine and the engine protocol to use.**

   In SAS, *library engines* represent the protocols to talk to different sources of data. Library engines are in two main categories: file-based or path-based engines and database engines.

   - *File-based* or *path-based engines* map to folders or files on your server file system and provide access to all the data files in those folders.

   - *Database engines* map to database server connections, providing access to external databases.

   In this example, you would select the file-based engine type, and then the ACCESS engine (for use with Microsoft Access databases).

5. **Specify the path to the database file, and then click Next.**

   Because your SAS administrator provided the file path to the database, you can simply type it in the Path field. If you would rather point-and-click your way to the path, click Browse to open the file selection window and then navigate to the correct path.

The database file path refers to the file system of the SAS server (SASApp in this example), not the file system on your local PC. If the SAS server is a remote machine that runs Microsoft Windows, the file path might look like a legitimate local file path. But it's the remote SAS session that will be accessing the file, so the path is defined in terms of that remote server machine.

6. **Enter additional options for the data source, and then click Next.**

   The third page of the wizard, as shown in Figure 15-6, provides a chance to specify any extra options that you might need to access the database. This is where that note from your database administrator, mentioned earlier, comes into play. Depending on the database and your particular setup, you might need to specify an option or two here. For example, if an administrator has applied user-level security, the USER option and PASSWORD option might apply to the Microsoft Access database.

   For this example, let's suppose that your administrator asked you to connect to the data with read-only access to avoid making inadvertent changes to the data. You can control that by setting the ACCESS option to READONLY, as shown in Figure 15-6.

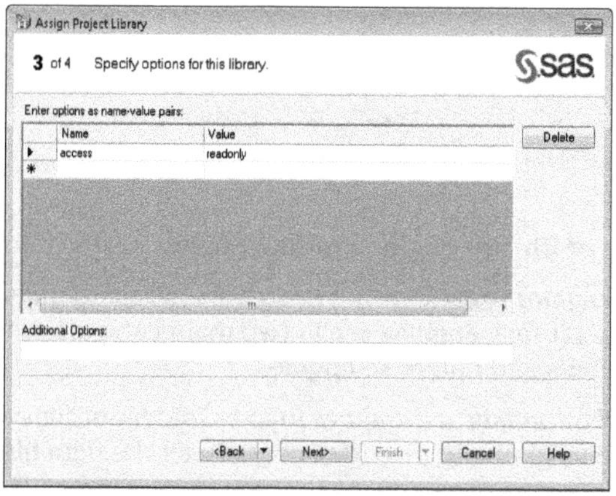

Figure 15-6:
The catchall
page for
any extra
options.

7. **Review the library summary, and then test the connection.**

   The final page of the wizard provides a summary of the library definition and an optional opportunity to test your library, as shown in Figure 15-7. If you click the Test Library button, SAS Enterprise Guide connects to the SAS server and submits the library statement with the options you specified. If all goes well, the status displays OK. If you run into a problem, click Show Log to get a hint of what might be missing or incorrect.

8. Click Finish.

The Assign Project Library task is added to your project and becomes part of the flow. When you next add data to the project (by choosing File⇨Open⇨Data), the new library should appear under the SASApp server, and all the tables in the database are available.

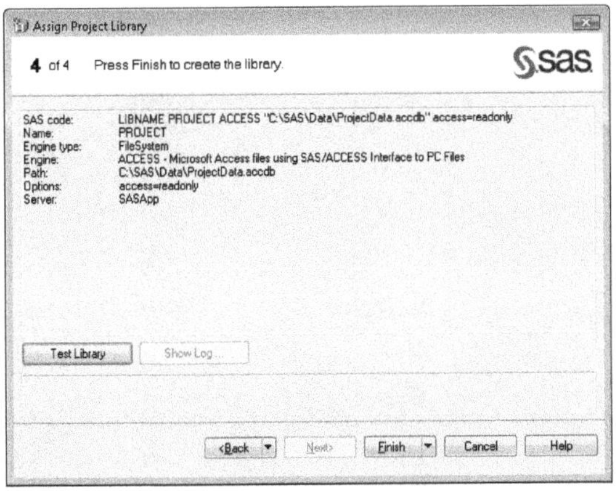

Figure 15-7:
It's a test!
We hope
you pass!

This is a project library, so it exists only within your project for the duration of your current session. The next time you use this project, you need to run the Assign Project Library task first before accessing any of the data that it points to.

To ensure that the Assign Project Library task is run before any data that needs it, create a link from the task to the first reference of the library data in your project. Here's how to create the link:

1. Select the Assign Library item in your Process Flow.

2. Right-click and choose Link Assign Library To from the contextual menu.

The Link window appears.

3. Click the first data table from this library that appears in your project, and then click OK.

Your project now shows a direct link between the Assign Project Library task and the data that you need from it. Figure 15-8 shows an example of this type of link. When you rerun your flow, the Assign Project Library task is guaranteed to run before the data reference is used.

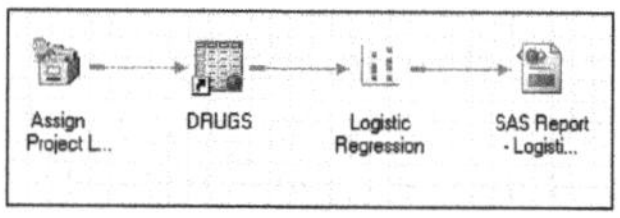

Figure 15-8:
Don't suffer
from a miss-
ing link.

Chapter 16

SAS Programming for the Faint of Heart

▶ Understanding the different types of SAS programs

▶ Using somebody else's SAS program to do your work

▶ Combining SAS statements to compose a SAS program

S AS has its roots as a programming language. Back in the late 1960s, before SAS was incorporated and the SAS System was a project at North Carolina State University, people were warming to the idea that computers were a useful tool for doing math. As difficult a task as programming a computer can be, it was still faster and more reliable than doing math yourself.

The goals of this chapter are to familiarize you with the content of typical SAS programs, teach you to read SAS log output, and show you how to run and modify programs. You won't become a SAS programming expert by reading this chapter, but it should provide a good foundation for further study. If you want to find out more, dozens of SAS programming books are available that cover every aspect of the craft. And yes, SAS programmers often do regard themselves as craftspeople, of a sort.

Demystifying the SAS Program

The SAS programming language began as a set of instructions to manipulate and analyze stacks of data. Arrange those instructions in a certain sequence, and you have a SAS program. Early SAS programs were encoded on punch cards and submitted as a batch of instructions. The results were hardly instantaneous — you often had to submit your program to the system and come back later, perhaps the next day, to get your answers and printed reports.

It's been more than 40 years since the first SAS programs were crafted, but today's SAS programmers still find meaning in many of those early concepts, such as cards, batch processing, submit, print, and report.

The building blocks of a SAS program are *steps*, which come in two main flavors: the DATA step and the procedure step. The DATA step is used to create, modify, merge, and transform data sources. Procedure steps perform, well, various procedures to analyze and report on that data.

In case you thought this was going to be easy, you need to be aware of additional constructs. SAS offers a macro language, which is a sort of glue to bind the DATA and procedures steps with sophisticated programming logic. In addition, some SAS procedures serve as a doorway into other programming languages. A prominent example is the SQL procedure, which allows a SAS programmer to dabble in SQL (structured query language) without having to leave the SAS environment.

When you have a SAS program that you want to reuse or refer to later, you save it on your disk with a .SAS file extension. Even though the contents are plain text, SAS applications recognize the .SAS file extension as a SAS program, which will make it easier to locate and process your programs.

Running (a Program) before Walking

Most beginning SAS programmers get their start by working with existing programs that others have supplied. In fact, you don't really need to know much about how to write a program to run one that's been written for you.

The example programs in this chapter are available at support.sas.com/ sasfordummies. If you want to follow along with the examples, visit the Web site and download the files to your PC. The steps provided in this chapter assume that you are using SAS Enterprise Guide to run SAS programs.

Let's walk through the steps for running a program in SAS Enterprise Guide:

1. **Choose File➪Open➪Program.**

   The Open Program window appears.

2. **Find the folder location where you saved the example programs for this chapter, select Chapter16_SampleProgram.sas, and then click Open.**

   The SAS program opens in a new program window, as shown in Figure 16-1.

3. **Click the Run button on the toolbar.**

SAS Enterprise Guide submits the SAS program to your default SAS server (for example, Local or SASApp), and then displays the results. Figure 16-2 shows an example of how the results appear.

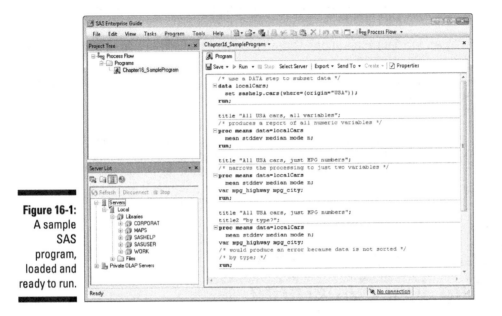

Figure 16-1: A sample SAS program, loaded and ready to run.

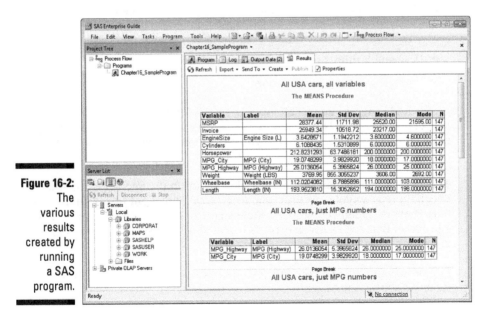

Figure 16-2: The various results created by running a SAS program.

When you run a SAS program, you can get a variety of results, many of which are delivered automatically into your SAS Enterprise Guide project. These results include

- SAS log output (on the Log tab), which shows how SAS processed the program and includes any errors or warnings.
- SAS data sets (on the Output Data tab) that were created or modified by the program.
- Report-style results (on the Results tab) generated by the SAS output delivery system (ODS). By default in SAS Enterprise Guide, these results use the SAS Report format.

These are the most common types of output that people expect from SAS programs. However, the SAS programming language offers so many features and so much flexibility that you can build almost anything in the SAS environment, including Web pages, e-mail messages, external text files, spreadsheets, and even network-based messages to other computers.

Reading the Log: SAS Is Telling You Something

The SAS log is your source for information if you want to know the following:

- What SAS did while running your program
- How much time it took to run the program
- What, if anything, went wrong

If your SAS program was a *CSI* episode, the SAS log would be like that magic black light that reveals the yucky evidence at the crime scene. When the program fails to run as expected and you need to know where things went awry, the SAS log is your primary forensics tool.

The most common element that people look for in the SAS log is the ERROR line. If there is a syntax or processing error, SAS spits out one or more ERROR lines that are usually colored a telltale shade of red. In SAS Enterprise Guide, a program that runs with an error is branded with a "scarlet X" on the program icon.

Here is an example of a common SAS error, caused by using the wrong name for a variable in a data set:

```
15         proc means data=sashelp.class;
16            var gender;
ERROR: Variable GENDER not found.
```

Most SAS error messages are self-explanatory. But if you encounter an error message that you can't decipher, don't despair! Visit the SAS support Web site at `support.sas.com` and paste the message into the search window. Chances are good that you'll find a few usage notes about the conditions that can cause the particular error.

After you've solved all the errors in your program, don't forget to investigate any WARNING lines that persist in the log. In SAS Enterprise Guide, a program that contains WARNING lines in the log shows a little yellow triangle (the international warning symbol) in the program icon. A warning is less severe than an error because your program ran to completion. However, the warning messages might reveal that things weren't processed as you expected. Here is an excerpt from a log that shows a misspelling that SAS has attempted to work around, generating a warning:

```
35          proc means data=localCars
36             mean stddev medion mode n;

                   ‾‾‾‾‾‾
                     1
WARNING 1-322: Assuming the symbol MEDIAN was misspelled as medion.
```

Finally, if everything is running well and you just want to dig into some of the processing details, SAS logs are peppered with NOTE lines that report on how much data was processed and how long the processing took. Here is an example of a typical note:

```
NOTE: There were 19 observations read from the data set SASHELP.CLASS.
NOTE: PROCEDURE MEANS used (Total process time):
      real time          0.06 seconds
      cpu time           0.03 seconds
```

To achieve consistent and correct results, you should ensure that your programs can run free of warnings and errors. Some SAS programmers who work in tightly regulated industries must show their SAS log output to prove that their programs run cleanly.

Dancing the DATA Step

Most SAS programmers cut their teeth with the DATA step. Although you can use the DATA step to perform almost any operation that reads and writes data files, the basic pattern of a DATA step program is something like this:

- A DATA statement names the data set to create.

- Statements identify input data sources, which can be other data sets, other files such as text files, or inline data records.

✔ Statements operate on the data values and influence the data values that are output. The statements can include functions and expressions to combine and dissect data values in almost every way imaginable. Each statement is applied to each observation (or record) in the data source.

All SAS statements are punctuated with a semicolon at the end. This separates one statement from another, like a pause between instructions. If you inadvertently forget the semicolon, SAS might generate some confusing messages in the log when running your program. Fortunately, the program editor windows in SAS and SAS Enterprise Guide provide coloring cues that can help you identify common syntax problems such as missing semicolons and mismatched quotes *before* you run your program.

Here is an example DATA step program that reads data about students:

```
data work.students;
  length student_name $ 14
         student_id $ 7
         birthday 8
         major $ 16
         current_age 8;
  informat birthday anydtdte20.;
  format birthday date9.;
  infile datalines dsd;
  input student_name
        student_id
        birthday
        major;
  /* this math calculates current age */
  current_age =
    round(yrdif(birthday,today(),'act/act'),1);
datalines;
Stephen Daniel,41968,21jun1988,SAS
Eileen Varnden,51970,08Nov1989,Ecology
Ann Gailey,61969,09mar1988,Spanish
Chris Dinger,71969,09aug1987,Computer Science
Jennie Tutone,8675309,02may1991,Fashion
;
run;
```

Let's read through the program statements and interpret what they mean:

✔ First, the DATA statement identifies the data file (Students) that will be created when the program runs. The file is in the WORK library, which means that the data file is temporary and will exist only during this SAS session.

✔ The LENGTH statement names the columns, or variables, that will be included in the output data. Each named column has a length and type. SAS offers only two data types: character and numeric. The character variables are identified by the dollar sign character ($) in the LENGTH statement.

✔ The FORMAT and INFORMAT statements describe how to treat the birthday column. The INFORMAT statement describes how to read and interpret the raw value. The FORMAT statement describes how the value should appear in reports. Note that the birthday column is stored in SAS as a number; that's important because we perform some calculations with it later.

✔ The INFILE statement specifies the location of the raw data to read. In this case, the data is included inline with the program, set off by a DATALINES section. However, many SAS programs are coded to read data from external files.

✔ The INPUT statement tells SAS to read the values into the columns that have been defined. Note that the order of the column names in the INPUT statement must match the sequence of the data values in the raw data.

✔ The next statement calculates the value of a new column, current_age, using the birthday value and three SAS functions: TODAY, YRDIF, and ROUND. You should read this line of code from the inside out. First, we calculate today's date using the TODAY function. The result is fed to the YRDIF function, along with the birthday value, to calculate the difference in years between the two dates. Because the result will most likely include some fraction of a year (such as 21.234), we then use the ROUND function to round the result to the nearest year.

✔ The remainder of the program, set off by the DATALINES statement, includes the raw data values to read into the data set.

Formats and lengths: The long and short of it

The column *length*, in SAS terms, is the amount of storage allocated in the data set to hold the column values. The length is specified in bytes. For numeric columns, the valid lengths are usually 3 through 8. The longer the length, the greater the precision allowed in the column values. For character columns, the length can be 1 through 32,767. For single-byte data values, that equates to the number of characters that the column can hold. For multibyte data values (encoded using DBCS, Unicode, or UTF-8), where a character can occupy more than one byte, the number of characters that fit might be less than the length value of the column.

The column *format*, in SAS terms, is an instruction for how to transform a raw value into an appearance that is suitable for a given purpose. A basic attribute of a format is the format length, which controls how much of the value is displayed. For example, a character column might have a storage length of 10 bytes but a format length of 5 characters ($5. format), so when you see the formatted values you will see at most 5 characters for each record.

Another attribute of the format is the precision. For example, the DOLLAR8. format will show you up to 8 characters of a value (including a currency symbol and thousands separator) in dollars, but no cents. DOLLAR8.2 will show you the decimal point and the value to the nearest cent (2 decimal spaces). In each case, the value displayed will not exceed 8 characters.

(continued)

(continued)

What happens if the formatted value runs into trouble squeezing into 8 characters? SAS drops the thousands separator and currency symbol to free up 2 slots first. If that's not enough, SAS begins to drop precision by lopping off the pennies and then the dimes. If that's still not enough, SAS rounds the value and uses scientific notation and other tricks to save space — all the while keeping the integrity of your original value for use in any calculations.

Following Procedures

The SAS language offers a procedure for just about everything: summary statistics, frequency counts, tabular reports, bar charts, and even loan amortization calculations. Whenever SAS developers want to add a new feature in support of a product offering or add a new analytic capability, they start by adding one or more procedures. These are often called *procs* for short, thanks to the PROC keyword that sets them off in a SAS program.

The name of the procedure usually suggests its purpose. For example, Table 16-1 lists a small sampling of SAS procedures and the work that they do.

Table 16-1	Examples of SAS Procedures
SAS Procedure	*Purpose*
PRINT	Creates a printed listing of your data.
SORT	Sorts your data by one or more columns and creates an output data set.
TRANSPOSE	Rearranges your data. For example, pivot the rows and columns to make it all topsy-turvy.
MEANS	Calculates summary statistics such as mean, standard deviation, mode, and median. Also an alias for the SUMMARY procedure.
FREQ	Calculates frequencies, percentages, and related statistics such as Chi-square tests.
REPORT	Creates a summary report of data including grouping variables and computed columns.
TABULATE	Creates cross-tabulation reports with a variety of statistics.
REG	Performs linear regression analysis.
GLM	Performs analysis of variance (ANOVA) and a large variety of statistical modeling techniques. (GLM stands for general linear models; this is one proc where the name is not obvious.)
GPLOT	Creates graphical line or scatter plots of your data.
GCHART	Creates bar charts or pie charts of your data.

The programming syntax used among SAS procedures is fairly consistent. It begins with a PROC statement, which usually includes a reference to a data set you're working with. This statement might include additional keywords to tweak the output of the procedure. Most procedures accept additional statements that allow you to modify how the data is processed or ask for additional output. You usually finish the procedure step with a RUN statement, or sometimes a QUIT statement, to close a series of operations in the procedure.

Here is a simple SAS program that runs a PROC MEANS step:

```
proc means data=sashelp.cars
   mean stddev median mode n;
run;
```

This program produces a report that lists five statistics for all the numeric variables in the Cars data set in the SASHELP library. If you want to modify the program so that it reports only on the variables related to mileage, simply add a VAR statement that names the variables to include:

```
proc means data=sashelp.cars
   mean stddev median mode n;
var mpg_highway mpg_city;
run;
```

Sometimes you want to create grouped output that's separated by the different values of a categorical variable. For example, you might want to group data records about automobiles according to their origin (United States, Europe, or Asia) or their model year. To tell SAS to group the data for analysis, you add a BY statement to the MEANS procedure. However, to calculate the grouped statistics, the procedure needs the data to be sorted by the grouping variable. To ensure that the data is sorted, you precede the MEANS procedure with a SORT procedure, as in this program:

```
proc sort data=sashelp.cars
   out=sortcars;
by origin;

proc means /* sortcars data is implied */
   mean stddev median mode n;
var mpg_highway mpg_city;
by origin;
run;
```

Figure 16-3 shows what the results look like when they are grouped by the ORIGIN column.

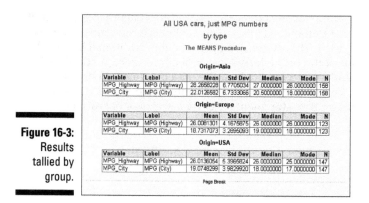

All USA cars, just MPG numbers

by type

The MEANS Procedure

Origin=Asia

Variable	Label	Mean	Std Dev	Median	Mode	N
MPG_Highway	MPG (Highway)	28.2658228	6.7705034	27.0000000	26.0000000	158
MPG_City	MPG (City)	22.0126582	6.7333066	20.5000000	18.0000000	158

Origin=Europe

Variable	Label	Mean	Std Dev	Median	Mode	N
MPG_Highway	MPG (Highway)	26.0081301	4.1675875	26.0000000	26.0000000	123
MPG_City	MPG (City)	18.7317073	3.2895093	19.0000000	18.0000000	123

Origin=USA

Variable	Label	Mean	Std Dev	Median	Mode	N
MPG_Highway	MPG (Highway)	26.0136054	5.3965824	26.0000000	25.0000000	147
MPG_City	MPG (City)	19.0748299	3.9829920	18.0000000	17.0000000	147

Page Break

Figure 16-3:
Results
tallied by
group.

Note that the sorted data is placed in a temporary data set. We then use this sorted data set (named SORTCARS in the example) in the MEANS procedure. Note also that in this example, the MEANS statement has no DATA= option. If you omit the DATA= option, SAS automatically uses the data set that was referenced most recently. This shorthand can help make your programs more reusable when using different data sets; however, you have to be careful to use the correct data set for the analysis.

You must presort SAS data sets before using BY groups because SAS reads data from data sets sequentially. But the rules are different when your data source resides in a database, such as Oracle or Teradata, instead of in a SAS data set. The SAS procedures and data access engines are smart enough to pass an implicit "order by" directive to the database. This means that using a BY statement in an analytical procedure such as PROC MEANS will work with database tables even if you don't presort the data. In fact, the act of presorting the data can result in a less efficient program because you'll be asking SAS to move data unnecessarily.

A Micro Look at Macro Programming

DATA steps and procedure steps can cover most of the work that you need to accomplish in a SAS program. However, you might know about other programming languages that also allow you to control program flow, offering constructs such as if-then-else logic and looping for repetitive operations. The SAS macro language fills this gap for SAS programs.

The macro language is the glue that controls how other steps are run. A SAS macro program is a named set of instructions that contains this control logic in addition to the DATA and procedures steps.

Macro magic revealed

Even many experienced SAS programmers still regard SAS macro programming as a sort of black art. A key to understanding SAS macros is to remember that macros simply generate text for SAS to interpret. Your macro programming statements, when processed by SAS, expand into text according to the directives and logic in your macros, and that text is subsequently processed by SAS as part of a larger program.

Consider this simple example:

```
options mprint;
%macro makedata(number);
  data out;
    %do i = 1 %to &number.;
      x&i. = &i. * &number.;
    %end;
  run;
%mend;

%makedata(4);
```

This program defines a macro function named makedata that generates as many statements as are indicated by the number argument. To see the SAS program that this routine generates, include the OPTIONS MPRINT; statement before using it. The MPRINT option tells SAS to reveal the generated text in the SAS log output. Running the preceding example yields

```
24          %makedata(4);
MPRINT(MAKEDATA):    data out;
MPRINT(MAKEDATA):    x1 = 1 * 4;
MPRINT(MAKEDATA):    x2 = 2 * 4;
MPRINT(MAKEDATA):    x3 = 3 * 4;
MPRINT(MAKEDATA):    x4 = 4 * 4;
MPRINT(MAKEDATA):    run;
```

Another option, MLOGIC, tells SAS to reveal the "thought process" of the macro processor when evaluating macro conditions such as %if-%then-%else and looping constructs. These SAS system options can serve as valuable debugging tools when you want to know what's going on in your macro programs. Here is the output from the same program with MLOGIC also enabled:

```
MLOGIC(MAKEDATA):  Beginning execution.
MLOGIC(MAKEDATA):  Parameter NUMBER has
           value 4
MPRINT(MAKEDATA):    data out;
MLOGIC(MAKEDATA):  %DO loop beginning;
           index variable I; start value is
           1; stop value is 4; by
        value is 1.
MPRINT(MAKEDATA):    x1 = 1 * 4;
MLOGIC(MAKEDATA):  %DO loop index
           variable I is now 2; loop will
           iterate again.
MPRINT(MAKEDATA):    x2 = 2 * 4;
MLOGIC(MAKEDATA):  %DO loop index
           variable I is now 3; loop will
           iterate again.
MPRINT(MAKEDATA):    x3 = 3 * 4;
MLOGIC(MAKEDATA):  %DO loop index
           variable I is now 4; loop will
           iterate again.
MPRINT(MAKEDATA):    x4 = 4 * 4;
MLOGIC(MAKEDATA):  %DO loop index
           variable I is now 5; loop will
           not iterate again.
MPRINT(MAKEDATA):    run;
```

Dipping your toe in with macro variables

The simplest way to begin using the SAS macro language is by assigning and using macro variables. A *macro variable* is like a reusable ink stamp onto which you can place any value that you want, and then reuse it later in your program. When you want to change the value that SAS uses, you simply change the value assigned to the macro variable in the first place, and your program behavior changes accordingly.

To *assign* a value to a macro variable, you use the %LET statement like this:

```
%let whichOrigin=USA;
```

This assigns the text value of USA to the whichOrigin macro variable. You can also use SAS functions to calculate the values that you want to assign to a macro variable. For example:

```
%let rightNow = %sysfunc(date(),date9.)
         %sysfunc(time(),timeampm.);
```

This code assigns the current date and time, as a formatted text value, to the rightNow variable. It uses the SAS date and time functions, plus the SAS date9. and timeampm. formats, to return the value 03OCT2009 12:37:41 PM (assuming that it's currently October 3, 2009 around lunch time).

To *use* a macro variable in your SAS program, you set it off with an ampersand symbol (&). For example, the following program creates a report of the subset of the CARS data set in which the ORIGIN column matches the assigned value of the whichOrigin macro variable. The report includes a footnote with the timestamp reflected in the rightNow variable:

```
footnote "Data as of &rightNow";
proc print data=sashelp.cars
    (where=(origin="&whichOrigin"));
run;
```

Going deeper with macro functions

If a macro variable is like a reusable ink stamp, a macro function is like an entire mimeograph machine. (Remember mimeographs? And the smell of that fresh ink on the ditto sheet?) With a macro function you can store a collection of statements or values that you can reuse later.

To define the body of a macro function, you use the %macro statement to begin the function and the %mend statement to end it. For example, this macro function contains the statements to run the MEANS procedure:

```
%macro runMeans;
   proc means data=sashelp.cars
      mean stddev n mode;
   run;
%mend;
```

When you submit these statements in SAS, the runMeans macro program is defined; but it won't run until you invoke it with another statement later in your program. To invoke a macro function, you use the percent sign (%) with the name of the macro. For example, to run the preceding example, you submit this statement:

```
%runMeans;
```

Macro functions become much more useful when they can accept *arguments* (sometimes called *parameters*) to change their behavior. By making a small change to the preceding example to add the whichData argument, the run-Means function can be used with any data set:

```
%macro runMeans(whichData);
   title "Output of MEANS for &whichData";
   proc means data=&whichData
      mean stddev n mode;
   run;
%mend;
```

Note that the whichData argument, after it's inside the body of the macro function, is simply a macro variable. The statements within the macro function can reference the variable by setting it off with an ampersand (&whichData).

Here are two statements that use this single macro function to report on two different data sets:

```
%runMeans(sashelp.class);
%runMeans(sashelp.cars);
```

Figure 16-4 shows the output of this program as it would appear in SAS Enterprise Guide.

Output of MEANS for sashelp.class

The MEANS Procedure

Variable	Mean	Std Dev	N	Mode
Age	13.3157895	1.4926722	19	12.0000000
Height	62.3368421	5.1270752	19	62.5000000
Weight	100.0263158	22.7739335	19	84.0000000

Page Break

Output of MEANS for sashelp.cars

The MEANS Procedure

Variable	Label	Mean	Std Dev	N	Mode
MSRP		32774.86	19431.72	428	13270.00
Invoice		30014.70	17642.12	428	14207.00
EngineSize	Engine Size (L)	3.1967290	1.1085947	428	3.0000000
Cylinders		5.8075117	1.5584426	426	6.0000000
Horsepower		215.8855140	71.8360316	428	200.0000000
MPG_City	MPG (City)	20.0607477	5.2382176	428	18.0000000
MPG_Highway	MPG (Highway)	26.8434579	5.7412007	428	26.0000000
Weight	Weight (LBS)	3577.95	758.9832145	428	3175.00
Wheelbase	Wheelbase (IN)	108.1542066	8.3118130	428	107.0000000
Length	Length (IN)	186.3621495	14.3579913	428	178.0000000

Page Break

Figure 16-4:
Two lines
of code
produce so
much infor-
mation!

Ask Your Data Questions Using SQL

The SQL procedure in SAS is a doorway to SQL (structured query language). SQL is an industry standard supported by every major database system. Like the DATA step, SQL lets you inspect and manipulate data sources. Because SAS (through its SAS/ACCESS modules) lets you interact with third-party database sources, SQL is a natural approach to working with data. In fact, when properly used, the SQL that you use in SAS can be passed down directly to the database you're working with, helping your programs to run much more efficiently.

Because the Query Builder task in SAS Enterprise Guide generates nothing but SQL programs, it can be a useful resource to understanding the basics about SQL. You can use Query Builder to generate simple or even complex queries, and then examine the generated SAS program to see how the statements fit together. Query Builder doesn't cover everything that SQL can do, but it's a great start.

Subsetting: Make your data smaller

The most common use of SQL is in subsetting data. Imagine that you have a data source with lots of rows and lots of columns. For any given report or analysis, you probably need to consider just a portion of those rows and columns. Because it's usually less expensive (in terms of time and computing resources) to analyze just the data you need and leave out the rest, you can use SQL to create a subset.

This example program uses the SQL procedure to select just two columns from the SASHELP.CARS data set and only those rows that have a value of "USA" for Origin. It stores the result in a new table named Example2:

```
proc sql;
create table example2 as
   select make, mpg_highway
   from sashelp.cars
   where origin="USA";
quit;
```

The PROC SQL and QUIT keywords are like slices of bread that sandwich the SQL statements that you want SAS to process. The "meat" of the program is in between, with one or more layers of statements to slice and dice your data into a delicious meal.

Do the math: calculate and group

SQL can also be used to create new columns by using functions and operators to manipulate the values in your tables. For example, if you have a table that contains a Height column and a Weight column for a group of people, you can use a simple formula to calculate a new column representing Body Mass Index (BMI). In the following example, the select * notation tells SQL to include all existing columns, plus the new bmi column that is calculated with the following formula:

```
proc sql;
create table classWithBMI as
   select *, (weight*703)/height as bmi
   from sashelp.class;
run;
```

You can also aggregate, or collapse, your data to create summarized groups. This creates many fewer records than the full detail data, and as a result makes it much easier to report on and understand what your data is telling you. Here is an example that takes our SASHELP.CARS data and calculates the average price-per-horsepower unit for each make of automobile:

```
proc sql;
create table perHorse as
   select make, avg(msrp/horsepower) as avg_ppp
       format dollar10.2 label="Price per pony"
   from sashelp.cars
   where origin = "USA"
   group by make
   order by avg_ppp desc;
quit;
```

Note a few other things about this example:

✔ In addition to standard SQL, this statement includes FORMAT and LABEL options to provide additional information to SAS, indicating how to format the data (see the sidebar titled "Formats and lengths: The long and short of it," earlier in this chapter).

✔ The GROUP BY clause tells SAS to collapse the detail data into groups according to the make of the automobile. Instead of producing one record per model of auto (Tahoe, Tracker, Astro, and so on), it creates one record per make (Chevrolet, Ford, Lincoln, and so on). The new column avg_ppp represents the average price-per-horsepower for each group.

✔ The ORDER BY clause tells SAS to sort the output data in descending order according to the value of avg_ppp from the most expensive to the least expensive.

Joining the crowd: combine tables

One of the most well-known uses of SQL is to combine data from multiple tables into a single table. In SQL parlance, this is called *joining* tables, and although it's very powerful, it can also be quite dangerous (in terms of computing resources) when performed without proper care. Chapter 5 covers the concept of joining data in much more detail.

Here is an example SQL program with a simple inner join; it combines two tables matching up only the records where custid in one table matches the value of customer in another table. This example uses an *alias* for each table name (t1 and t2). An alias is a convenient syntactical shortcut. Using aliases, we don't have to repeat the name of the input tables multiple times in the program.

```
proc sql;
   create table Combined as
      select t1.name, t2.units
      from candy.candy_customers as t1
      inner join candy.candy_sales_history as t2
         on (t1.custid = t2.customer);
quit;
```

Putting It All Together in a SAS Mashup

Here is a SAS program that shows many of the concepts we've covered in this chapter. It also has one of the most important features of a SAS program: comments! Whether you write your own programs or use programs written by someone else, comments (delimited by the /* and */ characters) are essential to understanding the program's purpose and keeping it maintained.

```
/* Putting it all together */
/* First, a macro variable that allows us to */
/* easily change the column we want to use   */
/* in just one place                         */
%let mpgVar = mpg_city; /* or mpg_highway */

/* Next, a PROC SQL step to calculate the */
/* average value across MAKEs             */
proc sql noprint;
create table work.example4 as
  select make,
         avg(&mpgVar) as avg_mpg format 4.2
  from sashelp.cars
  where origin="USA"
  group by make
  order by avg_mpg desc;

  /* new instruction: count the "makes" and store */
  /* in a macro variable named "howMany"          */
  select count(distinct make) into :howMany
  from sashelp.cars
  where origin="USA";
quit;

/* Now, use the new data table and macro values */
/* in a report                                  */
/* This title and PRINT step create a tabular   */
/* view of the data                             */
title "Analyzed %sysfunc(trim(&howMany)) values of Make";
proc print data=work.example4
    label noobs;
  var make avg_mpg;
  label avg_mpg="Average &mpgVar";
run;

/* This SGPLOT step creates a vertical bar   */
/* chart of the data                         */
title; /* clear title */
ods graphics / width=600 height=400;
proc sgplot data=work.example4;
  vbar make / response=avg_mpg;
  xaxis label="Make";
  yaxis label="Average &mpgVar";
run;
```

When you run this code, it produces a report that looks like the output in
Figure 16-5.

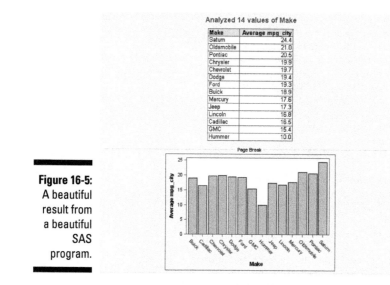

Analyzed 14 values of Make

Make	Average mpg_city
Saturn	24.4
Oldsmobile	21.0
Pontiac	20.5
Chrysler	19.9
Chevrolet	19.7
Dodge	19.4
Ford	19.3
Buick	18.9
Mercury	17.6
Jeep	17.3
Lincoln	16.8
Cadillac	16.5
GMC	15.4
Hummer	10.0

Figure 16-5:
A beautiful
result from
a beautiful
SAS
program.

Chapter 17

The New World Meets the Old: Programmers and SAS Enterprise Guide

. . . .

In This Chapter

▶ Working with projects

▶ Getting the most from SAS tasks

▶ Flexing your power with parameters

▶ Noting a few things that are different from traditional SAS

. . . .

*S*AS programmers can sometimes be . . . um (how to say this nicely?) . . . set in their ways. Although painting an entire class of people as having inflexible tendencies isn't fair, long-time SAS programmers tend to carry more legacy than folks who work in other areas of technology. After all, if the techniques you've been using to do your job for 20 years are still working, what's your incentive to change?

In this chapter, you read about the productivity gains that you can enjoy when you add SAS Enterprise Guide to your SAS programming toolbox. You see how to perform old tasks in a new way as well as how to accomplish some tasks that would be difficult — if not impossible — without the benefit of an integrated tool such as SAS Enterprise Guide.

The times, they are a-changin'

A woodworking show called *The Woodwright's Shop* airs on public television. It features an ambitious gentleman named Roy who completes woodworking projects using only turn-of-the-century tools (that is, turn-of-the-*last*-century). He is entertaining, and there is no question that he is an expert in his craft. Yet his progress in each episode is limited because he does everything by hand, the old-fashioned way. (He also occasionally has to dip into his first aid kit to patch up some minor injury.)

Another woodworking show, also on public television, is *The New Yankee Workshop*. This show features a familiar personality named Norm, who works in a state-of-the-art workshop with every modern power tool and woodworking convenience. Like Roy, Norm is an expert in carpentry and all things wood. However, Norm gets so much more accomplished in a single episode. Whereas Roy might build something small, such as a stool, Norm builds big projects, such as a dining room set.

Experienced SAS programmers can sometimes be like Roy. They are experts in their field, and they can accomplish quite a bit by using the traditional SAS tools, such as a plain text editor and the SAS Display Manager interface.

Tools such as SAS Enterprise Guide, however, can boost the productivity of even the most experienced SAS programmer. SAS Enterprise Guide provides easy methods to perform the more tedious tasks while allowing you to write SAS programs and integrate them into your overall processes. And SAS Enterprise Guide provides ways for you to share your work with others in new ways, making your SAS know-how more pervasive in your organization.

This is good news because many SAS programmers are finding that their old tools are becoming unavailable as their organizations adopt a distributed computing environment. Instead of allowing SAS to be installed on every PC, many companies install SAS in a centralized environment and supply SAS programmers with SAS Enterprise Guide as the tool to access that environment. As a result, some SAS programmers are reluctant converts to SAS Enterprise Guide. With some adjustment, these workers should enjoy increased productivity as a consolation prize.

Getting Organized with Projects

One of the biggest advantages that SAS Enterprise Guide offers is the capability to organize your work in project files. A SAS Enterprise Guide project is a great place to store related work together, including SAS programs, references to data, Output Delivery System (ODS) results such as HTML, and SAS logs. (See Chapter 10 for more details about the types of results you can work with.)

Project files do more than store all your work items, though. Project files also store the *relationships* among those work items. The process flow view of your project serves as a form of documentation for your work.

Figure 17-1 shows a sample process flow. You can read this project from left to right to easily see how it's put together. It begins with a SAS program (Make Customer Data) that builds a customer table. That table, along with two other tables, is used as input into a query task that joins the three tables to create an output table named JoinResult. JoinResult is then used as input to a scatter plot task.

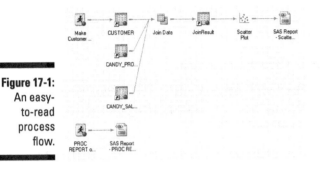

Figure 17-1:
An easy-
to-read
process
flow.

The only item that seems to be hanging out there is the SAS program at the bottom labeled PROC REPORT. Although the label might be informative, seeing how it relates to the other items is difficult.

Connecting the dots with links

The relationships described in this sample project so far, as shown by the arrow links in the process flow, are *implicit*. That is, SAS Enterprise Guide detects these relationships and illustrates them in the process flow view, with no intervention needed from you. SAS Enterprise Guide also lets you define your own links among items. This adds even more readability to your project and helps enforce the sequence in which items are run.

For example, suppose that the lone SAS program with the PROC REPORT label is meant to report on the JoinResult table. To build an explicit link from the data table to the SAS program, you could do the following:

1. **Right-click the JoinResult item and choose Link JoinResult To.**

   The Link window appears, showing a list of candidate items in the project to which you can link.

2. **Choose the PROC REPORT item from the list, and then click OK.**

   The process flow view updates to show the new relationship, as shown in Figure 17-2.

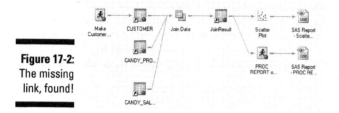

Figure 17-2:
The missing
link, found!

Another way to draw this link is to literally draw the link. You can

1. **Select an item in the flow by clicking it.**

2. **Position the mouse pointer near the edge of the item and click.**

3. **Drag an arrow to connect to another item, as if you were drawing a
   line segment in a paint application.**

This method is more intuitive in concept, but it can be a little tricky to
master.

When you link a data item to a SAS program item as input, SAS Enterprise
Guide automatically assigns the data reference to the &SYSLAST macro
variable before running the SAS program. Most SAS procedures will use the
&SYSLAST value as the DATA= value, if set. You can use this technique to
associate data tables with generic SAS programs without having to refer to the
data by name in the program.

Avoiding entropy with ordered lists

The process flow ties related tasks together and makes it easy to run them
all as a group, ensuring that tasks that produce output needed by other tasks
are run first. But what if you want to run just a subset of the tasks in your
project but still keep them in a certain sequence? The manual method would
have you selecting each task one at a time, running it, waiting while it completed, and repeating this for each task in order.

SAS Enterprise Guide has a hidden gem of a feature — ordered lists — which
lets you build simple lists of tasks from your project that you want to run in a
prescribed sequence. You can select these tasks *à la carte* from anywhere in
your project, including across multiple process flows, running them in whatever order you need.

To create an ordered list, follow these steps:

1. **Choose File⇨New⇨Ordered List.**

   The Ordered List window appears.

2. **Click Add.**

   The Select window appears, presenting you with a list of all the tasks in your project.

3. **Choose the tasks you want to include by clicking them; then click Open to add them to your list.**

   Press Ctrl while clicking to select multiple items at once.

   Figure 17-3 shows an example of the Ordered List window with a few tasks added. At this point, the tasks might not be in the correct order for your needs.

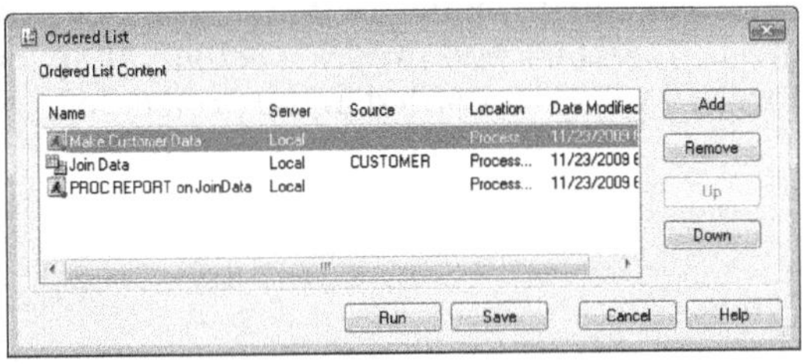

Figure 17-3:
Order SAS
around with
ordered
lists.

Ordered List						
Ordered List Content						
Name	Server	Source	Location	Date Modified		Add
Make Customer Data	Local		Process	11/23/2009 E		Remove
Join Data	Local	CUSTOMER	Process	11/23/2009 E		Up
PROC REPORT on JoinData	Local		Process	11/23/2009 E		Down
						Run Save Cancel Help

4. **To change the sequence for a task, select it in the list and click the Up or the Down button to move it within the list.**

5. **(Optional) If you want to run the tasks immediately, click Run.**

6. **When the list of tasks reflects the order that you want, click Save.**

   The ordered lists that you create appear in a special Ordered Lists section of your project view.

To run an ordered list after you create it, right-click the list item in the Ordered List section and choose Run Ordered List. SAS Enterprise Guide runs each task in the list in the correct order.

Generating project logs: Your work on record

Every task and SAS program that you run in SAS Enterprise Guide generates a log file as part of its output. SAS programmers rely on log files to show what work was performed, how long it took to complete, and whether any errors or warnings occurred.

The *project log* is an aggregated view of all the log files for all the tasks in your project. Every time you run your task or even the entire process flow, SAS Enterprise Guide adds the logs to the project log. The logs accumulate across *iterations,* meaning that the project log offers a history of every task you've run in your project. When you save your project, SAS Enterprise Guide saves your project log along with it.

The project log feature is not enabled by default, so if you want to build up this project history, you should turn it on when you create your project. To enable the project log, do the following:

1. **Choose View➪Project Log**

   The Project Log window appears in the project content area.

2. **Click Turn On.**

   The Project Log adds an entry to indicate that you "flipped the switch," as shown in Figure 17-4. All task and program activity that you perform from this point forward will be recorded in the project log.

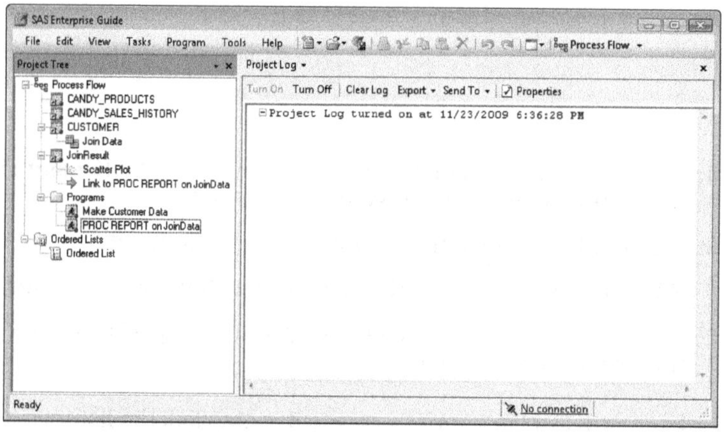

Figure 17-4: Project log — you have to flip the switch yourself.

Note that the project log won't contain any content until the first time you run tasks after turning it on.

The project log remains enabled for the life of the project. Because long-lived projects can accumulate large log files, SAS Enterprise Guide lets you clear the log as needed, saving it to an external file if you want to save it outside the project.

You can view the project log at any time by choosing View➪Project Log. If you want to pause the recording activity in the log or clear the log to start over, simply click the Turn Off or Clear Log button at the top of the Project Log view.

Letting SAS Tasks Do the Heavy Lifting

SAS Enterprise Guide supplies nearly 90 tasks that generate SAS program code for you, and all you have to do is point and click. The tasks cover basic data reporting, plots and charts, and advanced statistics.

You can use these tasks as a starting point for writing SAS programs, letting SAS Enterprise Guide generate as much of the code as possible.

SAS tasks cover the most popular options for SAS procedures. However, it doesn't take long for an experienced SAS programmer to discover that something is missing — some option or statement that hasn't surfaced in the point-and-click task interface.

There is a simple and obvious remedy: Use the SAS task to generate as many of the statements and options as possible, and then take a copy of the generated code and use it as the basis for your own SAS program. The disadvantage of this approach is that after you create your own SAS program from the task-generated version, you can no longer use the task user interface to maintain the program. You are on your own with the SAS program editor.

Here's a better way: Many SAS tasks allow you to insert your own statements and options at predefined points within the task user interface. By using this feature, you can have it both ways: point-and-click for the mainstream options with the capability to customize the generated SAS program with some extra statements.

Here are the steps to insert your own statements within a task, using the One-Way Frequencies task as an example:

1. **Choose Tasks⇨Describe⇨One-Way Frequencies, using the data of your choice.**

   The task window appears.

2. **Use the controls on the page to select the variables you want to analyze and any other options.**

3. **Click the Preview Code button (at the bottom left of the task window).**

   The Code Preview window appears with the SAS program code that reflects your selections thus far.

4. **On the top of the Code Preview window, click the Insert Code button.**

   The User Code window appears, as shown in Figure 17-5.

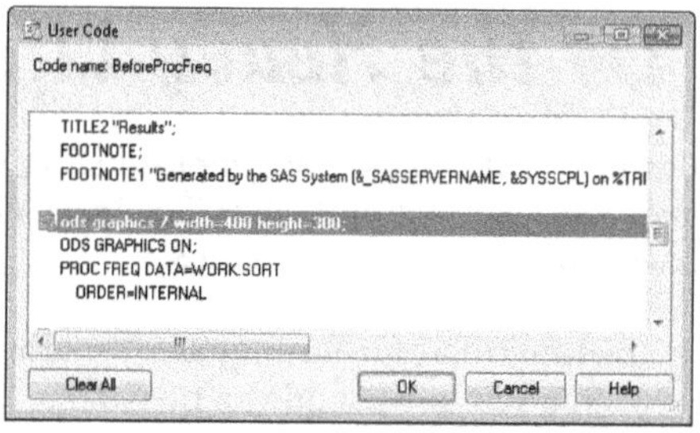

Figure 17-5:
Bend the
SAS tasks
to your will
with custom
code.

As you scroll through this user code view, note several lines labeled
`double-click to insert code`. These are the locations in the SAS
program that the task defines for you, allowing you to insert your own
statements and options.

5. **To insert your own code, double-click one of the indicated lines.**

    The Enter User Code window appears with a text field.

6. **Type your own SAS code segment into the text field.**

7. **After you add the options you want, click OK.**

8. **Click OK in the User Code window to close it.**

9. **Click the Preview Code button again in the task window to close the Code Preview window.**

    Clicking the Preview Code button toggles the Code Preview window on
    and off.

Note that whatever user code you enter is merged into the task-generated
code as is, so you need to take special care that the code you enter
is syntactically correct and makes sense at the insertion point you
selected. If you make a mistake, you'll see errors in the SAS log when
you run the task.

Being Flexible with Project Prompts

Like most software development, SAS programs tend to evolve. The first
stage of any given SAS program usually consists of DATA step code and procedure statements written to perform a task against a specific source of data.
Perhaps the program is required to meet a short-term goal or simply serve as
a prototype or proof of concept.

If you get good results with that first version of the program, chances are good that you or someone else will want to use your program to analyze a different data source or perhaps even a variety of data sources. It's at this point in the SAS program lifecycle that you might consider restructuring the program code to be more generic and reusable. Perhaps you would use macro variable substitution with %LET statements at the top of your program to assign values as needed, or you might devise a fancier version that contains a SAS macro program with parameters in the macro call.

SAS Enterprise Guide can integrate with your SAS programs using project prompts. You can think of prompts as SAS macro variables that SAS Enterprise Guide keeps track of, so that when you run your project, the application knows enough to prompt you for values. After gathering responses to the interactive prompts, SAS Enterprise Guide generates the %LET statements for you and submits them ahead of your program.

Prompts in SAS 9.2 were known as *parameters* in previous releases. In SAS programmer terms, though, you can think of them as fancy SAS macro variables.

Whereas macro variables are usually simple constructs in SAS, prompts can be much more sophisticated and provide a helpful prompting experience to an end user. You can create prompts to accept text strings, numbers (with range validation), single or multiple values from a predefined list of values, date or date-time values, and even variable names for use in SAS task roles.

To get started with project parameters, follow these steps:

1. **Choose View⇨Prompt Manager.**

   The Prompt Manager window appears. This window is a docked window in the SAS Enterprise Guide workspace.

2. **Click Add.**

   The Add New Prompt dialog box appears.

3. **Type a name for your prompt.**

   SAS Enterprise Guide automatically forms a valid SAS code name or macro variable name from the descriptive name you enter. You can change this code name if you want. You also have the option of adding a description to help document the prompt.

4. **Click the Prompt Type and Values tab.**

   This tab offers a list of prompt types to choose from, including text, numeric, and date. Figure 17-6 shows an example of what this dialog box might look like; its contents vary depending on the prompt type and data value type that you specify.

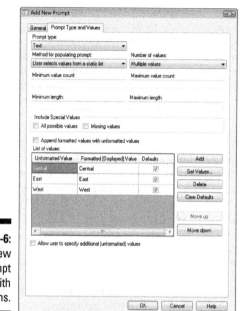

Figure 17-6:
Add a new
prompt
loaded with
options.

In this example, the prompt type is `text`, and the method for prompting is `User selects values from a static list`. With this list type, you have the opportunity to specify the contents of the list to present during a prompt. The Get Values button (to the right of the values list) offers an easy way to populate the list based on data values in a SAS data set or other data source.

Note that the Prompt Type and Values tab contains many options for how to treat this parameter. You can specify a default value, enclose the value in quotes, specify range checking options, and more. The window has too many options to describe here; you should be able to find a combination of options to fit your needs.

5. **When you finally settle on all your options, click OK to add the prompt to the project.**

The most natural place to use prompts in SAS Enterprise Guide is in Query Builder. You can make a query definition much more flexible by using prompts in filters. For example, instead of creating a filter that equates to `WHERE REGION="EAST"`, you can substitute a prompt value for the literal value `"EAST"` and prompt for the valid regions. Figure 17-7 shows an example of a query that references two prompts.

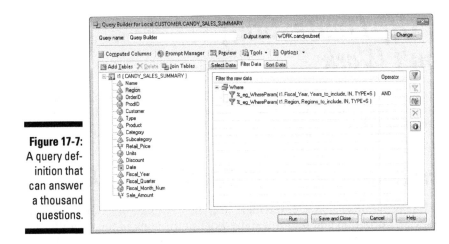

Figure 17-7:
A query definition that can answer a thousand questions.

Note that the filter definitions simply reference SAS macro calls with your selected prompts. Query Builder is smart enough to recognize when you use project prompts, so SAS Enterprise Guide presents a prompt for values each time the query is run. Figure 17-8 shows an example of the prompts that you would see when this query runs.

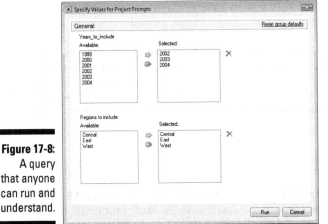

Figure 17-8:
A query that anyone can run and understand.

When you take a process flow and make it into a stored process, SAS Enterprise Guide is smart enough to promote your project prompts into stored process prompts with no extra work on your part. The prompting experience from a stored process is virtually identical to that of a process flow with project prompts.

Keeping Off-Limits: Stuff That Won't Work

Unfortunately, the world of SAS Enterprise Guide isn't completely Utopian. A handful of SAS programming practices simply won't work, at least not without a struggle.

X statements and SYSTASK (tsk, tsk)

Many SAS programs use the X statement and the SYSTASK function to escape from the SAS program and perform some work in the shell of the operating system where the program is running. For example, these techniques allow you to copy files among folders, query the contents of directories, and run batch files or shell scripts.

The default centralized SAS environment disables the use of the X statement and the SYSTASK function. The reason is that in a centralized environment accessed by dozens or hundreds of people, these types of shell-level commands can represent a security risk and introduce instability. SAS Enterprise Guide makes it easy for less-experienced users to have access to your SAS environment. Perhaps it isn't a good idea for those novice users to have unfettered access to your system shell environment as well.

You can work around this limitation with the cooperation of your system administrator. You can configure your SAS environment to allow these statements again, using the ALLOWXMD system option in the SAS startup command. However, use this approach with extreme caution, ensuring that everyone involved understands the potential risks of rogue SAS programs.

DDE is DOA

DDE, or Dynamic Data Exchange, is a 20-year-old protocol that Microsoft Windows applications can use to send messages and commands to each other. The SAS programming language includes a FILENAME statement access method for DDE to facilitate conversations between SAS for Microsoft Windows and other applications. For years, SAS programmers have used DDE to programmatically read and write data in Microsoft Excel worksheets. When the SAS program runs, it issues commands to start a Microsoft Excel process and establish a communication link, open workbook files, and access data in particular worksheet cells. It's interesting to watch such programs in action because Microsoft Excel windows pop up and values appear in cells as if typed by an invisible hand.

DDE technology works only under certain conditions, and these conditions often aren't met when you use SAS Enterprise Guide:

✔ **The two processes communicating via DDE must be running on the same machine.** In a distributed environment in which SAS runs on a remote server, the version of Microsoft Excel on your local PC is inaccessible to your SAS program. Remember that the DDE link is between Microsoft Excel and SAS, not SAS Enterprise Guide. The remote SAS session might even be running on a non-Windows system, such as UNIX, where DDE isn't supported at all.

✔ **The SAS session must run in a windowing environment.** Even if your SAS session is running on a PC that has Microsoft Excel installed, the SAS session is running *headless,* meaning that it has no visible windows. Without this window environment in place, DDE (which relies on Windows messages) is not effective.

SAS Enterprise Guide has built-in features to import and export data to and from Microsoft Excel, and you can use those features to regain some of the ground lost without DDE. However, SAS Enterprise Guide doesn't offer the same level of control at the cell level as DDE.

Nowhere to show: SAS/AF and %WINDOW

SAS/AF is a legacy application development environment that is built right into SAS. Using SAS/AF components, such as frames and screen control language (SCL), you can build applications that drive SAS processes. The user interface appears dated compared with most modern desktop applications and Web-based applications, but some companies continue to rely on their investment in these early, full-screen applications.

Because of the client/server nature of SAS Enterprise Guide and SAS, SAS/AF applications are not accessible in SAS Enterprise Guide. These are full-screen applications hosted in SAS; and with SAS operating as a server, there is no "screen" to host these windows. In fact, any SAS language feature that would normally produce a prompt or window in an interactive SAS session is off-limits with SAS Enterprise Guide. This includes %WINDOW statements, PROMPT options on LIBNAME statements, and interactive environments such as the REPORT window and the DATA step debugger.

In general, SAS statements that require user interaction and that would not work well in a SAS batch program won't work well in SAS Enterprise Guide either. Fortunately, SAS Enterprise Guide offers modern replacements for many of these interactive features. You can achieve much of the same experience (and more) through project parameters, Query Builder, and built-in tasks. In fact, you can even extend SAS Enterprise Guide with custom tasks, fulfilling the needs served by SAS/AF programs for so many years.

Ending control with ENDSAS

In the world of sophisticated batch SAS programs, using the ENDSAS statement to control program flow is common practice. The ENDSAS statement, as the name implies, ends the current SAS session. You might use this statement in a batch program to terminate processing when you encounter certain conditions.

However, in SAS Enterprise Guide, the SAS session is your lifeline to your results and SAS log. If your SAS program executes the ENDSAS statement, it's sort of like hanging up the phone before you've heard all the important information. Your results become disconnected and not retrievable from your SAS Enterprise Guide project.

Before you run such SAS programs with SAS Enterprise Guide, rework the logic to avoid using ENDSAS. Instead, you can change the structure, perhaps using macro statements, to conditionally execute just the code that you want instead of terminating the SAS session.

Part VI
The Part of Tens

The 5th Wave   By Rich Tennant

"Look-what if we just increase the size of the charts?"

In this part . . .

The Part of Tens is where we store those useful tips that would be pretty darn tough to figure out on your own. Even if you're an experienced SAS programmer or administrator, chances are good that you'll discover something new by reading this part. We offer tips on increasing your productivity, info for admins, and some extras to boot.

Chapter 18

Ten SAS Enterprise Guide Productivity Tips

. . . .

In This Chapter

▶ Using shortcut keys for quick action

▶ Multitasking with multiple sessions

▶ Sniffing out your server software

▶ Switching out your inputs

▶ Watching the log while code runs

▶ Moving data on the fast track

▶ Having fun with custom tasks

▶ Selecting, then running, your code

▶ Setting data performance options

▶ Scheduling projects

. . . .

SAS Enterprise Guide is a big application, sporting dozens of menu items and hundreds of windows and forms. The application is capable of so much, but many people who use it tend to spend all their time in a few focused areas related to their jobs.

This chapter offers a selection of ten helpful hints and tips to guide you while you explore SAS Enterprise Guide. Remember, it can be fun to try new things, so stray off the path occasionally and see what you can find.

Know the "Keys" to Success

In addition to the usual shortcut keys for copy, cut, paste, and so on, there are essential shortcut keys to quick action in your SAS Enterprise Guide session:

- ✔ **F4:** Takes you directly to the Process Flow view.
- ✔ **Ctrl+M:** Maximizes the view of the current document, whether showing data, code, or results. The view expands to occupy the entire SAS Enterprise Guide workspace. Use Ctrl+M again to restore the view to normal.
- ✔ **F8:** Submits the SAS program for processing when a code window is active. Experienced SAS programmers will remember this key because it's the same key used to submit programs in SAS Display Manager.

Don't Limit Yourself: Use More than One Session

SAS Enterprise Guide can open just one project file at a time, but nothing is stopping you from opening multiple SAS Enterprise Guide sessions to work on multiple projects at once.

With multiple sessions open, you can even copy and paste content among different projects, including tasks, queries, and data references.

See What's Installed on Your Server

To see the SAS products that your site has licensed and installed on your SAS server, do the following:

1. **In the Server List, connect to your SAS server by clicking its name to expand it.**

2. **Right-click the server icon and choose Properties.**

3. **In the Server Properties window that appears, click the Software tab and then click View SAS Server Products.**

   A window appears with the summary of products that were selected, showing which are licensed — and of those, which are installed for use.

Change the Input Data for a Task

Most tasks in SAS Enterprise Guide require a data source for input. After you select task options and run a task for one input data source, changing the task to use a different input data source but keeping all the other options you selected is easy.

To change the input data source for a task, follow these steps:

1. **If the new input data source isn't already referenced in your project, add it to your project.**

   Choose File⇨Open⇨Data to select data.

2. **Right-click the task in your process flow and choose Select Input Data.**

   A menu appears with a list of the other data sources in your project.

3. **Choose the input data source that you want to use.**

   The process flow automatically refreshes to show the new data source as flowing into the task.

   If the new data source doesn't contain all the columns referenced within the task (columns that might have been in the previous data), you have to open the task and correct any necessary column assignments.

Watch the Log Grow

If you're running a monster SAS program, you don't need to wait for it to finish to see its progress. Simply right-click the running task or program item in your Process Flow and choose Open Log. You can watch the SAS log scroll by, even as your SAS program runs on a remote SAS server.

If you open the project log (View⇨Project Log), you can monitor the progress of the entire project as one task leads into the next.

Copy Data from One SAS Server to Another

You can use the Upload and Download Data tasks to copy data files between servers. You can download the files from the source server to your local PC, and then upload the files from your PC to a destination server.

1. **Choose Tasks⇨Data⇨Download Data Files to PC.**

   The Download Data Files to PC window appears.

2. **Click Add to find the SAS data sources that you want to copy.**

3. **Select your data files (you can have several in the list), and then click Next.**

4. **Specify a destination file on your local PC to store the data files.**

   If you intend to use this folder only as a holding area before you upload the files, the folder can be a temporary area (such as C:\Temp).

5. **Click Finish to run the task and download the files.**

   This copies the files from the SAS server to your PC and might take a few moments to complete. The following steps let you then copy the files back to a different SAS server.

6. **Choose Tasks⇨Data⇨Upload Data Files to Server.**

   The Upload Data Files to Server window appears.

7. **Click Add to select the data files to upload.**

   The Select Data window appears.

8. **Navigate to the folder where you downloaded the data files in Step 4, select all the files, and then click Open.**

9. **Click Next.**

10. **Select the destination SAS server and SAS library.**

11. **If you want to work with these files immediately in your project, leave the Add Data Files to Your Current Project option selected.**

12. **Click Finish to upload the data.**

Although these steps have you move the data files *twice* (once from the source to your PC, and then once from the PC to the target server), this method is still much faster than other possible approaches. The reason that it's fast is that the upload and download operations are simple file transfers (similar to FTP) and don't involve opening, reading, and writing records of data, which can take much longer.

Expand Your Horizons with Custom Tasks

You can extend the capabilities of SAS Enterprise Guide with custom tasks. Developing new custom tasks is an advanced process requiring not only SAS programming skills but also Microsoft Windows programming skills. However, anyone can easily *use* custom tasks.

On the SAS support Web site, SAS provides a collection of custom task examples, many of which are useful just as they are. For example, tasks are available to merge data, create picture formats, and browse SAS catalog entries. To see the available custom tasks, visit support.sas.com/eguide.

Submit a Selection

If you have a large SAS program but need to run only a bit of it (for example, a single DATA step or a macro definition), you don't need to submit the entire program in SAS Enterprise Guide. To submit just a subset of the program, highlight the statements that you want to submit in the code editor. Then right-click and choose Submit Selection on *SAS Server,* where *SAS Server* is the name of your SAS server. SAS Enterprise Guide submits just the selected statements; the resulting log and output reflects the selected statements, not the entire program.

Don't Wait for Data to Open

When you add data to your project, SAS Enterprise Guide opens the data grid view so that you can see the first batch of records. This can take several seconds to complete, depending on the location and type of data.

If you're already familiar with your data and don't want to wait for the data view to open, you can turn off this behavior by default. To change this option, follow these steps:

1. **Choose Tools⇨Options.**

2. **In the Options window that appears, choose the Data: Data General category in the left pane.**

3. **Deselect the Automatically Open Data When Added to Project check box.**

4. **If you also want to save time by opening results from programs and tasks, choose the Results: Results General category and then clear the Automatically Open Data or Results when Generated check box.**

Schedule Your Project

After you get your SAS Enterprise Guide project running just the way you want it, you can schedule it to run unattended, even when you're not logged into your computer.

To schedule a project, choose File➪Schedule Project. SAS Enterprise Guide creates a script file and helps you to schedule the script through the Microsoft Windows Task Scheduler. The script, when run, automates SAS Enterprise Guide to open, run all tasks, and save your updated project.

Although the project can run while you're not logged into your computer, your computer does need to be turned on and plugged into a network connection to have access to any remote servers and data that it needs. Also, for a schedule task to run unattended, you must provide your Microsoft Windows user ID and password in the Task Scheduler interface.

Chapter 19

Ten Tips for Administrators

*U*p until just a few years ago, if you were a SAS administrator, your life was relatively uncomplicated (at least where SAS software was concerned). Your main duties included keeping the SAS license — SETINIT — current for the handful of SAS users in the organization. Perhaps you served as the SAS site representative, acting as a liaison between your SAS user community and SAS technical support staff. You might also have kept one or two SAS/SHARE servers running so that multiple SAS users could access your valuable SAS data simultaneously.

Today, SAS software comes in many shapes and sizes. It's in front of more users than ever, some of whom might not even realize they're using SAS. This chapter offers a selection of ten tips for the SAS administrator. These nuggets of knowledge are not obvious or well documented elsewhere, so they might prove very useful to you.

Determining When SASUSER Isn't Usable

The SASUSER library is sort of the My Documents location for output that you want to save across SAS sessions. Experienced SAS programmers know that SASUSER is a user-specific location that they can rely on for semipermanent storage. It's not exactly an enterprise-class storage repository, but it's not a temporary scratch space, either.

In this new world of SAS within a distributed environment, two common configurations make SASUSER unusable as a storage area that persists across sessions:

✔ **SAS running on IBM z/OS:** The first configuration is specific to the IBM z/OS (the mainframe system formerly known as OS/390, which in turn was formerly known as MVS). When accessing a z/OS SAS session from a client application such as SAS Enterprise Guide, the SAS session is created with the SASUSER library marked as temporary. This means that it behaves just like the WORK library; when the SAS session is over, anything stored in the library is deleted.

✔ **SASUSER is configured as read only:** This troublesome second configuration is common in SAS 9 deployments. Because some types of SAS 9 servers (such as the SAS Stored Process server) typically run under an administrative server account, the SASUSER library doesn't even really make sense.

As a result, the typical SAS 9 deployment includes the RSASUSER system option in all server configuration files. The RSASUSER option tells SAS to treat the SASUSER library as read-only, thereby rendering it off-limits for output from your SAS programs. Technically, you can remedy this by making sure that the configuration file used to launch your workspace servers doesn't contain the RSASUSER option. However, a better practice is to avoid the use of SASUSER in the distributed environment. This helps ensure that SAS programs behave correctly in stored processes as well as in interactive SAS and SAS Enterprise Guide sessions.

Managing Logins from SAS Enterprise Guide Explorer

In most organizations, resources such as databases and servers require credentials for a user to access them. In SAS, credentials are managed as logins, and logins are associated with your metadata identity.

Different types of resources require different logins, spread across a variety of authentication domains. Your metadata identity is like a key ring, and each login is like a key that unlocks a different resource.

For example, the login required to connect to a SAS workspace might be different than what is needed for an Oracle database. Your SAS workspace host and the Oracle database server have different authentication domains so that you can have distinct logins for each resource.

To see what logins you have on your key ring, you can do the following in SAS Enterprise Guide:

1. **Choose Tools⇨SAS Enterprise Guide Explorer.**

   The SAS Enterprise Guide Explorer window appears.

2. **Choose File⇨Manage Logins.**

   The Login Manager window appears, as shown in Figure 19-1.

This window offers a single view of the logins to which you have access. From here, you can add and delete logins, and also update the user ID and password values for the logins you already have. Some logins are inherited as group logins; you can't delete or change those from here. However, seeing which logins might affect your ability to access protected resources can be useful.

Disarming Application Features

You might have noticed that SAS Enterprise Guide Explorer is a useful tool for viewing and modifying your SAS environment. Some SAS administrators might say it's *too* useful — especially the part that lets you modify library definitions.

SAS Enterprise Guide offers such a wide range of capabilities that you might be looking for a way to keep your end users from becoming overwhelmed or straying into dangerous territory. Beginning with SAS 9.2, you can control which capabilities are available in certain SAS applications by using role-based settings.

In SAS Management Console, role definitions are part of the User Manager component. You can assign a collection of capabilities to each role; each SAS application exposes a set of capabilities that you can enable or disable. SAS Enterprise Guide and SAS Add-In for Microsoft Office currently offer the most control; they provide more than 100 capabilities (tasks and features) that an administrator can turn off.

What types of tasks might you want to restrict? Here are some examples:

✔ The ability to launch SAS Enterprise Guide Explorer (and thus access administrative functions)

✔ The ability to run the Query Builder task (which permits novice users to submit potentially expensive database queries), in favor of using the simpler Filter and Sort task

✔ The ability to run SAS tasks that use SAS products that are not available in your installation (for example, not all SAS customers have SAS/QC, which is required to use the p-Chart task)

When a user starts SAS Enterprise Guide in restricted mode, a subtle notification appears in the status bar, as shown in Figure 19-2. The user can click the Functions link to see a list of enabled and denied capabilities.

Figure 19-2:
What a
restricted
user sees.

Connection: sasdemo, win764-2610 | Functions: Restricted

Using METALIB to Synchronize Metadata with Reality

SAS libraries defined in metadata can contain definitions for tables (SAS data sets or views) that reside in those libraries. Some SAS applications (such as SAS Information Map Studio) require that those tables be registered in metadata before they can be used.

So if you have SAS programs that create data tables that you want to use later, how can you ensure that the metadata contains the table definitions? The easiest method is to use the METALIB procedure. PROC METALIB can report on existing library contents, create a report of the differences between the physical contents of the library and metadata, and synchronize the two.

SAS Enterprise Guide offers a user interface to help you run PROC METALIB; you can find it by choosing Tools⇨Update Library Metadata. You can access full documentation for the METALIB procedure from the SAS support Web site (support.sas.com).

Getting Better Performance from Information Maps

SAS Information Maps can simplify data access for end users, but ensuring good data access performance from all environments can be tricky. Here are two reasons why SAS Enterprise Guide and SAS Add-In for Microsoft Office need special consideration when accessing Information Maps:

✔ **These two products need access to the SAS server and libraries where Information Map data reside.** This is an issue only if more than one SAS server is defined in your environment. Data access is most efficient when you open the data using the server that is closest, in relative terms, to the data source definition. Think about the structure of Information Maps: Maps contain columns, which originate from tables, which reside in libraries, which are associated to a SAS server. Therefore, you achieve the best performance when you access the Information Map using the server that connects to the related library definitions.

✔ **SAS Enterprise Guide and SAS Add-In for Microsoft Office can access the detail data of the Information Map.** The detail data can be appropriate for these applications, which let you perform further ad hoc analysis with the data. Each application offers the option to retrieve an aggregated view. Because the detailed data is likely to have much more volume than the aggregated view, optimized access is even more important.

Making Your Database Work for You with Implicit Pass-Through

You can use SAS Enterprise Guide to build queries that run on any database. Query Builder generates SQL statements, and SAS/ACCESS components provide transparent access, using SAS libraries, to databases that are not part of SAS.

Every database vendor supports a different dialect of SQL and a different set of SQL functions. Still, Query Builder in SAS Enterprise Guide generates the same SQL statements, regardless of the target database. It can get away with this apparent lazy approach because SAS/ACCESS has a feature called *implicit pass-through,* which optimizes the SQL for the target database before passing it on. This means there is a better-than-even chance that the database server (instead of SAS) will process your generated query; having the database do all the work is the best scenario for optimum efficiency.

However, you can make selections in Query Builder that preclude pass-through, forcing SAS to pull large amounts of data from the database to process in your SAS session. For example, if you select to join two tables and narrow the result set with filters, and one of those tables is a SAS data set (not in the database), SAS might have to pull the entire second table from the database, perform the join, and then filter, instead of pulling only the matching records from the database.

Another way to break pass-through is to specify a filter expression that contains a function supported only in SAS (and there are plenty of those). If the database server doesn't have a corresponding function to match what is in your expression, SAS must pull the entire table from the database and then process it in your SAS session.

The key to success is an awareness of which query actions are database friendly. You might have to encourage some end users to break up a large complicated query into a few smaller ones, simply to ensure that the database server is used for the heavy lifting. For example, it might be more efficient to upload a small table to the database before joining it with a larger table — ensuring that the join operation can happen on the database server.

If you're concerned that your end users don't know enough about the database structure to use Query Builder efficiently, you can disable the feature or disable just the Join features. See "Disarming Application Features," presented previously in this chapter, for more information.

Publishing Reports from SAS Enterprise Guide

You can use SAS Enterprise Guide to build sophisticated reports, which you can then share with SAS Web Report Studio users. Here is a summary of how to make the planets align so that publishing can work:

1. **Create your output in SAS Enterprise Guide, using the SAS Report format.**

   You can't share HTML, PDF, RTF, or listing output with SAS Web Report Studio.

2. **If you want the shared report to be dynamic (refreshed each time you access it in SAS Web Report Studio), you must create a SAS stored process to produce the desired result.**

   See Chapter 11 for a description of SAS stored processes and how to create them.

3. **If you build a composite report with the built-in Report Builder (using File⇨New⇨Report), each part of the report must originate from a stored process (if you want all parts to be dynamic).**

4. **SAS Web Report Studio must be configured with Report Services enabled.**

   This allows SAS Enterprise Guide to communicate with SAS Web Report Studio. SAS Enterprise Guide connects to the Report Services through the Web infrastructure platform (informally called "the WIP" in some SAS notes and documentation.)

Catching and Killing a Runaway SAS Session

We've all made a mistake that we immediately regret. For SAS users, the mistake often takes the form of a foolhardy query that, if left unstopped, would run for days.

When you submit a query like this in SAS Enterprise Guide, you have two ways to atone for your mistake. In the task status window (accessed by choosing View⇨Task Status), you can right-click the query item in the list and choose Stop. With improvements in SAS 9.2, canceling a SAS job in this way stands a good chance of success. It's also the cleanest approach because it allows SAS to "reset the stage" for your next request (by cleaning up intermediate results and temporary data) and also terminate any related database queries.

Alternatively, you can right-click the item in the task status window and choose End SAS Process. That kills the SAS process, putting it out of its misery.

Killing the SAS process can have a few side effects. For example, any temporary data or results that you had in your SAS session are gone, following your SAS workspace process to the grave. Also, if your query request was accessing another database process via a SAS/ACCESS library, the database process might continue to process the request until you intervene further.

Telling One SAS.EXE from Another

The SAS Metadata Server, workspace server, OLAP server, stored process server, SAS/SHARE server, and other special SAS servers all have one basic thing in common: Namely, they all show up as SAS.EXE processes when running under Microsoft Windows. This can make it a challenge to determine which SAS processes are orphaned or consuming all your CPU cycles.

The *Process Explorer tool* from Microsoft (originally developed by Sysinternals) is a Task Manager replacement that offers more detail about running processes. With this tool, you can view details about SAS processes that are running on your server and discern the different SAS server processes.

Figure 19-3 shows an example of a system with several SAS processes. You can see from the command-line details column that one process represents the SAS Metadata Server (running as a service) and another is the SAS stored process server (judging from the `-config` option). The other two SAS.EXE processes are workspace sessions.

Figure 19-3:
Will the real SAS Metadata Server process please stand up?

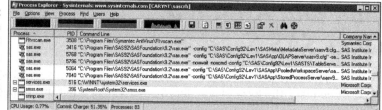

You can find Process Explorer and other useful process-sniffing tools at `technet.microsoft.com`.

Peering under the Covers with Process Logs

SAS programmers are familiar with *SAS logs,* which provide details about what happened during their SAS programs.

SAS administrators need to become familiar with server logs. Each class of SAS server offers its own style of log, providing appropriate information. Here is a summary of the popular log types:

- ✔ **SAS Metadata Server log:** Contains details of which users and processes connect to the SAS Metadata Server. It can also show when metadata is added, deleted, and modified — and by whom.

- ✔ **SAS object spawner log:** Contains initialization details for the servers that it controls. Also contains details about connections to workspace and stored process servers, how those processes were spawned (launched), who attempted to connect, whether they were successful, and error conditions if failures occurred.

- ✔ **SAS workspace server log:** Contains a snapshot of activity during a single SAS workspace session. This activity includes data access and SAS code processing. Usually, one workspace log file exists for each workspace process that is spawned. This means that the folder that contains the log files can become cluttered quickly, especially if many users are connecting to SAS sessions.

You can configure the logging activity of each server at a range of detail levels. The default is to show just the high-level activity, but you can tweak the options to get the nitty-gritty details, too. Much of the low-level details are useful only to SAS support staff to assist in diagnosing issues.

To configure the logging behavior for these SAS servers, you use the SAS logging facility (also known as Log4SAS). You can find more guidance about collecting such logs on the SAS support Web site at `support.sas.com`.

Chapter 20

Ten (or More) Web Resources for Extra Information

*O*kay, we lied! We're supposed to offer just ten resources, but we've given you more for your money with seventeen online resources. Read on for some helpful Web sites.

Where Do I Go For Support?

Just go to support.sas.com for technical support, online manuals, samples, user communities, software downloads (including service packs and hot fixes), and access to online and in-person training. You can search the same database that SAS Technical Support uses when you call with a problem. In addition, you can submit a problem online and view the status of your requests (called *tracks*) at any time.

What Else Does SAS Offer and How Are Others Succeeding with SAS?

Visit www.sas.com/software for details on SAS products and solutions by technology, by functional area, and by industry. For success stories with SAS in many industries and countries, go to www.sas.com/success/index.html. To attend a local, regional, national, or special-interest user conference, go to support.sas.com/usergroups and find one that you find useful.

How Can 1 Connect with other SAS Users?

SAS users are a well-connected, self-organizing bunch, and they love to meet with each other virtually and in person. Visit sasCommunity.org for the latest real-world techniques and events. Or try www.sasprofessionals.net, which is the Facebook for SAS users. If you want to find the trending SAS topics on Twitter, search for updates that use the #SAS hash tag.

Where Can 1 Get More Info on Making Effective Charts and Graphs?

Go to support.sas.com/sassamples/graphgallery and robslink.com/SAS/Home.htm for overviews, papers, and examples of the many graph types possible with SAS. Many of them can be used with the applications featured in this book; others require some SAS programming on your part to customize and adapt them for your needs.

For more background on charting data, see processtrends.com/ for a business slant and www.math.yorku.ca/SCS/Gallery/ for a more statistical bent on good and bad graphics.

Where Can I Ask Questions?

The SAS Discussion Forums at support.sas.com/forums are the perfect place to post your how-to questions and get answers from a knowledgeable community of SAS customers and employees. If you enjoy discussions via e-mail, consider subscribing to the SAS-L mailing list, hosted at www. listserv.uga.edu/archives/sas-l.html.

Where Can I Discover More about Statistics and Analytics?

For analytics help specific to SAS, see support.sas.com/statistics. Look up more specific topic papers on statistics with SAS at www.lexjansen. com/sugi/.

Where Can I Find Information That Didn't Fit in This Book?

The Web site for this book is at support.sas.com/sasfordummies. The site contains many of the SAS Enterprise Guide project files used in this book as examples, as well as sample data and SAS programs that you might find useful. In addition, check out the blogs maintained by the authors at blogs. sas.com/sasdummy and www.freakalytics.com.

Index

• T •

Business/Accounting & Bookkeeping

Bookkeeping For Dummies
978-0-7645-9848-7

eBay Business
All-in-One For Dummies,
2nd Edition
978-0-470-38536-4

Job Interviews
For Dummies,
3rd Edition
978-0-470-17748-8

Resumes For Dummies,
5th Edition
978-0-470-08037-5

Stock Investing
For Dummies,
3rd Edition
978-0-470-40114-9

Successful Time
Management
For Dummies
978-0-470-29034-7

Computer Hardware

BlackBerry For Dummies,
3rd Edition
978-0-470-45762-7

Computers For Seniors
For Dummies
978-0-470-24055-7

iPhone For Dummies,
2nd Edition
978-0-470-42342-4

Laptops For Dummies,
3rd Edition
978-0-470-27759-1

Macs For Dummies,
10th Edition
978-0-470-27817-8

Cooking & Entertaining

Cooking Basics
For Dummies,
3rd Edition
978-0-7645-7206-7

Wine For Dummies,
4th Edition
978-0-470-04579-4

Diet & Nutrition

Dieting For Dummies,
2nd Edition
978-0-7645-4149-0

Nutrition For Dummies,
4th Edition
978-0-471-79868-2

Weight Training
For Dummies,
3rd Edition
978-0-471-76845-6

Digital Photography

Digital Photography
For Dummies,
6th Edition
978-0-470-25074-7

Photoshop Elements 7
For Dummies
978-0-470-39700-8

Gardening

Gardening Basics
For Dummies
978-0-470-03749-2

Organic Gardening
For Dummies,
2nd Edition
978-0-470-43067-5

Green/Sustainable

Green Building
& Remodeling
For Dummies
978-0-470-17559-0

Green Cleaning
For Dummies
978-0-470-39106-8

Green IT For Dummies
978-0-470-38688-0

Health

Diabetes For Dummies,
3rd Edition
978-0-470-27086-8

Food Allergies
For Dummies
978-0-470-09584-3

Living Gluten-Free
For Dummies
978-0-471-77383-2

Hobbies/General

Chess For Dummies,
2nd Edition
978-0-7645-8404-6

Drawing For Dummies
978-0-7645-5476-6

Knitting For Dummies,
2nd Edition
978-0-470-28747-7

Organizing For Dummies
978-0-7645-5300-4

SuDoku For Dummies
978-0-470-01892-7

Home Improvement

Energy Efficient Homes
For Dummies
978-0-470-37602-7

Home Theater
For Dummies,
3rd Edition
978-0-470-41189-6

Living the Country Lifestyle
All-in-One For Dummies
978-0-470-43061-3

Solar Power Your Home
For Dummies
978-0-470-17569-9

Internet
Blogging For Dummies,
2nd Edition
978-0-470-23017-6

eBay For Dummies,
6th Edition
978-0-470-49741-8

Facebook For Dummies
978-0-470-26273-3

Google Blogger
For Dummies
978-0-470-40742-4

Web Marketing
For Dummies,
2nd Edition
978-0-470-37181-7

WordPress For Dummies,
2nd Edition
978-0-470-40296-2

Language & Foreign Language
French For Dummies
978-0-7645-5193-2

Italian Phrases
For Dummies
978-0-7645-7203-6

Spanish For Dummies
978-0-7645-5194-9

Spanish For Dummies,
Audio Set
978-0-470-09585-0

Macintosh
Mac OS X Snow Leopard
For Dummies
978-0-470-43543-4

Math & Science
Algebra I For Dummies,
2nd Edition
978-0-470-55964-2

Biology For Dummies
978-0-7645-5326-4

Calculus For Dummies
978-0-7645-2498-1

Chemistry For Dummies
978-0-7645-5430-8

Microsoft Office
Excel 2007 For Dummies
978-0-470-03737-9

Office 2007 All-in-One
Desk Reference
For Dummies
978-0-471-78279-7

Music
Guitar For Dummies,
2nd Edition
978-0-7645-9904-0

iPod & iTunes
For Dummies,
6th Edition
978-0-470-39062-7

Piano Exercises
For Dummies
978-0-470-38765-8

Parenting & Education
Parenting For Dummies,
2nd Edition
978-0-7645-5418-6

Type 1 Diabetes
For Dummies
978-0-470-17811-9

Pets
Cats For Dummies,
2nd Edition
978-0-7645-5275-5

Dog Training For Dummies,
2nd Edition
978-0-7645-8418-3

Puppies For Dummies,
2nd Edition
978-0-470-03717-1

Religion & Inspiration
The Bible For Dummies
978-0-7645-5296-0

Catholicism For Dummies
978-0-7645-5391-2

Women in the Bible
For Dummies
978-0-7645-8475-6

Self-Help & Relationship
Anger Management
For Dummies
978-0-470-03715-7

Overcoming Anxiety
For Dummies
978-0-7645-5447-6

Sports
Baseball For Dummies,
3rd Edition
978-0-7645-7537-2

Basketball For Dummies,
2nd Edition
978-0-7645-5248-9

Golf For Dummies,
3rd Edition
978-0-471-76871-5

Web Development
Web Design All-in-One
For Dummies
978-0-470-41796-6

Windows Vista
Windows Vista
For Dummies
978-0-471-75421-3